THE PREACHER'S HEBREW/GREEK COMPANION SERIES

General Editor / Old Testament Editor
Jonathan G. Kline, PhD
Senior Editor
Hendrickson Publishers

New Testament Editor
Sean M. McDonough, PhD
Professor of New Testament
Gordon-Conwell Theological Seminary

| The Preacher's Hebrew Companion Series |

Genesis 1–11

THE PREACHER'S HEBREW COMPANION TO

Genesis 1–11

A Selective Commentary for
Meditation and Sermon Preparation

Brian R. Doak

an imprint of Hendrickson Publishing Group

The Preacher's Hebrew Companion to Genesis 1–11:
A Selective Commentary for Meditation and Sermon Preparation

© 2023 by Hendrickson Publishers

Published by Hendrickson Academic
an imprint of Hendrickson Publishing Group
Hendrickson Publishers, LLC
P. O. Box 3473
Peabody, Massachusetts 01961-3473
www.hendricksonpublishinggroup.com

ISBN 978-1-68307-344-4

All rights reserved. No part of this book may be reproduced or transmitted in any form or by any means, electronic or mechanical, including photocopying, recording, or by any information storage and retrieval system, without permission in writing from the publisher.

Neither the publisher nor the author is responsible for, nor do they have any control over, the content of any third-party websites cited in this book, whether at the time of the book's publication or in the future.

All Scripture quotations marked NRSVue are from the *New Revised Standard Version Updated Edition*, copyright © 2021 National Council of the Churches of Christ in the United States of America. Used by permission. All rights reserved worldwide.

Printed in the United States of America

First Printing — February 2023

Library of Congress Control Number: 2022942107

CONTENTS

Series Editors' Preface   xi

Author's Introduction   xix

List of Abbreviations   xxi

GENESIS 1:1–5
THE FIRST ACTS OF CREATION
3

1:1 . . . . *4*
1:2 . . . . *7*
1:3–5 . . . . *10*
From Text to Sermon *16*

GENESIS 1:26–31
THE CREATION OF HUMANS
19

1:26–28 . . . . *20*
1:29–30 . . . . *31*
1:31 . . . . *38*
From Text to Sermon *41*

GENESIS 2:1–3
THE SABBATH
45

2:1–2 . . . . *46*
2:3 . . . . *50*
From Text to Sermon *53*

 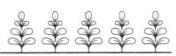

GENESIS 2:18–25

THE MAN, THE ANIMALS, AND THE WOMAN

57

2:18–19 58
2:20–24 66
2:25 78
From Text to Sermon 80

GENESIS 3:1–7

MAN, WOMAN, AND SERPENT

83

3:1–3 84
3:4–7 92
From Text to Sermon 103

GENESIS 3:14–21

CONSEQUENCES IN THE GARDEN

107

3:14–15 108
3:16 116
3:17–21 119
From Text to Sermon 129

GENESIS 4:1–16

BROTHER MURDERS BROTHER

133

4:1–2 134
4:3–7 139
4:8 148
4:9–15 151
4:16 166
From Text to Sermon 168

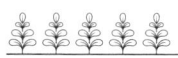 **GENESIS 6:1-22**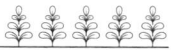

GOD DECIDES TO FLOOD THE EARTH

171

    6:1–10 . . . . *172*
    6:11–12 . . . . *184*
    6:13–16 . . . . *188*
    6:17–18 . . . . *198*
    6:19–21 . . . . *205*
    6:22 . . . . *212*
    From Text to Sermon *214*

 **GENESIS 8:20-9:7**

GOD RESTORES THE EARTH AFTER THE FLOOD

217

    8:20–22 . . . . *218*
    9:1–4 . . . . *228*
    9:5–7 . . . . *237*
    From Text to Sermon *244*

 **GENESIS 11:1-9**

THE TOWER OF CONFUSION

247

    11:1–2 . . . . *248*
    11:3–4 . . . . *252*
    11:5–7 . . . . *259*
    11:8–9 . . . . *266*
    From Text to Sermon *271*

Works Cited	275
Index of Biblical References	277
About the Author	281

SERIES EDITORS' PREFACE

Overview

Like many preachers, you may wish you could use the biblical languages in your sermon preparation, but the task seems daunting. Perhaps you lack confidence in your language skills—especially if it's been a long time since you studied Greek or Hebrew—and when you turn to technical commentaries, you feel overwhelmed. Or perhaps you simply don't have the time to do the laborious work of digging into the original-language texts. To help you overcome these challenges, we designed this series, the Preacher's Hebrew Companion (as well as its New Testament counterpart series, the Preacher's Greek Companion). In collaboration with the series authors, our goal as series editors is to gently guide you, the busy preacher, through the Hebrew text of select biblical passages in a way that will empower you to integrate original-language exegesis and homiletics. Our prayer is that you will find this book and the other volumes in this series spiritually and intellectually encouraging as well as pleasant to use. We hope your use of the series will make your sermon preparation a more profound and satisfying process and will invigorate your preaching.

Structure

Each volume in this series includes the following three features for a given biblical book (or portion of a book):

- **a curated selection of passages** we believe many preachers would likely choose to preach on from the biblical book (or portion of the book) in question; **or, for shorter biblical books, the entire book**, broken up into manageable passages

- all the basic **lexical and grammatical tools** you need (whatever your Hebrew skill level may be) **to work through and meditate on the Hebrew text** of these passages in a way that strengthens your sermon preparation and empowers you to preach more effectively

- **succinct, select comments** intended to help you responsibly and effectively bridge the gap between reading the Hebrew text and delivering a sermon on it

The Preacher's Hebrew Companion is not a traditional commentary series, as is reflected in its title and subtitle: "*Companion*" (not "Commentary") and "*Selected* Passages for *Meditation* and *Sermon Preparation*." That is, we conceived this series as a *supplement* to the wealth of fine commentaries that already exist, not as a replacement for any of them. We recommend using this series alongside traditional commentaries, which by design include helpful information that is not covered in ours.

The Selection of Passages

Each volume in the Preacher's Hebrew Companion series provides the Hebrew text of **approximately ten to twelve passages** from a particular biblical book (or portion thereof):

- In addition to having expertise in Hebrew and exegesis, our series authors typically have extensive preaching experience or are full-time preachers by vocation. Unless the biblical book in question is short enough to be included in full, they chose **passages** they think **preachers would most likely desire to preach**. In order to encourage preaching through the biblical book in an "expository" rather than a thematic manner, these passages are presented in canonical order. That said, for longer books (such as Isaiah or Matthew), we encouraged authors to choose passages that highlight or represent important themes found in the book; for such books, however, the chosen passages are still presented in canonical order. The curated, limited number of passages in each series volume allows you, if you wish, to use the passages as the basis for a "ready-made" sermon series of whatever length suits your schedule (e.g., for a series consisting of, say, four, seven, ten, or twelve sermons). Alternatively, you might choose to preach a series using some of the passages in a volume and then supplement these with passages from the biblical book in question that are not found in the volume.

- The aims of the series guided our decisions about passage length. On the one hand, we encouraged authors to choose **passages that are not too long**, so that the portions of text won't be daunting to you if your Hebrew skills are rudimentary; nor do we want you to be overwhelmed by wading through dozens of verses in Hebrew. For this reason, our ideal length for most passages has been approximately ten verses. On the other hand, in order to do justice to the natural boundaries of longer passages, we have taken care not to artificially truncate such texts. Consider, for example, the account of the crossing of the Red Sea (Exod 14–15) or the story of the raising of Lazarus (John 11). Although these texts are far too long to be included in full in a volume in this series, each constituent part of these texts is vital to understanding their narrative development and message. For such passages, we asked authors to focus—as a preacher might typically do when delivering a sermon on a lengthy passage—on what they consider to be the most salient verses from the passage. Accordingly, we have provided the Hebrew text for only these verses, with the author summarizing the other verses (in English).

- Finally, when authors deemed it helpful (especially for longer biblical books), they have indicated, on the first page devoted to each passage, the **larger literary unit to which the passage belongs**,[1] thus helping you see the passage in question as part of a larger whole rather than as an isolated pericope. In cases where this larger literary context is indicated, we encourage you to pick up a Bible and read and dwell on this context while using this volume to work through the passage.

The Presentation of Each Passage

This volume helps you work through each passage it contains by presenting the Hebrew text of the passage along with the lexical and grammatical information you need in order to dig into this original-language text. Designed to be highly accessible, this format is intended (1) to enable you to work through the text in manageable chunks and according to your abilities, regardless of your skill level in Hebrew; (2) to simultaneously facilitate both study and devotion; and (3) in conjunction with the author's commentary, to help you bridge the gap, as easily and seamlessly as possible, between the original-language text and preaching.

More specifically, this volume contains the following five sections for each passage:

- A **brief introduction** to the passage—typically comprising only a few sentences—is included in order to set the stage for the passage and highlight its important themes.

- For ease of reading and to encourage you to slow down and contemplate the text, the passage is typically divided into subunits. For each of these subunits, we provide the **Hebrew text** of each clause or phrase, along

---

1. Occasionally, such a literary unit is coterminous with the passage itself.

with **transliteration** (as a pronunciation help for those whose Hebrew is at a rudimentary level) and the author's **translation**.²

 Next, each clause or phrase from the subunit is presented in an interlinear fashion, notably with **a contextual gloss (or multiple contextual glosses) and parsing for each word**.³ For example:

1a	בְּרֵאשִׁית בָּרָא אֱלֹהִים		
	In the beginning, God created		
בְּרֵאשִׁית רֵאשִׁית	in beginning of/ when . . . began bə·rē·šît	CST W/ PREP בְּ	noun
בָּרָא ברא	(he) created bā·rā'	QAL PF 3MS	verb
אֱלֹהִים אֱלֹהִים	God 'ĕ·lō·hîm	ABS	noun

This formatting allows you to easily analyze each word in the clause or phrase (by helping you on the level of semantics and morphology) and to perceive how the words work together as a whole (by helping you on the level of syntax).

 A key feature of each volume in this series is the inclusion of **concise comments** to accompany some clauses and phrases. These have two primary goals: (1) to enable you to understand and exegete the text more deeply than might be possible from reading it in English, and (2) to equip

---

2. The Hebrew text used in this series has been taken from the Michigan-Claremont-Westminster Electronic Hebrew Bible, a popular electronic version based on the BHS that has been revised by its creators on the basis of comparison with the Leningrad Codex. This electronic text is in the public domain and has been made available courtesy of the J. Alan Groves Center for Advanced Biblical Research. For simplicity's sake, whenever there is a *ketiv-qere*, only the *qere* has been presented (without being marked as such). Interested readers should feel free to consult critical editions, such as the BHS, to see where instances of *ketiv-qere* or other text-critical issues occur.

3. The glosses are the author's own and intentionally err on the "literal" end of the spectrum, in order to help you apprehend the basic meaning(s) of each word in context. The parsings have been supplied by the team at Hendrickson. Naturally, some words can plausibly be parsed more than one way in context; in such cases, the parsing provided is the one we deemed to make the most sense, but other parsings could have been listed instead.

you with insights into the original-language text that will be of direct value for your preaching. To help you focus and not become overwhelmed with too much information, we encouraged our authors to comment only on those clauses and phrases for which they thought doing so would accomplish these two goals. In addition, because the volumes in this series are not only language aids but—ultimately and more importantly—preaching aids, we asked authors to highlight those features in the Hebrew text that bring out key themes, rhetorical and theological emphasis, narrative development, character development, connections with other biblical texts, and the like. Although noting various other features in the Hebrew text may have been intrinsically interesting from a grammatical perspective or helpful for strengthening your language skills, authors have generally refrained from commenting on such features when doing so would not be likely to aid you in moving from text to sermon in any substantial way.[4] In short, an author's brief, select comments are intended—in conjunction with the volume's language aids—to provide you both with *focus* and with *space* to slow down, meditate, wonder, and mature in your understanding and experience of the text, as you form your own judgments on it and prepare to proclaim the divine word to your hearers. The author's comments are not intended to circumscribe the possible interpretive options with one single answer (especially for texts whose interpretation is the particular subject of debate among Christian believers). Rather, they are meant to stimulate your thinking, to help you see features of the text (and connections with other texts) that you may not have perceived before, and to prompt you to ask questions that may not have previously occurred to you.

- Each passage ends with a brief section titled **"From Text to Sermon,"** in which our authors, building on their comments, suggest ways you can move from working through the Hebrew text to the task of homiletics, highlighting potential points of emphasis or particular insights you may wish to share with your audience. In this way, the authors provide you with possible ways to bring the text to life for your audience (e.g., types

---

4. Another way we have kept the presentation streamlined and uncluttered, so that you can achieve maximum focus, is by intentionally keeping source citations to a minimum. Authors' comments on a given passage are the fruit of their scholarly research on the passage, their personal reflection on it, and their experience preaching and teaching it. They cite secondary sources only when they draw a specific insight from one particular source or wish to point you to a particularly helpful resource for further reading. As stated above, we naturally encourage you to also use traditional commentaries (which typically provide more documentation) in your study and sermon preparation.

of illustrations you might use). Because individual preachers (and each of our series authors) bring their own particular skills, perspectives, backgrounds, and oratorical approaches to bear on the homiletical task, and because every biblical text has its own unique features, we encouraged our authors to structure the "From Text to Sermon" section as a free-form series of short paragraphs whose content and emphases are guided by their own personal judgment about what is most helpful for a variety of preachers in different places, cultures, and times. The remarks in this section are always grouped according to rubrics (in the form of inline headers); but rather than restrict authors with a "one-size-fits-all" set of rubrics, we allowed them to create their own rubrics and even, if helpful, to vary these rubrics across passages within their volume in light of the unique features and emphases of each passage.[5] We view the resulting diversity of approaches and emphases across this series (and even within a given volume) as a strength, and we hope this aspect of the series will encourage you to use your own judgment about how to preach each passage in a way that best suits you and your listeners, being sensitive to the promptings and guidance of the Spirit of God.

Audience and Theological Perspective

Since our hope is that many different kinds of people will find the volumes in this series useful, we have designed the Preacher's Hebrew Companion to be helpful to a broad spectrum of Christian preachers:

 Our intention is that the series will be **useful and accessible to a large and diverse group of preachers serving a variety of communities throughout the world.** For this reason, we encouraged authors to exercise sensitivity and broad-mindedness in their comments and particularly when writing the "From Text to Sermon" section, in which they could run the risk of being too culturally specific. In particular, we asked authors that any sermon illustrations they included in this section generally be as universal as possible or that, instead of providing specific illustrations, they point to themes from the passage you may wish to illustrate in one way or another. That said, because specificity is essential for good communication, we also allowed authors to suggest—when they deemed

---

5. That said, we suggested the following possible rubrics to authors as starting points to consider: theological themes, themes for application and illustration, integrating the broader historical and literary context, learning from the language, and (as deemed helpful and not reductionistic) "the big idea" of the passage.

it particularly helpful—concrete, culturally specific examples as springboards to help you think about examples that will be relevant for your own context.

- We asked our authors to express any **theological perspectives** in a way that is **consistent with the beliefs stated in the Apostles' Creed**. Because this series aims to meet the needs of Christian preachers of various theological viewpoints, we encouraged a diversity of theological perspectives within these bounds across the volumes in the series. In addition, because the series has a joint focus on exegesis (close attention to what a specific text says) and homiletics (how to preach said text), we advised authors when making any theological comments to let these flow naturally from the text at hand, rather than using the text as a springboard to discuss issues that would more properly fall under the rubric of systematic theology. Although we asked authors to avoid reading any given passage through the lens of a theological system grounded in other biblical texts, we also strongly encouraged them to discuss allusions to other biblical passages or other innerbiblical literary connections if they felt that doing so would help you understand the message of the text at hand and know how to preach it more effectively.

Acknowledgments

We would like to offer our heartfelt gratitude to the following individuals, who have played a central role in the creation of this series:

- Arley Kangas and Marco Resendes, for their excellent work on various aspects of the making of these volumes, especially transliterating, parsing, proofreading, and generating the indexes.

- Phil Frank, for his expert typesetting and for patiently working with us, in our capacity as series editors, to achieve the desired formatting and aesthetic for these volumes.

- The series authors, for joining us in this unique project and for sharing our vision and lending their considerable skills to the task. These volumes are the result of a fruitful collaboration between the Hendrickson team and the series authors (with both parties contributing to the content). We are truly grateful for the opportunity to have worked on this project together.

All of us—the series editors, the series authors, and the team at Hendrickson—pray that the volume you now hold in your hands will empower and encourage you to work through the Hebrew text of the Bible in order to deepen your sermon preparation and strengthen your proclamation of the word of God. We nurture a deep respect and appreciation for the challenging work that you as a preacher do on the "front lines," and we recognize the many challenges (logistical, mental, emotional, spiritual, and more) that you encounter on a weekly, indeed a daily, basis. We are honored to come alongside you and support you in your important labors, and we pray that your use of this book will bear much fruit for the kingdom of God.

JONATHAN G. KLINE
SEAN M. MCDONOUGH

AUTHOR'S INTRODUCTION

The grand story of salvation begins in Genesis. If Christians believe that God has divinely ordained the canon of Scripture, and even the order of the books, then they must also affirm this: God wanted us to hear Genesis first. And so we do. In particular, the first eleven chapters of Genesis, sometimes called the "primeval history," set a grand stage for all that is to come, defining the order of the created world before God, the status of humans in God's image, and the fallout of our struggle to survive in a broken world. The stunning interplay we find here between the cosmic and the personal, the universal and the particular, already anticipates the ultimate paradox and power of Christian faith, expressed most supremely in the incarnation of God in Jesus Christ. God and human. A savior who dies. Ultimate power and lowly weakness.

Because the opening chapters of Genesis are so familiar, we need to slow down and try to encounter them in a new way; otherwise, we run the risk of letting our eyes merely skim over the pages, certain that we already know the stories and the themes and the lessons. But do we already know them? We may not. Are we willing to take a risk to learn something new? Sometimes. But it is hard. Engaging with the text in ancient Hebrew forces us to truly focus, and as we linger over God's words, we will be changed and we will learn. We will find that creation of the natural world and people, so majestically described in the iconic opening phrase of the book, is a continual process in Genesis. We will learn that our most shameful, base desires—to kill, to dominate, to boast, to make idols—already have a mysterious origin in our spiritual ancestors. We will also rediscover that our most wonderful longings—for God, for meaningful work, for acceptance, for knowing—have their origin in the divine order of all things. Genesis 1–11 tells the story of our own choices and our own world today.

I started working on this volume in 2020, during the early days of the COVID-19 pandemic, a time of global anxiety and change. These anxieties and changes were personal and professional for me as well—one of my closest friends and colleagues (Javier Garcia), who had been among the first to read parts of this book in progress, died in 2021, and my role as a professor in the classroom shifted to administrative and leadership responsibilities at my university. My wife and I battled surgeries and setbacks of various normal kinds, and our daughters seemed to grow up too quickly before our eyes. As I worked on this project, I saw my own family, my own personality, and my own struggle reflected in these early chapters of Genesis, and I was reminded that it is Scripture that best tells the story of my own life.

I am so honored and grateful that my friend and colleague since our time as students at Harvard together, Jonathan Kline, reached out to me to undertake this project, and I thank him for his patience and help. His work as an editor made this volume much better than it would have been otherwise.

I dedicate this book to the memory of Professor Javier A. Garcia (1987–2021): "The believer . . . lauds the Creator, the Redeemer, God, Father, Son and Holy Spirit, for the bodily presence of a brother" (Dietrich Bonhoeffer, *Life Together* [London: SCM, 2015 (orig. 1954)], 9).

LIST OF ABBREVIATIONS

1	first person	indef	indefinite
2	second person	INF	infinitive
3	third person	INTERR/interr	interrogative
ABS	absolute	JUSS	jussive
ADJ	adjective	M	masculine
ADV	adverb	NIPH	Niphal
ATTR	attributive	P	plural
C	common	PASS	passive
COHORT	cohortative	PF	perfect
CONJ/conj	conjunction	PRED	predicative
CST	construct	PREP/prep	preposition
DEF. ART.	definite article	PRON/pron	pronoun
demonstr	demonstrative	PTCP	participle
F	feminine	S	singular
HIPH	Hiphil	SUBST	substantive
HITH	Hithpael	SX	suffix
HOPH	Hophal	w/	with
IMPF	imperfect	WAYY	wayyiqtol
IMPV	imperative		

NOTE: *All verse numbers in this volume refer to the Hebrew text; when the English verse numbering differs, it is listed in brackets following the Hebrew numbering.*

GENESIS 1:1–5

THE FIRST ACTS OF CREATION

The Bible begins at the beginning—with the creation of the world. Repeated readings of this powerful text, especially in its original language, yield new meanings and possibilities. The text is at once bold and enigmatic. Some of the terminology requires explanation far beyond what a single term in translation can convey, while in other cases the declarations are simple and profound and stand without comment: "Let there be light!"

LARGER LITERARY CONTEXT ▸ 1:1–2:3

1:1

1a

בְּרֵאשִׁית בָּרָא אֱלֹהִים
bərēšît bārā' ĕlōhîm

In the beginning, God created

1b

אֵת הַשָּׁמַיִם וְאֵת הָאָרֶץ:
'ēt haššāmayim wə'ēt hā'āreṣ.

the heavens and the earth.

1a	בְּרֵאשִׁית בָּרָא אֱלֹהִים		
	In the beginning, God created		
בְּרֵאשִׁית	in beginning of/ when . . . began	CST W/ PREP בְּ	noun
רֵאשִׁית	*bə·rē'·šît*		
בָּרָא	(he) created	QAL PF 3MS	verb
ברא	*bā·rā'*		
אֱלֹהִים	God	ABS	noun
אֱלֹהִים	*'ĕ·lō·hîm*		

בְּרֵאשִׁית has most frequently been translated "In the beginning," and indeed there is reasonable evidence supporting the accuracy of this translation. Others have opted to read the preposition בְּ here as temporal: "When God began . . ." This translation draws attention to the fact that the grammar in Hebrew doesn't quite say "in *the* beginning" (presumably בָּרֵאשִׁית in Hebrew). All translations are inherently interpretations; theological affirmation clearly plays a role in one's interpretative process here, as God's status as creator *ex nihilo* would be strongly affirmed by "In the beginning . . ." but left open to question with "When God began . . ." In the latter rendering, the text describes not the very first spark of time before which there was nothing—notice the (potentially) physical elements already there in v. 2—but rather a moment when God began creating a particular set of things. Even so, the creation of what we understand as time itself (in the form of light and dark, the sun and other celestial bodies) occurs later, in vv. 3–5, 14–19, so one need not fear losing all elements of the *ex nihilo* theology either way.

The first two words of Genesis, בְּרֵאשִׁית and בָּרָא, involve wordplay—both begin with the same three letters in Hebrew (*bet, resh, aleph*)—and the first seven words of Scripture form a pleasing poetic balance:

bərēšît bārā' 'ĕlōhîm
'ēt haššāmayim wə'ēt hā'āreṣ

The verb ברא appears for the most part to be a special term related to divine action, describing only God's own acts of creating; both humans and God can עשׂה ("make, do, act"), יצר ("fashion, mold"), and בנה ("build"), but only God can ברא. The language of God as "creator" (using this verb ברא) plays a prominent role in Isa 40–55, where the prophet encourages his community to remember that the same God who created them can create new things in their world.

The term for "God" here in Gen 1, אֱלֹהִים, is at once a generic term for a deity (formed on the common Semitic base word for "deity," אֵל), yet also with a flourish—the plural ending ים . What does the plural mean? Some attribute the form to Israel's God's status above and beyond every other (i.e., the "plural of majesty"), and Christians will obviously see a hint at multiplicity within divine unity (the Trinity). Notice also the first-person plural address uttered by אֱלֹהִים in 1:26 and 11:7.

1b	אֵת הַשָּׁמַיִם וְאֵת הָאָרֶץ:		
	the heavens and the earth.		
	אֵת (direct object marker) אֵת *'ēt*	---	particle
	הַשָּׁמַיִם the heavens/skies/ air above שָׁמַיִם *haš·šā·mayim*	ABS W/ DEF. ART.	noun
	וְאֵת and (+ direct object marker) אֵת *wə·'ēt*	--- W/ CONJ ו	particle
	הָאָרֶץ: the earth/land below אֶרֶץ *hā·'ā·reṣ*	ABS W/ DEF. ART.	noun

The paired terminology for "heavens" (שָׁמַיִם) and "earth" (אֶרֶץ) here and elsewhere in the Hebrew Bible describes what is high and low, the totality of things—not necessarily a Christian conception of "heaven" as an otherworldly place. שָׁמַיִם can describe the place where birds fly and the place where God is; אֶרֶץ can describe the land on which one stands or even the underworld as a place where the dead rest.

1:2

2a
וְהָאָ֗רֶץ הָיְתָ֥ה תֹ֙הוּ֙ וָבֹ֔הוּ
wəhā'āreṣ hāyətâ tōhû wāvōhû

And the earth was all chaos and chaotic,

2b
וְחֹ֖שֶׁךְ עַל־פְּנֵ֣י תְה֑וֹם
wəḥōšek 'al-pənê təhôm

with darkness over the face of the sea,

2c
וְר֣וּחַ אֱלֹהִ֔ים מְרַחֶ֖פֶת עַל־פְּנֵ֥י הַמָּֽיִם׃
wərûaḥ 'ĕlōhîm məraḥefet 'al-pənê hammāyim

and the breath of God rippled across the face of the waters.

2a	וְהָאָ֗רֶץ הָיְתָ֥ה תֹ֙הוּ֙ וָבֹ֔הוּ		
	And the earth was all chaos and chaotic,		
וְהָאָ֗רֶץ אָרֶץ *wə·hā·'ā·reṣ*	now/and the earth	ABS W/ CONJ וְ + DEF. ART.	noun
הָיְתָ֥ה היה *hā·yə·tâ*	(it) was	QAL PF 3FS	verb
תֹ֙הוּ֙ תֹהוּ *tō·hû*	wasteland/chaos/void	ABS	noun
וָבֹ֔הוּ בֹּהוּ *wā·vō·hû*	and wasteland/ chaos/void	ABS W/ CONJ וְ	noun

Mystery surrounds the state of the uncreated אָרֶץ. The term תֹהוּ, rendered here as "chaos," elsewhere in the Hebrew Bible describes a wasteland (Deut 32:10), something that is useless or unprofitable (1 Sam 12:21), and that which makes justice go astray (Isa 29:21). The word paired with it, בֹּהוּ, rendered here as "chaotic," appears only one other time—in Jer 4:23, perhaps quoting Gen 1:2—and it is probably not an independent term with its own meaning but rather a wordplay on תֹהוּ. Common translations, such as "formless and void," do not capture the fact that בֹהוּ plays off the word תֹהוּ, while others, such as Robert Alter's elegant "welter and waste," capture the sound repetition nicely (see Alter 1997:3). "Chaos and chaotic" may also convey the idea that what the text describes is not technically "nothing"; rather, we have a spirit or wind from God, darkness, and a saltwater sea (תְהוֹם, on which see below).

2b	וְחֹשֶׁךְ עַל־פְּנֵי תְהוֹם		
	with darkness over the face of the sea,		
וְחֹשֶׁךְ חֹשֶׁךְ	and darkness wə·ḥō·šek̲	ABS W/ CONJ ו	noun
עַל־ עַל	over/upon/above 'al-	---	prep
פְּנֵי פָּנֶה	face/surface of pə·nê	CST	noun
תְהוֹם תְּהוֹם	sea/saltwater/deep tə·hôm	ABS	noun

In the Hebrew Bible, the term חֹשֶׁךְ is used with roughly the same range of meaning that "darkness" has in English. Many times, חֹשֶׁךְ indicates the darkness of natural patterns, i.e., the darkness of night that alternates with the day, or even the darkness of night invoked by divine punishment (e.g., Exod 10:15; Ezek 32:8). At other points, חֹשֶׁךְ takes on a physical, personified quality, as in 2 Sam 22:12: "He [God] set חֹשֶׁךְ around him as a canopy . . ." In most cases, darkness is quite undesirable—it is a place where prisoners sit (Isa 42:7) and where people go to be forgotten (Isa 45:7), and it is a spiritual or intellectual state where people lack guidance (Mic 3:6; Eccl 2:13).

פָּנִים (in construct, פְּנֵי) idiomatically refers to a "surface," though its primary (bodily) reference is to the human face.

תְהוֹם is at once a technical term for a saltwater sea (as opposed to a freshwater lake, stream, and so on) and a broader indication of the waters of the "deep," that is, waters that are presumed to be far underground, welling up as though from the core of the earth (e.g., Gen 7:11; Deut 8:7). In the Semitic Akkadian language of the Babylonian creation story called Enuma Elish (perhaps composed roughly during the same time period in which the book of Genesis took written form), one of the primary characters is named "Tiamat," which is the Akkadian term for "saltwater sea" that is equivalent to Hebrew תְהוֹם. In that story, Tiamat threatens the cosmic order, forcing a conflict with another deity (Marduk), who must defeat her with gruesome acts of violence. We could read the invocation of תְהוֹם here in Genesis as a direct challenge to the Babylonian myth: the very next verse indicates that God dismisses the chaos of the uncreated disorder with mere words. No battle. No opposition. No other gods.

2c	וְרוּחַ אֱלֹהִים מְרַחֶפֶת עַל־פְּנֵי הַמָּיִם:		
	and the breath of God rippled across the face of the waters.		
וְרוּחַ / רוּחַ / wə·rû·aḥ	and wind/spirit/breath of	CST W/ CONJ וְ	noun
אֱלֹהִים / אֱלֹהִים / ĕ·lō·hîm	God	ABS	noun
מְרַחֶפֶת / רחף / mə·ra·ḥe·fet	hovered/fluttered/flashed	PIEL PTCP FS	verb
עַל־ / עַל / 'al-	over/upon/above	---	prep
פְּנֵי / פָּנֶה / pə·nê	(the) face/surface of	CST	noun
הַמָּיִם: / מַיִם / ham·māyim	the waters	ABS W/ DEF. ART.	noun

The "breath" or "spirit" of God, רוּחַ אֱלֹהִים (also referred to as רוּחַ יְהוָה "breath/spirit of the LORD" in some contexts), is a creative, powerful force in the Old Testament—inspiring dream interpretation (Gen 41:38), warfare (repeatedly in Judges), art/design (Exod 31:3), prophecy and visions (Ezek 11:5), and more. Here at the beginning of creation, this divine breath, spirit, or wind "ripples," "flashes," or "hovers" over the water. The verb רחף (at the base of the unique form מְרַחֶפֶת) is quite rare in the Bible; in its two other appearances (Deut 32:11; Jer 23:9), this verb describes the way a mother eagle will "hover over" (or perhaps "rustle up"?) her young, and the way a person's bones might "shake" or "quiver" when the person is in a state of being totally dismayed or even drunk. As a physical image, one might think of being out on a boat in the middle of a lake or out on the open ocean, feeling a breeze—perhaps frighteningly strong, perhaps gentle—rippling through one's clothes and across the water. Here the common term for "water," מַיִם, could be read as poetically interchangeable with תְהוֹם in the previous clause.

1:3–5

3a
וַיֹּאמֶר אֱלֹהִים
wayyōʾmer ʾĕlōhîm

And God said,

3b
יְהִי אוֹר
yəhî ʾôr

"Let there be light!"

3c
וַיְהִי־אוֹר׃
wayəhî-ʾôr.

—and there was light.

4a
וַיַּרְא אֱלֹהִים אֶת־הָאוֹר כִּי־טוֹב
wayyarʾ ʾĕlōhîm ʾet-hāʾôr kî-ṭôv

And God saw the light, that it was good,

4b
וַיַּבְדֵּל אֱלֹהִים בֵּין הָאוֹר וּבֵין הַחֹשֶׁךְ׃
wayyavdēl ʾĕlōhîm bên hāʾôr ûvên haḥōšek.

and God divided between the light and the darkness.

5a
וַיִּקְרָא אֱלֹהִים ׀ לָאוֹר יוֹם
wayyiqrāʾ ʾĕlōhîm lāʾôr yôm

And God called the light "Day,"

5b
וְלַחֹשֶׁךְ קָרָא לָיְלָה
wəlaḥōšek qārāʾ lāylâ

and the darkness he called "Night."

5c
וַיְהִי־עֶרֶב
wayəhî-ʿerev

And it was evening,

5d	וַֽיְהִי־בֹ֖קֶר
	wayəhî-vōqer
	and it was morning,
5e	י֥וֹם אֶחָֽד׃
	yôm 'eḥād.
	day one.

3a	וַיֹּ֣אמֶר אֱלֹהִ֔ים
	And God said,

וַיֹּ֣אמֶר	and (he) said	QAL WAYY 3MS	verb
אמר	*way·yō'·mer*		
אֱלֹהִ֔ים	God	ABS	noun
אלהים	*'ĕ·lō·hîm*		

3b	יְהִ֣י א֑וֹר
	"Let there be light!"

יְהִ֣י	let there be/may (it) be	QAL JUSS 3MS	verb
היה	*yə·hî*		
א֑וֹר	light	ABS	noun
אור	*'ôr*		

The succinctness of this first divine proclamation is loaded with meaning: God's creative acts are unopposed, quick, and simple. Indeed, readers of Hebrew can see that in the original language the first command is only two words (comprising three syllables total); whereas in English the standard rendition, followed here, is four words (comprising four syllables). A more idiomatic translation such as "Light—now!" or "Let's have light!" would better capture the brevity. That said, the English rendering "let there be" for יְהִ֣י, which continues throughout this first chapter for God's creative pronouncements, offers the archaic and dignified feel of a king making a decree.

3c	וַיְהִי־אוֹר:		
	—and there was light.		
וַיְהִי־ היה	and there was *wa·yə·hî-*	QAL WAYY 3MS	verb
אוֹר: אור	light *'ôr*	ABS	noun

The result of creation follows the command with equal brevity. The distance on the page between יְהִי אוֹר and וַיְהִי־אוֹר speaks volumes: nothing intervenes between God's pronouncement and its accomplishment. The presence of the darkness and the potential for an allusion to Babylonian mythology in the word תְהוֹם has set up at least the possibility that a battle could follow—perhaps early listeners to a passage like this in biblical Israel might have expected just such a battle, based on other ancient creation stories. None occurs.

4a	וַיַּרְא אֱלֹהִים אֶת־הָאוֹר כִּי־טוֹב		
	And God saw the light, that it was good,		
וַיַּרְא ראה	and (he) saw *way·yar'*	QAL WAYY 3MS	verb
אֱלֹהִים אֱלֹהִים	God *'ĕ·lō·hîm*	ABS	noun
אֶת־ את	*(direct object marker)* *'et-*	---	particle
הָאוֹר אור	the light *hā·'ôr*	ABS W/ DEF. ART.	noun
כִּי־ כי	that/for/because/since *kî-*	---	conj
טוֹב טוב	good/pleasant *ṭôv*	MS PRED	adj

Genesis 1 repeats this pattern of God's seeing (רָאָה) followed by the proclamation of goodness (טוֹב). In English, "good" is a rather broad term; the usage of טוֹב in Hebrew is similar, as טוֹב can indicate health, physical attractiveness, positive emotional or spiritual impressions, or upright behavior. Note that Gen 1 does not include a term opposite to טוֹב, such as רַע/רָעָה ("bad, evil"). The first sense that anything is other than טוֹב occurs in 2:9, with the presence of the "tree of טוֹב וָרָע [good and evil]," and in 2:18, where God declares that it is "not good [לֹא־טוֹב] that the man should be alone."

4b	וַיַּבְדֵּל אֱלֹהִים בֵּין הָאוֹר וּבֵין הַחֹשֶׁךְ׃
	and God divided between the light and the darkness.

וַיַּבְדֵּל בדל	and (he) divided/separated way·yav·dēl	HIPH WAYY 3MS	verb
אֱלֹהִים אֱלֹהִים	God ʾĕ·lō·hîm	ABS	noun
בֵּין בֵּין	between bên	---	prep
הָאוֹר אוֹר	the light hā·ʾôr	ABS W/ DEF. ART.	noun
וּבֵין בֵּין	and between û·vên	--- W/ CONJ וּ	prep
הַחֹשֶׁךְ׃ חֹשֶׁךְ	the darkness ha·ḥō·šeḵ	ABS W/ DEF. ART.	noun

The verb בדל is common in texts dealing with priestly and ritual concerns, often indicating the separation that should occur between opposed concepts, such as clean and unclean or holy and unholy (e.g., Lev 10:10; Ezek 22:26), and divisions between groups of people (Num 8:14; Neh 9:2). Here, "night" and "day" are both named and then the text moves on without any comment on the superiority of either natural state.

5a

וַיִּקְרָ֨א אֱלֹהִ֤ים ׀ לָאוֹר֙ י֔וֹם

And God called the light "Day,"

וַיִּקְרָ֨א קרא	and (he) called/named way·yiq·rā'	QAL WAYY 3MS	verb
אֱלֹהִ֤ים ׀ אֱלֹהִים	God 'ĕ·lō·hîm	ABS	noun
לָאוֹר֙ אוֹר	to the light lā·'ôr	ABS W/ PREP לְ + DEF. ART.	noun
י֔וֹם יוֹם	day yôm	ABS	noun

יוֹם most frequently indicates a single or specific day (e.g., "the third day," "on this very day," etc.), especially when paired with a number. In the plural, יוֹם can indicate many days or even years. In this clause, יוֹם describes what seems to be the concept of a "day" as opposed to "night," which is mentioned in the next clause.

5b

וְלַחֹ֖שֶׁךְ קָ֣רָא לָ֑יְלָה

and the darkness he called "Night."

וְלַחֹ֖שֶׁךְ חֹשֶׁךְ	and to the darkness wə·la·ḥō·šek	ABS W/ CONJ וְ + PREP לְ + DEF. ART.	noun
קָ֣רָא קרא	he called/named qā·rā'	QAL PF 3MS	verb
לָ֑יְלָה לַיְלָה	night lāy·lâ	ABS	noun

5c

וַֽיְהִי־עֶ֥רֶב

And it was evening,

וַֽיְהִי־ היה	and it was wa·yə·hî-	QAL WAYY 3MS	verb
עֶ֥רֶב עֶרֶב	evening/dusk 'e·rev	ABS	noun

The sequence of evening first, and then morning, may have some significance—though readers are left to guess what that might be. In some areas of the world (e.g., in many parts of the West), the day "begins" with the morning and ends in the evening, while Jewish tradition (based on this verse) considers a day to begin and end at sunset. The author seems unconcerned with the question of how "day" and "night" or "evening" and "morning" would have any significance without the sun to mark that passing on earth.

5d	וַֽיְהִי־בֹ֖קֶר		
	and it was morning,		
וַֽיְהִי־ היה	and it was wa·yə·hî-	QAL WAYY 3MS	verb
בֹ֖קֶר בֹּקֶר	morning/dawn vō·qer	ABS	noun

5e	י֥וֹם אֶחָֽד׃		
	day one.		
י֥וֹם יוֹם	day yôm	ABS	noun
אֶחָֽד׃ אֶחָד	one 'e·ḥād	ABS	cardinal number

From Text to Sermon

As you meditate on this passage and contemplate
how you might teach or preach it to others,
consider the following areas of emphasis.

 Historical and Literary Context. When thinking about the broader historical and literary context, you might find it helpful to read some of the other creation stories that circulated in ancient Israel. Although doing so may seem counterintuitive, this can be a fascinating way of considering how the biblical account challenged other, competing stories in its historical context—and also how it might challenge us today in a world of confusing and competing narratives about life and its meaning. For example, try reading the Babylonian "Enuma Elish" story, or an Egyptian narrative such as the "Memphite" creation story (both are available in several translations through simple searches online). What themes and plot points do you notice in these other stories? For example, in Enuma Elish, stunning violence and a titanic struggle precede the creation event, and humans are created as an afterthought out of the blood of a dead rebel god—to serve as slaves. How might an early Israelite audience have experienced the narrative of Gen 1 compared to a story like this? Readers might also notice that the Bible has other creation stories, too, some of which emphasize different themes from the ones present in Gen 1 (e.g., note the images of violence associated with creation in Ps 74 and Job 26). Ancient Israelites apparently had many images with which to think about the mystery and grandeur of God's creation; why does the Bible begin, then, exactly with the imagery found in Gen 1?

 Bridge to the Gospel. As a bridge to the preaching of the gospel in the New Testament, notice the repetition of the word "good" in Gen 1. Our word "gospel" derives ultimately from the Greek term *euangelion*, "good news" or "happy proclamation." Sin and human corruption are of course also prominent themes we will find in Gen 1–11, not to mention throughout the Bible. Why begin exactly this way, with this proclamation of the fundamental goodness of creation? Notice also the way that the opening of John 1 quotes (in Greek) the Bible's first phrase, "in the beginning," and later in John (ch. 20) and in Acts 2 God's spirit or wind (compare with God's רוּחַ, "spirit" or "breath" or "wind," in Gen 1:2) changes Jesus' disciples forever.

Some significant Hebrew words in Gen 1 to consider for deeper exploration could include ברא, "create," a verb only used to describe God's creative activity, and the often-repeated terms for "light" (אוֹר), "darkness" (חֹשֶׁךְ), "day" (יוֹם), and "night" (לַיְלָה). Compare, for example, with the way the poet in Ps 139 uses these terms in an intimate manner to speak of personal creation.

 Illustrations. As we think about how to illustrate the themes of Gen 1 with more contemporary literature, we might consider a poem like T. S. Eliot's famous *Four Quartets* and its meditation on how the past and future are woven together. In Isa 40–55, the prophet repeatedly uses the language of creation to talk about *new* creation—specifically, the way God will re-create Israel as a new nation after their painful experience in exile. In the story of the Passover in Exod 12, God tells the Hebrew slaves that they are to reorient time itself, declaring the day of their freedom to be the first day of the year. And at the Bible's conclusion, in the book of Revelation, the language of the Garden of Eden comes back with full force: the tree of life returns, and humans are invited back to the place they once called home. These biblical invocations of creation demand that we always ask: What is God creating in my community today? How can I recognize and affirm God's creative movements in my own life and in the lives of those around me? In film, consider watching Terrence Malick's 2011 *The Tree of Life* and exploring not only the experimental imagery used to show creation but also the dual themes of "law" and "grace" set alongside these creation themes.

GENESIS 1:26–31

THE CREATION OF HUMANS

Although the story of origins in Genesis certainly places the creation of humans alongside of—and subsequent to—the creation of earth itself and other living creatures, the language used in this passage concerning the creation of humans is certainly special. God bursts forth with a poem about men and women and the "image of God," and he orders humans to organize the world in a particular way that invites us to think about our place within nature.

LARGER LITERARY CONTEXT ▸ 1:1–2:3

1:26–28

26a

וַיֹּ֖אמֶר אֱלֹהִ֑ים
wayyōʾmer ʾĕlōhîm

And God said,

26b

נַֽעֲשֶׂ֥ה אָדָ֛ם בְּצַלְמֵ֖נוּ כִּדְמוּתֵ֑נוּ
naʿăśe ʾādām bəṣalmēnû kidmûtēnû

"Let us make humanity in our image, according to our likeness.

26c

וְיִרְדּוּ֩ בִדְגַ֨ת הַיָּ֜ם
wəyirdû vidgat hayyām

And let them rule over the fish of the sea

26d

וּבְע֣וֹף הַשָּׁמַ֗יִם
ûvəʿôf haššāmayim

and over the birds of the air

26e

וּבַבְּהֵמָה֙
ûvabbəhēmâ

and over the beasts

26f

וּבְכָל־הָאָ֔רֶץ
ûvəkol-hāʾāreṣ

and over all the earth

26g

וּבְכָל־הָרֶ֖מֶשׂ הָֽרֹמֵ֥שׂ עַל־הָאָֽרֶץ׃
ûvəkol-hāremeś hārōmēś ʿal-hāʾāreṣ.

and over all the creeping things that creep upon the earth."

27a

וַיִּבְרָ֨א אֱלֹהִ֤ים ׀ אֶת־הָֽאָדָם֙ בְּצַלְמ֔וֹ
wayyivrāʾ ʾĕlōhîm ʾet-hāʾādām bəṣalmô

So God created humanity in his image;

27b	בְּצֶ֥לֶם אֱלֹהִ֖ים בָּרָ֣א אֹת֑וֹ
	bəṣelem ʾĕlōhîm bārāʾ ʾōtô
	in the image of God he created them;
27c	זָכָ֥ר וּנְקֵבָ֖ה בָּרָ֥א אֹתָֽם׃
	zāḵār ûnəqēvâ bārāʾ ʾōtām.
	male and female he created them.
28a	וַיְבָ֣רֶךְ אֹתָם֮ אֱלֹהִים֒
	wayəvāreḵ ʾōtām ʾĕlōhîm
	And God blessed them,
28b	וַיֹּ֨אמֶר לָהֶ֜ם אֱלֹהִ֗ים
	wayyōʾmer lāhem ʾĕlōhîm
	and God said to them,
28c	פְּר֥וּ וּרְב֛וּ
	pərû ûrəvû
	"Be fruitful and multiply
28d	וּמִלְא֥וּ אֶת־הָאָ֖רֶץ
	ûmilʾû ʾet-hāʾāreṣ
	and fill the earth!
28e	וְכִבְשֻׁ֑הָ
	wəḵivšūhā
	Subdue it—
28f	וּרְד֞וּ בִּדְגַ֤ת הַיָּם֙
	ûrədû bidgat hayyām
	and rule over the fish of the sea
28g	וּבְע֣וֹף הַשָּׁמַ֔יִם
	ûvəʿôf haššāmayim
	and over the birds of the air

28h	וּבְכָל־חַיָּה הָרֹמֶשֶׂת עַל־הָאָרֶץ׃
	ûvəkol-ḥayyâ hārōmeśet 'al-hā'āreṣ.
	and over all the living things that creep upon the earth."

26a	וַיֹּאמֶר אֱלֹהִים
	And God said,

וַיֹּאמֶר	and (he) said	QAL WAYY 3MS	verb
אמר	way·yō'·mer		
אֱלֹהִים	God	ABS	noun
אֱלֹהִים	'ĕ·lō·hîm		

26b	נַעֲשֶׂה אָדָם בְּצַלְמֵנוּ כִּדְמוּתֵנוּ
	"Let us make humanity in our image, according to our likeness.

נַעֲשֶׂה	let us make	QAL COHOR⁻ 1CP	verb
עשׂה	na·'ă·śe		
אָדָם	human/humanity/humans/man/person	ABS	noun
אָדָם	'ā·dām		
בְּצַלְמֵנוּ	in our image/crafted image/physical representation	CST W/ PREP בְּ + 1CP SX	noun
צֶלֶם	bə·ṣal·mē·nû		
כִּדְמוּתֵנוּ	according to/as in our likeness/pattern	CST W/ PREP כְּ – 1CP SX	noun
דְּמוּת	kid·mû·tē·nû		

Despite the first-person singular forms used up to this point, אֱלֹהִים now switches to the first-person *plural* form נַעֲשֶׂה. Why? Perhaps we can discern some clue in the term אָדָם, which here must be translated as "humanity" or "humans" (taking the singular as a collective term for a plurality). If אָדָם is a plurality, created in God's image and likeness, then must God also be a plurality of some sort? Indeed, it is important that, however we translate אָדָם, we translate it in a way that is inclusive of both men and women, for we find in v. 27 that clearly more is meant than just a "man" or "men." Moreover, we probably should not translate אָדָם here as "Adam," precisely because of the elaboration of "male and female" in v. 27 (unless one is prepared to take "Adam" as a joint male-female personal name). Granted, the lack of the definite article (הַ-) with אָדָם, in contrast to v. 27's הָאָדָם, could invite some other shade of meaning to the use of אָדָם here—but that shade of meaning seems not to be a personal name. The first time אָדָם is used as a clearly personal name ("Adam") is in Gen 4:25. Up to that point, the phrase הָאָדָם must be translated as "the man" or "humanity," as context dictates (in Hebrew, personal names by rule cannot have the definite article).

The terms צֶלֶם and דְּמוּת, which in English translation ("image" and "likeness") might appear to mean nearly the same thing, have occasioned no small amount of attention. Does the term צֶלֶם refer to a physical image, like a sculpture, and then דְּמוּת to something more personal or spiritual, a "pattern" or "likeness" in some other sense? Perhaps. We know that צֶלֶם is used elsewhere in the Old Testament to refer to physical representations other nations might make of their deities or other associated religious items (e.g., Num 33:52; 1 Sam 6:5; 2 Kgs 11:18). The creation of images of deities was in fact quite common in the Bible's ancient Near Eastern world; the physical image of a god or goddess was viewed as that deity's physical presence on earth—the image participated and shared in the identity of that deity. To steal that image in battle, for example, could be seen as a serious defeat for the deity (or perhaps the deity had voluntarily chosen, in this theology, to allow his/her image to be taken as a punishment). For Israel, all images of the deity were officially forbidden (see Exod 20:1–6; Deut 4–5). Thus, in a potentially surprising move here in the Bible's first chapter, God casts *humans* as his only "image" on earth.

26c	וְיִרְדּוּ בִדְגַת הַיָּם		
	And let them rule over the fish of the sea		
	וְיִרְדּוּ	and let them/may they rule/have dominion	QAL JUSS 3MP W/ CONJ וְ verb
	רדה	wə·yir·dû	

	בִּדְגַת	over (the) fish of	CST	noun
	דָּגָה	vid·gat	W/ PREP בְּ	
	הַיָּם	the seas/waters	ABS	noun
	יָם	hay·yām	W/ DEF. ART.	

The verb רדה is a bold term to describe the human relationship over animals and nature. It can refer to the dominion a king might have over a kingdom (1 Kgs 5:4 [4:24]; Ps 110:2), bosses overseeing conscripted labor (1 Kgs 5:30 [16]), the leadership a priest might exercise in the temple (Jer 5:31), and even the mastery a slave owner has over a slave (Lev 25:43). The tone throughout Gen 1–2 is certainly one of caring responsibility and flourishing—yet humans must be empowered to organize, guard, and take ownership of the world.

26d	וּבְעוֹף הַשָּׁמַיִם			
	and over the birds of the air			
	וּבְעוֹף	and over (the) bird/birds of	CST	noun
	עוֹף	û·vəʿôf	W/ CONJ וְ + PREP בְּ	
	הַשָּׁמַיִם	the heavens/skies/air above	ABS	noun
	שָׁמַיִם	haš·šā·mayim	W/ DEF. ART.	

26e	וּבַבְּהֵמָה			
	and over the beasts			
	וּבַבְּהֵמָה	and over the beasts/animals	ABS	noun
	בְּהֵמָה	û·vab·bə·hē·mâ	W/ CONJ וְ + PREP בְּ + DEF. ART.	

26f	וּבְכָל־הָאָרֶץ			
	and over all the earth			
	וּבְכָל־	and over/in all/ (the) entirety of	CST	noun
	כֹּל	û·və·ḵol-	W/ CONJ וְ + PREP בְּ	

הָאָ֑רֶץ	the earth/land	ABS	noun
אֶרֶץ	hā·'ā·reṣ	W/ DEF. ART.	

26g	וּבְכָל־הָרֶ֖מֶשׂ הָרֹמֵ֥שׂ עַל־הָאָֽרֶץ׃
	and over all the creeping things that creep upon the earth."

וּבְכָל־	and over/in all/(the) entirety of	CST W/ CONJ וְ + PREP בְּ	noun
כֹּל	û·və·ḵol-		
הָרֶ֖מֶשׂ	the creeping/crawling things	ABS W/ DEF. ART.	noun
רֶמֶשׂ	hā·**re**·meś		
הָרֹמֵ֥שׂ	the ones that creep/crawl	QAL PTCP MS W/ DEF. ART.	verb
רמשׂ	hā·rō·**mēś**		
עַל־	upon/on	---	prep
עַל	'al-		
הָאָֽרֶץ׃	the earth/land	ABS W/ DEF. ART.	noun
אֶרֶץ	hā·'ā·reṣ		

Such lengthy lists, repeating all categories and types of animal and environments a person could possibly imagine, show the comprehensive nature of God's domain. The list has a special emphasis on animals; note that trees and mountains, though also surely included in the scope of וּבְכָל־הָאָרֶץ ("and over all the earth," v. 26f), are not specifically mentioned in the way that the fish, birds, "beasts," and creeping things are. One imagines a vibrant living world, teeming with movement, over which humans are to exercise their ability to רדה ("rule, have dominion"). As we will see in the next chapter, humans will till the earth, but perhaps the focus on animals here gestures toward the role of animal husbandry and acknowledges the fact that humans cannot control the weather, seas, or mountains very effectively.

THE CREATION OF HUMANS

27a

וַיִּבְרָ֨א אֱלֹהִ֤ים ׀ אֶת־הָֽאָדָם֙ בְּצַלְמ֔וֹ

So God created humanity in his image;

וַיִּבְרָ֨א ברא	and/so (he) created way·yiv·rā'	QAL WAYY 3MS	verb
אֱלֹהִ֤ים ׀ אלהים	God 'ĕ·lō·hîm	ABS	noun
אֶת־ את	(direct object marker) 'et-	---	particle
הָֽאָדָם֙ אדם	the man/human hā·'ā·dām	ABS W/ DEF. ART.	noun
בְּצַלְמ֔וֹ צלם	in his image/crafted image/ physical representation bə·ṣal·mô	CST W/ PREP בְּ + 3MS SX	noun

27b

בְּצֶ֥לֶם אֱלֹהִ֖ים בָּרָ֥א אֹתֽוֹ

in the image of God he created them;

בְּצֶ֥לֶם צלם	in the image/crafted image/ physical representation of bə·ṣe·lem	CST W/ PREP בְּ	noun
אֱלֹהִ֖ים אלהים	God 'ĕ·lō·hîm	ABS	noun
בָּרָ֥א ברא	he created bā·rā'	QAL PF 3MS	verb
אֹתֽוֹ את	(direct object marker +) him 'ō·tô	--- W/ 3MS SX	particle

Notice the masculine singular pronominal suffix in אֹתוֹ, which grammatically matches the singular אָדָם in v. 26b. See v. 27c immediately below, however—the אָדָם is inherently double, "male and female," as already observed above. To translate "he created *him*," though woodenly correct in Hebrew, would not capture the plain sense of the narrative action. And then in v. 28, the pronoun suffix switches to plural: אֹתָם ("he blessed *them*"). Perhaps through this mixture of the singular and the plural we are to infer a deeper spiritual "oneness" to all humanity that transcends our categories of sex and gender.

27c	זָכָ֥ר וּנְקֵבָ֖ה בָּרָ֥א אֹתָֽם׃
	male and female he created them.

זָכָ֥ר	male	ABS	noun
זָכָר	zā·kār		
וּנְקֵבָ֖ה	and female	ABS	noun
נְקֵבָה	û·nə·qē·vâ	W/ CONJ ו	
בָּרָ֥א	he created	QAL PF 3MS	verb
ברא	bā·rā'		
אֹתָֽם׃	(direct object marker +) them	---	particle
אֵת	'ō·tām	W/ 3MP SX	

The terms זָכָר and נְקֵבָה seem to refer particularly to physical sex.

The poem in v. 27 has a balanced structure and puts special emphasis on humans and the "image" relationship, repeated twice in the poem:

> So God created humanity in his image;
> > in the image of God he created them;
> > > male and female he created them.

In fact, we find short poems like this embedded within larger structures throughout Gen 1–11 (see also 2:23; 4:23–24; 9:6–7; and a longer example in 3:14–19).

28a	וַיְבָ֣רֶךְ אֹתָם֮ אֱלֹהִים֒
	And God blessed them,

וַיְבָ֣רֶךְ	and (he) blessed	PIEL WAYY 3MS	verb
ברך	wa·yə·vā·rek		
אֹתָם֮	(direct object marker +) them	---	particle
אֵת	'ō·tām	W/ 3MP SX	
אֱלֹהִים֒	God	ABS	noun
אֱלֹהִים	'ĕ·lō·hîm		

This is not the first "blessing" in the Bible, and it is not reserved for humans alone—God blesses (ברך) the fish and birds in v. 22. As a blessing upon humans, combined with the command to multiply, וַיְבָ֣רֶךְ in this verse foreshadows the use of ברך as a keyword in the call of Abraham in Gen 12:1–3.

THE CREATION OF HUMANS

28b

	וַיֹּאמֶר לָהֶם אֱלֹהִים		
	and God said to them,		
וַיֹּאמֶר אמר	and (he) said way·yōʾ·mer	QAL WAYY 3MS	verb
לָהֶם לְ	to them lā·hem	--- W/ 3MP SX	prep
אֱלֹהִים אֱלֹהִים	God ʾĕ·lō·hîm	ABS	noun

28c

	פְּרוּ וּרְבוּ		
	"Be fruitful and multiply		
פְּרוּ פרה	bear fruit/be fruitful pə·rû	QAL IMPV MP	verb
וּרְבוּ רבה	and be many/multiply û·rə·vû	QAL IMPV MP W/ CONJ וְ	verb

The command here to "be fruitful" parallels the command to the fish in v. 22. Though God's act of creation by speech is something God alone does, the emphasis moves to the power within creation itself to extend the story beyond the initial seven-day frame we find in Gen 1. Indeed, God repeats the "be fruitful" command, using this same verb פרה, throughout the flood narrative (8:17; 9:1, 7), and this specific language of fruitfulness resounds throughout the stories of the ancestors and God's promise that they will have numerous descendants (17:6, 20; 26:22; 28:3; 35:11; 41:27; 48:4). פרה also describes plant growth (e.g., Isa 11:1 and Ps 128:3, both of which employ plant metaphors to talk about human flourishing).

28d

	וּמִלְאוּ אֶת־הָאָרֶץ		
	and fill the earth!		
וּמִלְאוּ מלא	and fill û·mil·ʾû	QAL IMPV MP W/ CONJ וְ	verb
אֶת־ אֵת	(direct object marker) ʾet-	---	particle

| הָאָרֶץ | the earth/land | ABS | noun |
| אֶרֶץ | hā·'ā·reṣ | W/ DEF. ART. | |

28e וְכִבְשֻׁהָ

Subdue it—

| וְכִבְשֻׁהָ | and subdue/subjugate it | QAL IMPV MP | verb |
| כבשׁ | wə·ḵiv·šu·hā | W/ CONJ וְ + 3FS SX | |

In v. 26, humans have already been given the command to "rule over" (רדה) fish, birds, beasts, and the entire earth. Here God introduces a new term, כבשׁ, with a semantic range similar to that of רדה, again with stark usage elsewhere in the Bible to describe subduing a land through warfare (Num 32:22; Josh 18:1; 2 Sam 8:11) and subjugating slaves (Jer 34:11, 16; Neh 5:5; 2 Chr 28:10). Translators must, however, be careful to avoid what the Hebrew linguist James Barr termed "illegitimate totality transfer," that is to say, assuming any given word could or must bear any of its possible meanings in any given circumstance (Barr 1961). In this instance, for example, we would not want to rush to assume that because verbs like כבשׁ and רדה describe slavery in some contexts, they must be understood with explicit reference to slavery here in this verse. Careful consideration of context and the range of meanings a word can have, combined with deeper study as needed, will usually help steer us toward faithful results.

28f וּרְדוּ בִּדְגַת הַיָּם

and rule over the fish of the sea

וּרְדוּ	and rule/have dominion	QAL IMPV MP	verb
רדה	û·rə·dû	W/ CONJ וְ	
בִּדְגַת	over (the) fish of	CST	noun
דָּגָה	biḏ·ḡat	W/ PREP בְּ	
הַיָּם	the seas/waters	ABS	noun
יָם	hay·yām	W/ DEF. ART.	

See comments above on רדה at v. 26c.

28g

	וּבְע֣וֹף הַשָּׁמַ֔יִם	
	and over the birds of the air	
וּבְע֣וֹף	and over (the) bird/birds of	CST W/ CONJ וְ + PREP בְּ — noun
ע֣וֹף	û·və·'ôf	
הַשָּׁמַ֔יִם	the heavens/skies/air above	ABS W/ DEF. ART. — noun
שָׁמַיִם	haš·šā·**mayim**	

28h

	וּבְכָל־חַיָּ֥ה הָֽרֹמֶ֖שֶׂת עַל־הָאָֽרֶץ׃	
	and over all the living things that creep upon the earth."	
וּבְכָל־	and over/in all/(the) entirety of	CST W/ CONJ וְ + PREP בְּ — noun
כֹּל	û·və·ḵol-	
חַיָּ֥ה	(the) animal(s)/beast(s)/ living thing(s)	ABS — noun
חַיָּה	ḥay·yâ	
הָֽרֹמֶ֖שֶׂת	the (ones) that creep/crawl	QAL PTCP FS W/ DEF. ART. — verb
רמשׂ	hā·rō·**me**·śet	
עַל־	upon/on	--- prep
עַל	'al-	
הָאָֽרֶץ׃	the earth/land	ABS W/ DEF. ART. — noun
אֶרֶץ	hā·'ā·reṣ	

1:29–30

29a
וַיֹּאמֶר אֱלֹהִים
wayyōʾmer ʾĕlōhîm

Then God said,

29b
הִנֵּה נָתַתִּי לָכֶם אֶת־כָּל־עֵשֶׂב ׀ זֹרֵעַ זֶרַע
hinnē nātattî lākem ʾet-kol-ʿēśev zōrēaʿ zeraʿ

"See, I have given you every green thing sprouting seeds

29c
אֲשֶׁר עַל־פְּנֵי כָל־הָאָרֶץ
ʾăšer ʿal-pənê kol-hāʾāreṣ

that is upon the face of all the earth,

29d
וְאֶת־כָּל־הָעֵץ אֲשֶׁר־בּוֹ פְרִי־עֵץ זֹרֵעַ זָרַע
wəʾet-kol-hāʿēṣ ʾăšer-bô fərî-ʿēṣ zōrēaʿ zāraʿ

and every tree that has the fruit of the tree in it, sprouting seeds—

29e
לָכֶם יִהְיֶה לְאָכְלָה׃
lākem yihye ləʾoklâ.

it is for you, for food.

30a
וּלְכָל־חַיַּת הָאָרֶץ
ûləkol-ḥayyat hāʾāreṣ

And to every living thing of the earth,

30b
וּלְכָל־עוֹף הַשָּׁמַיִם
ûləkol-ʿôf haššāmayim

and to every bird of the air,

30c
וּלְכֹל ׀ רוֹמֵשׂ עַל־הָאָרֶץ
ûləkōl rômēś ʿal-hāʾāreṣ

and to everything that creeps upon the earth

30d	אֲשֶׁר־בּוֹ נֶפֶשׁ חַיָּה
	ʾăšer-**bô** nefeš ḥayyâ

that has the breath of life in it—

30e	אֶת־כָּל־יֶרֶק עֵשֶׂב לְאָכְלָה
	ʾet-kol-yereq ʿēśev ləʾoḵlâ

every piece of green vegetation as food.

30f	וַיְהִי־כֵן׃
	wayəhî-**ḵēn**.

And it was so.

29a	וַיֹּאמֶר אֱלֹהִים

Then God said,

וַיֹּאמֶר	and (he) said	QAL WAYY 3MS	verb
אמר	way·**yō**ʾ·mer		
אֱלֹהִים	God	ABS	noun
אֱלֹהִים	ʾĕ·lō·**hîm**		

29b	הִנֵּה נָתַתִּי לָכֶם אֶת־כָּל־עֵשֶׂב ׀ זֹרֵעַ זֶרַע

"See, I have given you every green thing sprouting seeds

הִנֵּה	see/look/behold	---	particle
הִנֵּה	hin·**nē**		
נָתַתִּי	I give/have given	QAL PF 1CS	verb
נתן	nā·**tat**·tî		
לָכֶם	to you	---	prep
ל	lā·**ḵem**	W/ 2MP SX	
אֶת־	(direct object marker)	---	particle
אֵת	ʾet-		

כָּל־	all/all of/every	CST	noun
כֹּל	kol-		
עֵ֫שֶׂב ׀	green thing/shrub/grass/vegetation	ABS	noun
עֵ֫שֶׂב	'ē·śev		
זֹרֵ֫עַ	sowing/sprouting/yielding	QAL PTCP MS	verb
זרע	zō·rē·a'		
זֶ֫רַע	seed	ABS	noun
זֶ֫רַע	ze·ra'		

29c — אֲשֶׁר֙ עַל־פְּנֵי כָל־הָאָ֑רֶץ

that is upon the face of all the earth,

אֲשֶׁר֙	that/which	---	relative pron
אֲשֶׁר	'ă·šer		
עַל־	upon/on	---	prep
עַל	'al-		
פְּנֵי	(the) face/surface of	CST	noun
פָּנֶה	pə·nê		
כָל־	all/(the) entirety of	CST	noun
כֹּל	kol-		
הָאָ֫רֶץ	the earth/land	ABS W/ DEF. ART.	noun
אֶ֫רֶץ	hā·'ā·reṣ		

29d — וְאֶת־כָּל־הָעֵ֛ץ אֲשֶׁר־בּ֥וֹ פְרִי־עֵ֖ץ זֹרֵ֣עַ זָ֑רַע

and every tree that has the fruit of the tree in it, sprouting seeds—

וְאֶת־	and (+ direct object marker)	--- W/ CONJ וְ	particle
אֵת	wə·et		
כָּל־	all/all of/every	CST	noun
כֹּל	kol-		
הָעֵץ	the tree/trees	ABS W/ DEF. ART.	noun
עֵץ	hā·'ēṣ		

THE CREATION OF HUMANS

אֲשֶׁר־ אֲשֶׁר	that/which 'ă·šer-	---	relative pron
בּוֹ בְּ	in/within/upon it bô	--- W/ 3MS SX	prep
פְּרִי־ פְּרִי	fruit of fə·rî-	CST	noun
עֵץ עֵץ	tree 'ēṣ	ABS	noun
זֹרֵעַ זרע	sowing/sprouting/yielding zō·rē·a'	QAL PTCP MS	verb
זֶרַע זֶרַע	seed zā·ra'	ABS	noun

The narrator repeats this concept of trees having their own seeds in them, both here and earlier on the third day of creation (1:9–13), in a way that could mark a point of emphasis. God has imbued nature with a mechanism for its own reproduction: the day-to-day growth of plants does not rely on divine capriciousness or any vegetative rituals dedicated to fertility deities. Rather, it is a "built-in" feature, given over to the care and use of humans.

29e	לָכֶם יִהְיֶה לְאָכְלָה:		
	it is for you, for food.		
לָכֶם לְ	to/for you lā·ḵem	--- W/ 2MP SX	prep
יִהְיֶה היה	it will be yih·ye	QAL IMPF 3MS	verb
לְאָכְלָה: אָכְלָה	as/for food/sustenance lə·'oḵ·lâ	ABS W/ PREP לְ	noun

30a	וּלְכָל־חַיַּת הָאָרֶץ		
	And to every living thing of the earth,		
וּלְכָל־ כֹּל	and to/for every/each/all û·lə·ḵol-	CST W/ CONJ וְ + PREP לְ	noun

חַיַּת חַיָּה	animal/beast/living thing of ḥay·yat	CST	noun
הָאָרֶץ אֶרֶץ	the earth/land hā·'ā·reṣ	ABS W/ DEF. ART.	noun

30b וּלְכָל־עוֹף הַשָּׁמַיִם

and to every bird of the air,

וּלְכָל־ כֹּל	and to/for every/each/all û·lə·ḵol-	CST W/ CONJ וְ + PREP לְ	noun
עוֹף עוֹף	bird/birds of 'ôf	CST	noun
הַשָּׁמַיִם שָׁמַיִם	the heavens/skies/air above haš·šā·*mayim*	ABS W/ DEF. ART.	noun

30c וּלְכֹל ׀ רוֹמֵשׂ עַל־הָאָרֶץ

and to everything that creeps upon the earth

וּלְכֹל ׀ כֹּל	and to/for every/each/all û·lə·ḵōl	CST W/ CONJ וְ + PREP לְ	noun
רוֹמֵשׂ רמשׂ	one that creeps/crawls rô·*mēś*	QAL PTCP MS	verb
עַל־ עַל	upon/on 'al-	---	prep
הָאָרֶץ אֶרֶץ	the earth/land hā·'ā·reṣ	ABS W/ DEF. ART.	noun

30d אֲשֶׁר־בּוֹ נֶפֶשׁ חַיָּה

that has the breath of life in it—

אֲשֶׁר־ אֲשֶׁר	that/which 'ă·šer-	---	relative pron

THE CREATION OF HUMANS

בּוֹ בְּ	in/upon it bô	--- W/ 3MS SX	prep
נֶ֫פֶשׁ נֶ֫פֶשׁ	breath/life/soul ne·feš	ABS	noun
חַיָּה חַי	living/alive ḥay·yâ	FS ATTR	adj

The phrase נֶ֫פֶשׁ חַיָּה literally means "living breath/life/soul," or perhaps (if חַיָּה is understood as a substantive) "breath/life/soul of a living thing." The English idiom "breath of life" conveys the sense well.

30e	אֶת־כָּל־יֶ֫רֶק עֵ֫שֶׂב לְאָכְלָה		
	every piece of green vegetation as food.		
אֶת־ אֵת	*(direct object marker)* ʾet-	---	particle
כָּל־ כֹּל	every/each/all kol-	CST	noun
יֶ֫רֶק יֶ֫רֶק	herb/green/greenery of ye·req	CST	noun
עֵ֫שֶׂב עֵ֫שֶׂב	green thing/shrub/grass/vegetation ʿē·śev	ABS	noun
לְאָכְלָה אָכְלָה	as/for food/sustenance lə·ʾok̲·lâ	ABS W/ PREP לְ	noun

In this final phrase of v. 30, the verb נָתַ֫תִּי ("I have given") from v. 29 is implied—that is, "[*I have given*] every piece of green vegetation as food" to all the creatures previously mentioned in v. 30. (Most translations supply this verb here in v. 30 to make this clear.) The effect of grouping humans, birds, and other animals together under this provision of food shows all living things in a state of receiving God's gift of sustenance. This food is explicitly plant life (marked by several different terms for plants and green things), and notably not meat acquired by way of predation or scavenging. (See also the commentary below on ch. 9.)

30f	וַיְהִי־כֵֽן׃
	And it was so.

וַיְהִי־	and it was	QAL WAYY 3MS	verb
היה	wa·yə·hî-		
כֵֽן׃	so/thus	---	adv
כֵּן	kēn		

This short phrase encodes a simple and profound message about God's power. God's declarations are followed by no drama, no discussion, and no opposition. It was so.

1:31

31a וַיַּ֤רְא אֱלֹהִים֙ אֶת־כָּל־אֲשֶׁ֣ר עָשָׂ֔ה
wayyar' 'ĕlōhîm 'et-kol-'ăšer 'āśâ
And God saw all that he did—

31b וְהִנֵּה־ט֖וֹב מְאֹ֑ד
wəhinnē-ṭôv mə'ōd
indeed, it was very good.

31c וַֽיְהִי־עֶ֥רֶב
wayəhî-'erev
And it was evening,

31d וַֽיְהִי־בֹ֖קֶר
wayəhî-vōqer
and it was morning,

31e י֥וֹם הַשִּׁשִּֽׁי׃
yôm haššiššî.
day six.

31a	וַיַּרְא אֱלֹהִים אֶת־כָּל־אֲשֶׁר עָשָׂה		
	And God saw all that he did—		
וַיַּרְא	and (he) saw	QAL WAYY 3MS	verb
ראה	*way·yar'*		
אֱלֹהִים	God	ABS	noun
אֱלֹהִים	*'ĕ·lō·hîm*		
אֶת־	(direct object marker)	---	particle
אֵת	*'et-*		

כָּל־ kol-	all/everything	ABS	noun
אֲשֶׁר 'ă·šer-	that which	---	relative pron
עָשָׂה 'ā·śâ	he made/did	QAL PF 3MS	verb

The phrase "God saw" (וַיַּרְא אֱלֹהִים) is a key concept in Gen 1–11; God does not create and turn away, but rather creates and sees—and continues seeing. This final seeing on the sixth day includes the proclamation (in the next phrase in this verse) that creation is not only "good" but, in summation of the chapter, "*very* good."

31b — וְהִנֵּה־טוֹב מְאֹד

indeed, it was very good.

וְהִנֵּה־ wə·hin·nē-	and see/look/behold	W/ CONJ וְ	particle
טוֹב ṭôv	good	MS PRED	adj
מְאֹד mə·'ōd	very	---	adv

In older translations, הִנֵּה was often rendered "behold," drawing attention (as the Hebrew term most often does) to the "hereness and nowness" of what follows. In the classical Hebrew of Genesis and in much other biblical Hebrew prose, הִנֵּה can function much like the interjection "look" or "right" currently functions in English; e.g., "*Look*, I want to tell you what I think . . . ," or "I'm thinking about all of this, *right*, and I've come to the conclusion that . . ." The challenge for the contemporary translator—as with all language—is to consider how the term is used in context and to render it in an artful way. With הִנֵּה, sometimes this can be done through the leading word "look," or even "here." At other times, one can use "indeed." And in some cases (or for some translators, in nearly all cases), the term can be omitted.

31c	וַיְהִי־עֶרֶב
	And it was evening,

	וַיְהִי־	and it was	QAL WAYY 3MS	verb
	היה	wa·yə·hî-		
	עֶרֶב	evening/dusk	ABS	noun
	עֶרֶב	'e·rev		

31d	וַיְהִי־בֹקֶר
	and it was morning,

	וַיְהִי־	and it was	QAL WAYY 3MS	verb
	היה	wa·yə·hî-		
	בֹקֶר	morning/dawn	ABS	noun
	בֹּקֶר	vō·qer		

31e	יוֹם הַשִּׁשִּׁי:
	day six.

	יוֹם	day	ABS	noun
	יוֹם	yôm		
	הַשִּׁשִּׁי:	the sixth	---	ordinal
	שִׁשִּׁי	haš·šiš·šî	W/ DEF. ART.	number

From Text to Sermon

*As you meditate on this passage and contemplate
how you might teach or preach it to others,
consider the following areas of emphasis.*

 Historical and Literary Context. Notice two other specific places in Gen 1–11 where the affirmation of human identity as being in God's "image" and "likeness" appears: in Gen 5:1, God redeclares human identity in his likeness (דְּמוּת) directly after "the fall" in ch. 3 and the first murder in ch. 4, and Gen 9:6 redeclares the image (צֶלֶם) after the horrible destruction of the flood. In the latter case, the narrator cites the image of God as the basis for the "reckoning" that must be paid if one person kills another. God radically owns his creative decision, even in the face of the worst humanity has to offer. How might Christians predicate their engagement with all issues of justice on this profound truth of human identity in the image of God?

Even though no explicit distinction between "right and wrong" has yet been introduced at this point in the narrative, and no commands have been given from Mount Sinai, we find the spark of a moral world alive and well already in the Bible's first chapter—even beyond the implications of the *imago Dei*. Humans are asked to "rule over" and "subdue" the animal world (vv. 26, 28). This position requires enormous responsibility and suggests a relationship of mutual dependency and care. God then blesses humanity and offers the first explicit command to humans, in the imperative grammatical form: "Be fruitful and multiply and fill the earth" (v. 28). Think about how such a primal command invites us to consider what our task is today on this front, and also what other primal, simple commands God has given us. The language of "blessing," combined with the imperative to "be fruitful," echoes forward into the refilling of the earth after Noah (Gen 9:1, 7) and God's choice of Abraham and Sarah and the other ancestors in Gen 12–50 (e.g., Gen 12:1–3; 17:6; 28:3; 35:11). Moreover, notice how the prophet Jeremiah echoes the same phrase "be fruitful and multiply" in Jer 23:3 to speak of return and the reestablishment of the land after the Babylonian destruction and exile in the sixth century BCE. Here we have occasion to meditate upon how, in the biblical vision, creation is not merely about the past. Creation is an *ongoing reality*. Creation predicts our future.

❦ *Bridge to the Gospel.* Christians look to Jesus as our model for what it looks like to live a life that fully shows God's image to the world. Deliberately invoking the language of creation, Paul puts it this way in 2 Cor 4:4–6: Jesus Christ is

> the image [Greek: *eikōn*] of God. . . . For it is the God who said, "Light will shine out of darkness," who has shone in our hearts to give the light of the knowledge of the glory of God in the face of Christ. (NRSVue)

Jesus reached out and literally touched the blind, the skin-diseased, the deaf, and those whose mental state or political situation put them outside the bounds of polite company. Failure to follow Jesus' example in this regard puts us out of compliance with Scripture's first and perhaps most profound statement on human identity, the one found in Gen 1:26–27.

The emphasis on food—not just for humans, but for all animal life—in vv. 29–30, preceding the final pronouncement that all God's work was "very good," focuses our attention on the primal cycle of life in which we participate. To be sure, Christian ethics around "table fellowship" address the core of human community—when we eat together, we can understand and love each other more fully. Eating together was a mark of early Christian community, as portrayed in the book of Acts and referenced in the letters of Paul. Jesus modeled this practice when he shared food as a method of teaching and as an act of love (Mark 2:13–17). In what ways do we participate in the goodness of creation and follow Jesus' practice when we share our food, our homes, and our resources with others?

 Illustrations. As we consider how to illustrate the themes of Gen 1 within our contemporary world, we can think about this situation of being created in "God's image" in terms of the many attempts our media, corporations, politicians, and marketing campaigns make to re-form us into their image. Which of these image-making attempts around us honor the God who created the world—and which do not? How will we know the difference?

Consider also the significance of humanity's image-bearing connection to God for the way that we treat one another. As a prayer experiment, for example, we might call to mind the faces of selected people we know—not only the faces of those we love, those we find beautiful and friendly and kind, but also . . . others. Those we despise. Those we find "ugly" in every sense. Those who oppose us at work, in the political arena, or in our daily relations. World leaders. Family members. Celebrities. Criminals. Every ability and disability. *All of these are made in God's*

image. Acknowledging this profound truth does not mean that they (or we) do not sin, nor does it mean we must approve of everyone's actions. However, it does mean that we must all look at one another in the light of God's creation, God's goodness, and our innate, always-present function as image-bearers on earth. In a politically divided world, this radical declaration in the Bible's first book has the power to make any of us uncomfortable at the possibilities.

GENESIS 2:1–3

THE SABBATH

The formal creation narrative ends not with the creation of humans on the sixth day, but rather with the seventh day—the Sabbath. God rests and blesses the work he has completed, adding a crowning achievement to creation and instituting the formal pattern of the seven-day week.

LARGER LITERARY CONTEXT ▸ 1:1–2:3

2:1–2

1 וַיְכֻלּ֛וּ הַשָּׁמַ֥יִם וְהָאָ֖רֶץ וְכָל־צְבָאָֽם׃
wayəkullû haššāmayim wəhā'āreṣ wəkol-ṣəvā'ām.

**Then the heavens and the earth
and all their host were completed.**

2a וַיְכַ֤ל אֱלֹהִים֙ בַּיּ֣וֹם הַשְּׁבִיעִ֔י
wayəkal 'ĕlōhîm bayyôm haššəvî'î

So God completed on the seventh day

2b מְלַאכְתּ֖וֹ אֲשֶׁ֣ר עָשָׂ֑ה
məla'ktô 'ăšer 'āśâ

his work that he did.

2c וַיִּשְׁבֹּת֙ בַּיּ֣וֹם הַשְּׁבִיעִ֔י
wayyišbōt bayyôm haššəvî'î

And he rested on the seventh day

2d מִכָּל־מְלַאכְתּ֖וֹ אֲשֶׁ֥ר עָשָֽׂה׃
mikkol-məla'ktô 'ăšer 'āśâ.

from all his work that he did.

1	וַיְכֻלּ֛וּ הַשָּׁמַ֥יִם וְהָאָ֖רֶץ וְכָל־צְבָאָֽם׃
	Then the heavens and the earth and all their host were completed.

וַיְכֻלּ֛וּ	and (they) were finished/completed	PUAL WAYY 3MP	verb
כלה	*wa·yə·kul·lû*		

הַשָּׁמַ֖יִם šā·mayim	the heavens/skies/air above haš·šā·mayim	ABS W/ DEF. ART.	noun
וְהָאָ֑רֶץ 'ā·reṣ	and the earth wə·hā·'ā·reṣ	ABS W/ CONJ וְ + DEF. ART.	noun
וְכָל־ kōl	and all of wə·kol-	CST W/ CONJ וְ	noun
צְבָאָֽם׃ ṣā·ḇā	their host/army/unit ṣə·ḇā·'ām	CST W/ 3MP SX	noun

The word צְבָא, here translated "host," is noteworthy in that it is most often associated with a *military* host (i.e., an army). Why refer to all that falls under the rubric of "the heavens and the earth" as an army here? Perhaps צְבָא was a figure of speech in the ancient Israelite world, similar to how in English we might say something like, "Yes, you're invited—you and your whole crew," where "crew," which etymologically may refer to a military detachment of reinforcements, has come to mean "those with you" more generally. Thus, צְבָא indicates the totality of things that come along with the heavens and earth. Still, צְבָא gives creation an embodied, personified sense—God orchestrates a host of powerful characters to act on his behalf.

2a	וַיְכַ֤ל אֱלֹהִים֙ בַּיּ֣וֹם הַשְּׁבִיעִ֔י
	So God completed on the seventh day

וַיְכַ֤ל כלה	and (he) finished/completed wa·yə·kal	PIEL WAYY 3MS	verb
אֱלֹהִים֙ אֱלֹהִים	God 'ĕ·lō·hîm	ABS	noun
בַּיּ֣וֹם יוֹם	on the day bay·yôm	ABS W/ PREP בְּ + DEF. ART.	noun
הַשְּׁבִיעִ֔י שְׁבִיעִי	the seventh haš·šə·vî·'î	--- W/ DEF. ART.	ordinal number

THE SABBATH

2b	מְלַאכְתּוֹ אֲשֶׁר עָשָׂה
	his work that he did.

מְלַאכְתּוֹ	his work	CST W/ 3MS SX	noun
מְלָאכָה	*məlak̲·tô*		
אֲשֶׁר	that/which	---	relative pron
אֲשֶׁר	*'ă·šer*		
עָשָׂה	he did/acted/made	QAL PF 3MS	verb
עשׂה	*'ā·śâ*		

2c	וַיִּשְׁבֹּת בַּיּוֹם הַשְּׁבִיעִי
	And he rested on the seventh day

וַיִּשְׁבֹּת	and he stopped/ceased/rested	QAL WAYY 3MS	verb
שׁבת	*way·yiš·bōt*		
בַּיּוֹם	on the day	ABS W/ PREP בְּ + DEF. ART.	noun
יוֹם	*bay·yôm*		
הַשְּׁבִיעִי	the seventh	--- W/ DEF. ART.	ordinal number
שְׁבִיעִי	*haš·šə·vî·'î*		

The verb שׁבת here, for "rested" (i.e., "stopped, ceased"), is the basis for the term שַׁבָּת, "Sabbath." The text here does not explicitly declare a "Sabbath," with rules and consequences, as first appears in the Ten Commandments (Exod 20:9–10; Deut 5:13–14). Even before those commandments are specified, however, we do find Israel engaged in a formal Sabbath practice (by name) in the story of gathering manna in Exod 16. Why rest or stop on this seventh day? Why should God rest or stop at all? The text does not say; it only tells us that God does this, thus setting up the pattern of the week of work, culminating in rest. Leviticus 23 also features a seven-day pattern for certain ritual observances in addition to the Sabbath pattern (see also Num 28–29).

2d	מִכָּל־מְלַאכְתּוֹ אֲשֶׁר עָשָׂה:		
	from all his work that he did.		
מִכָּל־ כֹּל *mik·kol-*	from all of	CST W/ PREP מִן	noun
מְלַאכְתּוֹ מְלָאכָה *mə·laḵ·tô*	his work	CST W/ 3MS SX	noun
אֲשֶׁר אֲשֶׁר *ʾă·šer*	that/which	---	relative pron
עָשָׂה: עשׂה *ʿā·śâ*	he did/acted/made	QAL PF 3MS	verb

God's activity is only rarely referred to by means of this precise term, מְלָאכָה, "work" (perhaps the only other case is Jer 50:25). This does not need to imply, of course, that God does not continue to do things throughout Scripture, but the use of this term here does highlight God's activity during the seven-day creation event in a special way. Throughout the Old Testament, we find clusters of the term מְלָאכָה appearing in passages devoted to the "work" of worship in designated holy places—the tabernacle (Exod 35–36) and the temple (1 Kgs 7; 1 Chr 28–29)—and, additionally, for the work of building the wall around Jerusalem in the book of Nehemiah (esp. in ch. 6).

2:3

3a וַיְבָ֤רֶךְ אֱלֹהִים֙ אֶת־י֣וֹם הַשְּׁבִיעִ֔י
wayəvārek ʾĕlōhîm ʾet-yôm haššəvîʿî
So God blessed the seventh day

3b וַיְקַדֵּ֖שׁ אֹת֑וֹ
wayəqaddēš ʾōtô
and made it holy,

3c כִּ֣י ב֤וֹ שָׁבַת֙ מִכָּל־מְלַאכְתּ֔וֹ
kî vô šāvat mikkol-məlaʾktô
for on it he rested from all his work

3d אֲשֶׁר־בָּרָ֥א אֱלֹהִ֖ים לַעֲשֽׂוֹת׃
ʾăšer-bārāʾ ʾĕlōhîm laʿăśôt.
of creation that he did
[lit., that God created by doing].

3a	וַיְבָ֤רֶךְ אֱלֹהִים֙ אֶת־י֣וֹם הַשְּׁבִיעִ֔י		
	So God blessed the seventh day		
	וַיְבָ֤רֶךְ ברך	and (he) blessed *wa·yə·vā·rek*	PIEL WAYY 3.MS	verb
	אֱלֹהִים֙ אֱלֹהִים	God *ʾĕ·lō·hîm*	ABS	noun
	אֶת־ אֵת	*(direct object marker)* *ʾet-*	---	particle
	י֣וֹם יוֹם	day *yôm*	ABS	noun

הַשְּׁבִיעִי šəbîʿî	the seventh haš·šə·vî·ʾî	--- W/ DEF. ART.	ordinal number

Scripture now reveals God's third blessing—the first was for sea creatures and birds (1:22), the second was for humans (1:28), and now the third is for the Sabbath day itself. In fact, analysis of the approximately three hundred uses of the term ברך ("bless") throughout not only Genesis but also the entirety of the Old Testament shows that this is the only place where ברך is used to bless a day (note, however, Jer 20:14, where the speaker wishes that a day *not* be blessed). The object of the verb ברך is overwhelmingly either people (individuals, families, nations) or God, and then only occasionally objects, land, work, or sacrifices (e.g., Deut 28:5; 33:13; 1 Sam 9:13; Job 1:10; Prov 20:21).

3b	וַיְקַדֵּשׁ אֹתוֹ		
	and made it holy,		
	וַיְקַדֵּשׁ and he consecrated/ made holy קדשׁ wa·yə·qad·dēš	PIEL WAYY 3MS	verb
	אֹתוֹ (*direct object marker +*) it אֵת ʾō·tô	--- W/ 3MS SX	particle

The term קדשׁ frequently appears in the Old Testament to speak of consecration, but this is the term's only appearance in Genesis. The act of making things holy plays a prominent ritual role in Exodus, Leviticus, and Numbers, and for this reason many scholars have connected the institution of the Sabbath here to the priestly codes and ritual formulations that come later in the Torah. Indeed, some have speculated that Gen 1–2 may have played a formal role—perhaps through recitation, singing, or other enactment—in a weekly Sabbath ritual in the temple.

3c	כִּי בוֹ שָׁבַת מִכָּל־מְלַאכְתּוֹ		
	for on it he rested from all his work		
	כִּי for/because/since כִּי kî	---	conj

בוֹ בְּ	on it/in it vô	--- W/ 3MS SX	prep
שָׁבַת֙ שבת	he stopped/ceased šā·vat	QAL PF 3MS	verb
מִכָּל־ כֹּל	from all/(the) entirety of mik·kol-	CST W/ PREP מִן	noun
מְלַאכְתּ֖וֹ מְלָאכָה	his work məlaḵ·tô	CST W/ 3MS SX	noun

3d אֲשֶׁר־בָּרָ֥א אֱלֹהִ֖ים לַעֲשֽׂוֹת׃

of creation that he did
[lit., that God created by doing].

אֲשֶׁר־ אֲשֶׁר	that/which ʾă·šer-	---	relative pron
בָּרָ֥א ברא	(he) created bā·rāʾ	QAL PF 3MS	verb
אֱלֹהִ֖ים אֱלֹהִים	God ʾĕ·lō·hîm	ABS	noun
לַעֲשֽׂוֹת׃ עשׂה	to do/act/make la·ʿă·śôt	QAL INF CST W/ PREP לְ	verb

From Text to Sermon

*As you meditate on this passage and contemplate
how you might teach or preach it to others,
consider the following areas of emphasis.*

 Historical and Literary Context. Examine Scripture to find other passages in the Old Testament that deal with the Sabbath. As we read beyond Genesis, we find a stunning and even sobering truth: God takes the Sabbath *very* seriously. In God's first declaration of law from Mount Sinai, the "Ten Commandments" (Exod 20), God includes a command about the Sabbath: no living thing—not even cattle, foreigners residing in the land, or slaves—is to do any work. Later in Exodus (31:14–15; 35:2), God repeats the Sabbath command and clarifies the penalty for disobedience: death. Numbers 15:32–36 narrates a story of a man found merely gathering sticks, presumably for a fire, on the Sabbath. His penalty? He is stoned to death. Even in Old Testament texts where authors do not invoke the death penalty as the Torah does, the importance of the Sabbath is still crucial, such as in the prophets Jeremiah (17:21–27) and Isaiah (56:6; 58:13–14). Isaiah in particular offers Sabbath observance as something that anyone can do to please God:

> If you refrain from trampling the Sabbath, from pursuing your own interests on my holy day; if you call the Sabbath a delight and the holy day of the LORD honorable; if you honor it, not going your own ways, serving your own interests or pursuing your own affairs; then you shall take delight in the LORD, and I will make you ride upon the heights of the earth.
>
> (Isa 58:13–14 NRSVue)

 Bridge to the Gospel. We find in the New Testament not an abolishment of the Sabbath but a reframing and a refocusing by Jesus of the Sabbath's purpose. In a central passage on this topic in the Gospel of Mark (2:23–3:6), Jesus debates with Pharisees who accuse the disciples of violating the Sabbath by picking pieces of grain from a field. Jesus tells them that "the Sabbath was made for humankind and not humankind for the Sabbath" (NRSVue). In other words, Jesus claims, the Sabbath was instituted by God for the benefit of people—to give rest and sustenance from the weariness of the workweek. Later in the passage, Jesus heals a man's withered hand on the Sabbath, asking, "Is it lawful to do good or to do harm on the Sabbath, to save life or to kill?" (NRSVue). This observation comports well with the reason given for the Sabbath in the slight restatement of the Ten Commandments found in Deut 5. Here, God gives an explanation for Sabbath observance that is different from what we find in Exod 20, where the creation pattern is cited. In Deuteronomy, the observation of the Sabbath comes with a memory: "Remember that you were a slave in the land of Egypt" (Deut 5:15 NRSVue).

 Relevance for Today. As we think about how to further understand the Sabbath in our own world, consider the fact that nature provides no exact mathematical rationale for the cycle of the seven-day week as a unit of measuring time. The cycle of the earth around the sun (365 days) does not neatly divide into a seven-day week; the lunar cycle works in patterns of approximately 29.5 days; and a single rotation of the earth lasts just under 24 hours. None of these are divisible by seven, though a seven-day week, with a series of more or less irregular months, can be used to approximate a cycle that gives us a full solar year. Rather than trying to rationalize the use of sevens or find some mathematical meaning to it, we could also see it as a free innovation by God—a spiritual law placed upon the universe. One may compare, for example, the stark command found at the beginning of the Passover event in Exod 12, where, as the Hebrew slaves prepare to leave Egypt, God declares their current month to now be the first month of a new year, a new way of counting, and a new holiday. So, too, at the end of the first week of creation, God has created something new in the cosmos. God does not adhere to the world's patterns—he creates and sustains them. Our task, then, is to ask what is real in God's accounting and to adjust our world according to it. As Jesus famously taught his disciples to pray: *Thy will be done, on earth as it is in heaven*. How might we adjust our lives to God's Sabbath reality?

For many of us, work is our life and our identity. The story in Genesis of creation and work in the Garden of Eden suggests that God created work for us, before sin or grief had entered the picture, and thus work, when practiced rightly, is holy and ordained by God. However, it is spiritually instructive to consider the connection between Sabbath and release from slavery in Deuteronomy. *No one is created to be a slave*. No one is created to work constantly. All of us need time and space to give ourselves back to our families, and to reclaim time even for our own selves. This is the break from striving that the Sabbath offers. The Sabbath was made for us—for observance, for rest, and even for celebration. What would it look like, in your own life, to set down the scheming and the emails and the phone calls for one day each week to recognize your true source of life? What would it look like to truly celebrate and enjoy the gifts of God on the Sabbath—in the words of the famous seventeenth-century Westminster Confession, to recognize our chief end as humans as being to "glorify God and enjoy him forever"?

GENESIS 2:18–25

THE MAN, THE ANIMALS, AND THE WOMAN

Although God has already created humans and animals in chapter 1, creation continues in chapter 2—focusing in on an emotionally complex and earthy sequence in which man and woman are further created, are differentiated from each other and other animals, and begin relating to each other.

LARGER LITERARY CONTEXT ▸ 2:4–25

2:18–19

18a וַיֹּ֙אמֶר֙ יְהוָ֣ה אֱלֹהִ֔ים
wayyōʾmer YHWH ʾĕlōhîm

Then the Lord God said,

18b לֹא־ט֛וֹב הֱי֥וֹת הָֽאָדָ֖ם לְבַדּ֑וֹ
lōʾ-ṭôv hĕyôt hāʾādām ləvaddô

"It is not good for the man to be alone;

18c אֶֽעֱשֶׂהּ־לּ֥וֹ עֵ֖זֶר כְּנֶגְדּֽוֹ׃
ʾeʿĕśeh-lô ʿēzer kənegdô.

I will make a helper for him, alongside him."

19a וַיִּצֶר֩ יְהוָ֨ה אֱלֹהִ֜ים מִן־הָֽאֲדָמָ֗ה
wayyiṣer YHWH ʾĕlōhîm min-hāʾădāmâ

So the Lord God crafted from the earth

19b כָּל־חַיַּ֤ת הַשָּׂדֶה֙
kol-ḥayyat haśśāde

every living creature of the field

19c וְאֵת֙ כָּל־ע֣וֹף הַשָּׁמַ֔יִם
wəʾēt kol-ʿôf haššāmayim

and all the birds of the air,

19d וַיָּבֵא֙ אֶל־הָ֣אָדָ֔ם
wayyāvēʾ ʾel-hāʾādām

and he brought (them) to the man

19e לִרְא֖וֹת מַה־יִּקְרָא־לֽוֹ
lirʾôt mah-yiqrāʾ-lô

to observe what he would call each of them.

19f	וְכֹל אֲשֶׁר יִקְרָא־לוֹ הָאָדָם נֶפֶשׁ חַיָּה
	wəkōl 'ăšer yiqrā'-lô hā'ādām nefeš ḥayyâ

And whatever the man would call each of the living things,

19g	הוּא שְׁמוֹ:
	hû' šəmô.

that was its name.

18a	וַיֹּאמֶר יְהוָה אֱלֹהִים
	Then the LORD God said,

וַיֹּאמֶר	then (he) said	QAL WAYY 3MS	verb
אמר	way·yō'·mer		
יְהוָה	the LORD/YHWH	ABS	noun
יהוה	YHWH		
אֱלֹהִים	God	ABS	noun
אֱלֹהִים	'ĕ·lō·hîm		

Beginning in 2:4, the title for the deity switches from "God" (אֱלֹהִים), which was used in ch. 1, to this expanded title, "the LORD God." The so-called tetragrammaton, the four-letter name of God, יְהוָה, is a name unique to Israel's God (whereas אֱלֹהִים, "God," is a form of the common Semitic word for God/god, divine being, deity, etc.). Scholars have posited various theories regarding the meaning of the word יְהוָה, to no definite conclusion; the name seems to be based on the verb היה, "to be," and most have assumed the name must mean something like "The One Who Exists" or "The One Who Will Be," or something along those lines (review Exod 3:13–15 for the story in which the Lord reveals this name to Moses). The use of the name here and throughout Genesis (e.g., Gen 4:1; 9:26; 15:1)—even in the mouths of characters in dialogue (as opposed to the third-person narrator)—far prior to God's official revelation of the name to Moses at the burning bush, would seem to indicate some kind of "retrospective understanding" on the part of the narrator in Genesis.

Hebrew readers will notice that the vowel pointing around יְהוָה mostly replicates the vowel points for another word, אֲדֹנָי, which literally means "my lords." Note that most English translations, including ours here, omit "my," render "lords" (a so-called plural of majesty) in the singular, and use capital and small capital letters for "Lord" when translating the divine name יהוה, and then normal capitalization as appropriate when translating אֲדֹנָי. (For the full vowel pointing reflecting the אֲדֹנָי pronunciation, including the *holem* above the *waw*, which is almost always omitted, see, e.g., Exod 13:15 in the standard Masoretic ["Traditional"] Hebrew tradition, at least as printed in many Hebrew formats of the Bible, or Exod 14:8, where the *holem* is placed above the first *heh*.) Using the vowel pointing of אֲדֹנָי ("my lords") for יְהוָה is no accident, as a Jewish tradition beginning at some time before the medieval period—when the Masoretic text was produced—respected the name of God to such a degree that it wanted to discourage readers from trying to pronounce it. Thus, the vowels for אֲדֹנָי provided around the word יְהוָה alert the reader to pronounce the word aloud as אֲדֹנָי (and not "Yahweh," which many suspect is at least close to the way the name would have originally been pronounced). Indeed, this is the reading tradition among Jewish readers, and most Christian readers of the Hebrew text, to this day.

The term "Jehovah" arose centuries ago in some Christian circles based on a misunderstanding of this convention. Some readers of the Latin version of the Bible mistakenly took the vowels in אֲדֹנָי and pronounced them with the consonants in יהוה, with the result (after taking account of the fact that in Latin there was overlap between the sounds produced by the written letters *j* and *y*) that the hybrid term "Jehovah" was born. The name "Jehovah" is not a name at all; it is grammatically nonsensical, though it is perhaps a beautiful word and has made its way into hymns, worship, and popular spiritual discourse in various ways.

Aside from the issues of pronouncing the name, the introduction of the longer title "the Lord God" also provides a new, more intimate style of narration in this chapter. If Gen 1 could be viewed as a "high-level," cosmic presentation of creation, Gen 2 offers a "zoomed-in" view, giving God a more intimate (i.e., personal) name and narrating the creation of animals and people in more earthy, intimate terms. Whereas in ch. 1 God created all things by ethereal speech alone, in ch. 2 the Lord God creates man from the earth, woman from the rib of the man, and all animal life from the earth after the creation of the man (but before the creation of the woman).

18b

לֹא־ט֛וֹב הֱי֥וֹת הָֽאָדָ֖ם לְבַדּ֑וֹ

"It is not good for the man to be alone;

לֹא־ lō'-	no/not	---	particle
ט֛וֹב ṭôv	good/pleasing/fitting	MS PRED	adj
הֱי֥וֹת hĕ·yôt	to be	QAL INF CST	verb
הָֽאָדָ֖ם hā·'ā·dām	the man/human	ABS W/ DEF. ART.	noun
לְבַדּ֑וֹ lə·vad·dô	to/by his own/alone	--- W/ 3MS SX	adv

In Gen 2:7, God created the man out of the dust of the ground, breathing life into his nostrils. Still, things are not yet good. The use of "not good" here is jarring, as the narrator of ch. 1 had repeatedly used an unqualified טוֹב to describe the results of the created order. In 1:30, God declared the situation of man and women together, supervising the created order, as "very good." The man's isolation now marks a reversion—perhaps a flashback—to a state of "not good." Note that the term הָֽאָדָם is not a name (e.g., "Adam"), since (as noted above with respect to 1:26b) in Hebrew proper nouns as a rule cannot take the definite article.

18c

אֶֽעֱשֶׂהּ־לּ֥וֹ עֵ֖זֶר כְּנֶגְדּֽוֹ׃

I will make a helper for him, alongside him."

אֶֽעֱשֶׂהּ־ 'e·'ĕ·śəh-	I will make/do/act	QAL COHORT 1CS	verb
לּ֥וֹ lô	to/for him	--- W/ 3MS SX	prep
עֵ֖זֶר 'ē·zer	help/helper	ABS	noun
כְּנֶגְדּֽוֹ׃ kə·neg·dô	as/like/according to his side/opposite	--- W/ PREP כְּ + 3MS SX	prep

God proposes a "helper" (עֵזֶר) as the solution to the man's loneliness. In English, the bare word "helper" could indicate a younger or inferior partner—e.g., a "little helper" or someone whose task is subordinated to the primary actor. In the Hebrew Bible, עֵזֶר appears around fifteen times, and over half of these uses describe God as the עֵזֶר. Consider, for example, Ps 121:1–2 (NRSVue):

> I lift up my eyes to the hills—
> from where will my help [עֶזְרִי] come?
>
> My help [עֶזְרִי] comes from the Lord,
> who made heaven and earth.

עֵזֶר also has military connotations and describes help in the face of enemies (Exod 18:4; Deut 33:7, 29; Ezek 12:14). The "help" God has in mind here in Gen 2:18 must be strong indeed.

19a	וַיִּצֶר יְהוָה אֱלֹהִים מִן־הָאֲדָמָה		
	So the Lord God crafted from the earth		
	וַיִּצֶר — and (he) formed/crafted/molded יצר — *way·yi·ṣer*	QAL WAYY 3MS	verb
	יְהוָה — the Lord יהוה — YHWH	ABS	noun
	אֱלֹהִים — God אֱלֹהִים — *ʾĕ·lō·hîm*	ABS	noun
	מִן־ — from מִן — *min-*	---	prep
	הָאֲדָמָה — the earth/ground/soil אֲדָמָה — *hā·ʾă·dā·mâ*	ABS W/ DEF. ART.	noun

יצר is the same term that was used in 2:7 to describe the "crafting" of the man from the dust of the earth. More than other terms for creating, such as עשה and ברא, which can trend toward abstraction, יצר is decidedly earthy and physical—often elsewhere describing the crafting, forming, or fashioning of a physical object, like pottery, or an anthropomorphic image from earth, wood, or stone (Isa 64:7 [8]; Jer 18:11; Hab 2:18), and also used to depict the forming of a baby in the womb (Isa 49:5; Jer 1:5). The author of Isa 40–55 treasures יצר as a favorite verb, repeatedly using the term to describe God's fashioning of Israel and contrasting this with the actions of those who craft material images of idols.

The use of אֲדָמָה here harks back to the wordplay in 2:7, where God crafts the אָדָם ("man") from the אֲדָמָה ("earth"), prefiguring the linked fate of humans and the earth—they will work it and also return to it at death.

19b	כָּל־חַיַּת הַשָּׂדֶה֙		
	every living creature of the field		
	כָּל־ all/every כֹּל kol-	CST	noun
	חַיַּת animal/beast/living thing of חַיָּה ḥay·yat	CST	noun
	הַשָּׂדֶה the field שָׂדֶה haś·śā·de	ABS W/ DEF. ART.	noun

19c	וְאֵת֙ כָּל־עוֹף הַשָּׁמַיִם		
	and all the birds of the air,		
	וְאֵת and (+ direct object marker) אֵת wə·ēt	--- W/ CONJ וְ	particle
	כָּל־ all/every כֹּל kol-	CST	noun
	עוֹף bird/birds of עוֹף 'ôf	CST	noun
	הַשָּׁמַיִם the heavens/skies/air above שָׁמַיִם haš·šā·mayim	ABS W/ DEF. ART.	noun

19d	וַיָּבֵא אֶל־הָאָדָם		
	and he brought (them) to the man		
	וַיָּבֵא and he brought בּוֹא way·yā·vē'	HIPH WAYY 3MS	verb

THE MAN, THE ANIMALS, AND THE WOMAN

אֶל־ 'el-	to/toward	---	prep
הָאָדָם hā·'ā·dām	the man/human	ABS W/ DEF. ART.	noun

19e   לִרְאוֹת מַה־יִּקְרָא־לוֹ

to observe what he would call each of them.

לִרְאוֹת ראה lir·'ôt	to see/observe	QAL INF CST W/ PREP לְ	verb
מַה־ מָה mah-	what	---	interr pron
יִּקְרָא־ קרא yiq·rā'-	he will/would call	QAL IMPF 3MS	verb
לוֹ לְ lô	to/for it/him	--- W/ 3MS SX	prep

The action here presents the relationship between God and the man, as well as the emerging power of the man, in fascinating terms. God is observing, watching the man as he names every living thing. Why, or how, is God observing this process? Presumably we are to imagine God observing everything that occurs, so what is it about this process that draws God's attention in a particular way? Again, we find a link back to ch. 1: As God had announced (קרא) night and day and sky and earth in ch. 1, now the man announces (קרא) the names of all the animals. In light of the limited use of קרא to describe God's invocation of physical, cosmic elements in ch. 1, it is significant that the man now has the task to קרא living things. What God does on a cosmic scale the man now does on an intimate scale, imitating God. The two opening chapters of Genesis thus make a powerful statement on the joint responsibility God and humans are to take in terms of not only earth-care but also creativity—the act of naming and thus even creation itself.

19f

וְכֹל אֲשֶׁר יִקְרָא־לוֹ הָאָדָם נֶפֶשׁ חַיָּה

And whatever the man would call each of the living things,

וְכֹל כֹּל	and all/everything wə·ḵōl	ABS W/ CONJ	noun
אֲשֶׁר אֲשֶׁר	that/which 'ă·šer	---	relative pron
יִקְרָא־ קרא	he will/would call yiq·rā'-	QAL IMPF 3MS	verb
לוֹ לְ	to/for it/him lô	--- W/ 3MS SX	prep
הָאָדָם אָדָם	the man/human hā·'ā·ḏām	ABS W/ DEF. ART.	noun
נֶפֶשׁ נֶפֶשׁ	soul/living thing/breath ne·p̄eš	ABS	noun
חַיָּה חַי	living ḥay·yâ	FS ATTR	adj

19g

הוּא שְׁמוֹ׃

that was its name.

הוּא הוּא	it/he hû'	---	personal pron
שְׁמוֹ׃ שֵׁם	his/its name šə·mô	CST W/ 3MS SX	noun

To give something a "name," in the basically shared theological understanding of Israel's ancient Near Eastern world, was to give it existence. For example, the Babylonian creation account Enuma Elish begins by stating: "When on high the heavens had not been *named* . . ." One could draw a parallel to the way we think of naming children today—there seems to be some special connection (even if purely emotional) between giving a baby a name and its coming into existence. The common practice of naming a homestead, a car, or even a band of friends, also reflects this practice—names formalize existence, solidify personality, and create identity.

2:20–24

20a
וַיִּקְרָ֨א הָֽאָדָ֜ם שֵׁמ֗וֹת לְכָל־הַבְּהֵמָה֙
wayyiqrā' hā'ādām šēmôt ləkol-habbəhēmâ

So the man gave names to all the beasts

20b
וּלְע֣וֹף הַשָּׁמַ֔יִם
ûləʻôf haššāmayim

and to all the birds of the air

20c
וּלְכֹ֖ל חַיַּ֣ת הַשָּׂדֶ֑ה
ûləkōl ḥayyat haśśāde

and to all living things of the field,

20d
וּלְאָדָ֕ם לֹֽא־מָצָ֥א עֵ֖זֶר כְּנֶגְדּֽוֹ׃
ûləʼādām lōʼ-māṣāʼ ʻēzer kənegdô.

but for the man no one could find a helper alongside him.

21a
וַיַּפֵּל֩ יְהוָ֨ה אֱלֹהִ֧ים ׀ תַּרְדֵּמָ֛ה עַל־הָאָדָ֖ם
wayyappēl YHWH ʼĕlōhîm tardēmâ ʻal-hāʼādām

So the Lord God caused a deep sleep to fall upon the man,

21b
וַיִּישָׁ֑ן
wayyîšān

and he slept,

21c
וַיִּקַּ֗ח אַחַת֙ מִצַּלְעֹתָ֔יו וַיִּסְגֹּ֥ר בָּשָׂ֖ר תַּחְתֶּֽנָּה׃
wayyiqqaḥ 'aḥat miṣṣalʻōtāyw wayyisgōr bāśār taḥtennâ.

and he took one of his ribs and closed the flesh back over it,

22a
וַיִּ֩בֶן֩ יְהוָ֨ה אֱלֹהִ֧ים ׀ אֶֽת־הַצֵּלָ֛ע
wayyiven YHWH ʼĕlōhîm ʼet-haṣṣēlāʻ

and the Lord God built from the rib

22b		אֲשֶׁר־לָקַח מִן־הָאָדָם לְאִשָּׁה
		'ăšer-lāqaḥ min-hā'ādām lə'iššâ

that he took from the man a woman.

22c		וַיְבִאֶהָ אֶל־הָאָדָם׃
		wayəvî'ehâ 'el-hā'ādām.

He brought her to the man,

23a		וַיֹּאמֶר הָאָדָם
		wayyō'mer hā'ādām

and the man said,

23b		זֹאת הַפַּעַם עֶצֶם מֵעֲצָמַי
		zō't happa'am 'eṣem mē'ăṣāmay

"This, at last, is bone from my bone

23c		וּבָשָׂר מִבְּשָׂרִי
		ûvāśār mibbəśārî

and flesh from my flesh;

23d		לְזֹאת יִקָּרֵא אִשָּׁה
		ləzō't yiqqārē' 'iššâ

this one will be called 'woman,'

23e		כִּי מֵאִישׁ לֻקֳחָה־זֹּאת׃
		kî mē'îš luqŏḥâ-zō't.

for from 'man' this one was taken."

24a		עַל־כֵּן יַעֲזָב־אִישׁ
		'al-kēn ya'ăzov-'îš

For this reason, a man leaves

24b		אֶת־אָבִיו וְאֶת־אִמּוֹ
		'et-'āvîw wə'et-'immô

his father and his mother

THE MAN, THE ANIMALS, AND THE WOMAN

24c	וְדָבַק בְּאִשְׁתּוֹ
	wədāvaq bə'ištô
	and clings to his wife,
24d	וְהָיוּ לְבָשָׂר אֶחָד׃
	wəhāyû ləvāśār 'eḥād.
	and they become one flesh.

20a	וַיִּקְרָא הָאָדָם שֵׁמוֹת לְכָל־הַבְּהֵמָה
	So the man gave names to all the beasts

וַיִּקְרָא	and (he) called	QAL WAYY 3MS	verb
קרא	way·yiq·rā'		
הָאָדָם	the man/human	ABS	noun
אדם	hā·'ā·dām	W/ DEF. ART.	
שֵׁמוֹת	names	ABS	noun
שם	šē·môt		
לְכָל־	to/for all/each/every	CST	noun
כל	lə·kol-	W/ PREP לְ	
הַבְּהֵמָה	the beast	ABS	noun
בהמה	hab·bə·hē·mâ	W/ DEF. ART.	

20b	וּלְעוֹף הַשָּׁמַיִם
	and to all the birds of the air

וּלְעוֹף	and to/for (the) bird/birds of	CST	noun
עוף	û·lə·'ôf	W/ CONJ וְ + PREP לְ	
הַשָּׁמַיִם	the heavens/skies/air above	ABS	noun
שמים	haš·šā·mayim	W/ DEF. ART.	

20c

וּלְכֹל חַיַּת הַשָּׂדֶה

and to all living things of the field,

וּלְכֹל כֹּל	and to/for all/each/every û·lə·ḵōl	CST W/ CONJ וּ + PREP לְ	noun
חַיַּת חַיָּה	(the) animal/beast/ living thing of ḥay·yat	CST	noun
הַשָּׂדֶה שָׂדֶה	the field haś·śā·ḏe	ABS W/ DEF. ART.	noun

20d

וּלְאָדָם לֹא־מָצָא עֵזֶר כְּנֶגְדּוֹ׃

but for the man no one could find a helper alongside him.

וּלְאָדָם אָדָם	and/but to (the) man/human û·lə·'ā·ḏām	ABS W/ CONJ וּ + PREP לְ	noun
לֹא־ לֹא	no/not lō'-	---	particle
מָצָא מצא	he finds/found mā·ṣā'	QAL PF 3MS	verb
עֵזֶר עֵזֶר	help/helper 'ē·zer	ABS	noun
כְּנֶגְדּוֹ׃ נֶגֶד	as/like/according to his side/opposite kə·neḡ·dô	--- W/ PREP כְּ + 3MS SX	prep

The initial process ends without full resolution. The ambiguity of the third-person singular here—"he found" (מָצָא)—leaves open the question of who it was that could not find the helper for the man. Are we to think that God enacted the animal parade with the intention of finding the helper but could not figure it out? Was the parade for the man's sake only, to cause him frustration and show him his differences from the animals? Whatever the case, the text creates a distinct emotional effect: Drama builds, and for a moment the man's loneliness threatens to be unending.

Notice that וּלְאָדָם could also be translated "but for Adam," as the phrase lacks a definite article (the presence of the definite article would otherwise indicate the noun is not a name). See comment below at 3:17a.

21a

וַיַּפֵּל֩ יְהוָ֨ה אֱלֹהִ֧ים ׀ תַּרְדֵּמָ֛ה עַל־הָאָדָ֖ם			

So the LORD God caused a deep sleep to fall upon the man,

Hebrew	Gloss	Parsing	Part of Speech
וַיַּפֵּל֩ / נפל	and (he) caused to fall/cast / *way·yap·pēl*	HIPH WAYY 3MS	verb
יְהוָ֨ה / יהוה	the LORD / *YHWH*	ABS	noun
אֱלֹהִ֧ים ׀ / אלהים	God / *ĕ·lō·hîm*	ABS	noun
תַּרְדֵּמָ֛ה / תרדמה	sleep/deep sleep / *tar·dē·mâ*	ABS	noun
עַל־ / על	on/upon / *'al-*	---	prep
הָאָדָ֖ם / אדם	the man/human / *hā·'ā·dām*	ABS W/ DEF. ART.	noun

The Old Testament authors only rarely use the particular term found here for "deep sleep," תַּרְדֵּמָה—it occurs only seven times in total. In six of these instances (including the present one), the deep sleep described is divinely induced or involves a mysterious process of visionary dreaming (Gen 15:12; 1 Sam 26:12; Isa 29:10; Job 4:13; 33:15).

21b

וַיִּישָׁ֑ן	

and he slept,

Hebrew	Gloss	Parsing	Part of Speech
וַיִּישָׁ֑ן / ישׁן	and he slept / *way·yî·šān*	QAL WAYY 3MS	verb

21c

וַיִּקַּ֗ח אַחַת֙ מִצַּלְעֹתָ֔יו וַיִּסְגֹּ֥ר בָּשָׂ֖ר תַּחְתֶּֽנָּה׃	

and he took one of his ribs and closed the flesh back over it,

Hebrew	Gloss	Parsing	Part of Speech
וַיִּקַּ֗ח / לקח	and he took / *way·yiq·qaḥ*	QAL WAYY 3MS	verb
אַחַת֙ / אֶחָד	one / *'a·ḥat*	ABS	cardinal number

מִצַּלְעֹתָיו צֵלָע	from his ribs *miṣ·ṣalʿō·tāyw*	CST W/ PREP מִן + 3MS SX	noun
וַיִּסְגֹּר סגר	and he shut/closed over *way·yis·gōr*	QAL WAYY 3MS	verb
בָּשָׂר בָּשָׂר	flesh/meat *bā·śār*	ABS	noun
תַּחְתֶּנָּה׃ תַּחַת	under/instead of it *taḥ·ten·nâ*	--- W/ 3FS SX	prep

The term here for "ribs" can also refer to the "side" of something generally, and so could conceivably refer to some piece of the man's side (though almost all interpreters have understood this as a "rib bone"). In normal cases, men and women have the same number of ribs, so there is no reason to stretch the text here to attempt to explain anatomical differences between the sexes to make this an etiology for some feature of male ribs. Continuing our observation earlier (regarding v. 19) on the pottery-like crafting method by which the Lord God creates the man, here again we are asked to envision the deity carefully stitching up the flesh to cover the wound from the lost rib or side part.

22a	וַיִּבֶן יְהוָה אֱלֹהִים ׀ אֶת־הַצֵּלָע
	and the Lord God built from the rib

וַיִּבֶן בנה	and (he) built/created *way·yi·ven*	QAL WAYY 3MS	verb
יְהוָה יהוה	the Lord *YHWH*	ABS	noun
אֱלֹהִים ׀ אֱלֹהִים	God *ʾe·lō·hîm*	ABS	noun
אֶת־ אֵת	(direct object marker) *ʾet-*	---	particle
הַצֵּלָע צֵלָע	the rib/side *haṣ·ṣē·lāʿ*	ABS W/ DEF. ART.	noun

22b

	אֲשֶׁר־לָקַח מִן־הָאָדָם לְאִשָּׁה		
	that he took from the man a woman.		
אֲשֶׁר־ 'ă·šer-	that/which	---	relative pron
לָקַח lā·qaḥ	he took	QAL PF 3MS	verb
מִן־ min-	from	---	prep
הָאָדָם hā·'ā·dām	the man/human	ABS W/ DEF. ART	noun
לְאִשָּׁה lə·'iš·šâ	to/into/for a woman/wife	ABS W/ PREP לְ	noun

22c

	וַיְבִאֶהָ אֶל־הָאָדָם:		
	He brought her to the man,		
וַיְבִאֶהָ wa·yə·vī·'e·hâ	and he brought her	HIPH WAYY 3MS W/ 3FS SX	verb
אֶל־ 'el-	to/toward	---	prep
הָאָדָם: hā·'ā·dām	the man/human	ABS W/ DEF. ART.	noun

Another intimate scene: the Lord God, having crafted the man like an earthen vessel and stitched together a woman from the raw body of the man, now personally leads the woman to the man and presents her. The exact process by which the Lord God creates the woman, however, remains mysterious. How are we to envision it as a physical act?

23a

	וַיֹּאמֶר הָאָדָם		
	and the man said,		
וַיֹּאמֶר way·yō'·mer	and (he) said	QAL WAYY 3MS	verb

הָאָדָם֙	the man/human	ABS	noun
אָדָם	hā·ʾā·**dām**	W/ DEF. ART.	

23b

זֹאת הַפַּ֗עַם עֶ֚צֶם מֵֽעֲצָמַ֔י

"This, at last, is bone from my bone

זֹאת	this	---	demonstr
זֹאת	zōʾt		pron
הַפַּעַם	(the) time	ABS	noun
פַּעַם	hap·**pa**·ʿam	W/ DEF. ART.	
עֶצֶם	bone	ABS	noun
עֶצֶם	ʿe·ṣem		
מֵעֲצָמַי	from my bone	CST	noun
עֶצֶם	mē·ʿă·ṣā·**may**	W/ PREP מִן + 1CS SX	

Adam erupts with a poem, the first words spoken by a human in the Bible. It is as if, before having an equal partner to speak with, he had nothing to say. His words here, recognizing the woman as "bone from my bone, and flesh from my flesh," simultaneously acknowledge the way in which she was created (she was taken from his body) and their fundamental equality.

23c

וּבָשָׂ֖ר מִבְּשָׂרִ֑י

and flesh from my flesh;

וּבָשָׂר	and flesh/meat	ABS	noun
בָּשָׂר	û·vā·**śār**	W/ CONJ וְ	
מִבְּשָׂרִי	from my flesh/meat	CST	noun
בָּשָׂר	mib·bə·śā·**rî**	W/ PREP מִן + 1CS SX	

23d

לְזֹאת֙ יִקָּרֵ֣א אִשָּׁ֔ה

this one will be called 'woman,'

לְזֹאת	to/for this	---	demonstr
זֹאת	lə·zōʾt	W/ PREP לְ	pron

THE MAN, THE ANIMALS, AND THE WOMAN

יִקָּרֵא קרא	it will be called *yiq·qā·rē'*	NIPH IMPF 3MS	verb
אִשָּׁה אשׁה	woman/wife *'iš·šâ*	ABS	noun

This clause literally reads, "*It [masc.] will be called* [יִקָּרֵא] *to this [fem.] a woman/wife*"; a more natural translation is "this one will be called a woman/wife." The same grammatical construction appears elsewhere in the Hebrew Bible: e.g., in Isa 1:26, where "*It [masc.] will be called* [יִקָּרֵא] *to you [fem.] the city of righteousness*" means "You shall be called the city of righteousness" (NRSVue; see also Isa 32:5; 35:8; 62:4, 12; Jer 19:6).

23e	כִּי מֵאִישׁ לֻקֳחָה־זֹּאת׃		
	for from 'man' this one was taken."		
	כִּי כי	for/since *kî*	---	conj
	מֵאִישׁ אישׁ	from man *mē·'îš*	ABS W/ PREP מִן	noun
	לֻקֳחָה־ לקח	(she) was taken *lu·qŏ·ḥâ-*	PUAL PF 3FS	verb
	זֹאת׃ זאת	this *zō't*	---	demonstr pron

The titles "man" (אִישׁ) and "woman" (אִשָּׁה) sound almost identical except for the final feminine *-â* syllable at the end for "woman." From the perspective of historical Semitic linguistics, most scholars believe the etymologies of these words are more complex. It may well be the case that these words for "man" and "woman" in Hebrew, despite sounding similar, actually come from distinct and unrelated noun roots (similar to how, in English, the words "male" and "female" are probably not etymologically related despite both containing the element "male"). Whatever the case, the Hebrew-speaking author of Genesis here uses the similar sounds of the words אִישׁ and אִשָּׁה to serve the rich symbolism of the story, relating the bodies and experience of man and woman to each other.

24a	עַל־כֵּן יַעֲזׇב־אִישׁ		
	For this reason, a man leaves		
עַל־כֵּן 'al-kēn	therefore [lit., on/upon thus]	---	adv
יַעֲזׇב־ עזב ya·'ă·zov-	(he) leaves/will leave/ should leave/may leave [alternatively: "forget"]	QAL IMPF 3MS	verb
אִישׁ 'îš	man/husband	ABS	noun

The phrase עַל־כֵּן frequently introduces "etiological" information, that is, an account of how an institution or practice began, or how a place or person received their name (for other etiological phrases like this within Genesis alone, see 10:9; 11:9; 16:14; 19:22; 21:31; 25:30; 26:33; 29:34–35; 30:6; 31:48; 32:33 [32]; 33:17; 50:11). The notion that the man would be the one to leave father and mother—rather than the other way around—is distinctive, for it is most often assumed to be the case that traditional societies (like ancient Israel) were not only patrilineal (lineage, name, and property are passed down mostly along male lines) but also patrilocal (that is, women would leave their homes and dwell at the location of the man to whom they were married). Broadly speaking, we know that although patrilineality and patrilocality were the rule in the ancient world, some societies were indeed matrilocal, even as patrilocality was the predominant custom (see Schloen 2001).

Moreover, at this point it is helpful to remember two things: (1) The verb עזב can also mean "forget" or "forsake," thus suggesting not so much a physical separation as some other sense in which the man will change his primary allegiance from his family of origin to his wife. (2) The imperfect/prefix-conjugation term יַעֲזׇב־ could also be translated as "leaves," "will leave," "should leave," "could leave," "may leave," and so on. Presumably, the choice one makes here in terms of how to translate יַעֲזׇב־ would also affect how one translates the verbs דָּבַק and וְהָיוּ below (in vv. 24c and 24d).

24b — אֶת־אָבִיו וְאֶת־אִמּוֹ

his father and his mother

אֶת־ אֵת	(direct object marker) 'et-	---	particle
אָבִיו אָב	his father ʾā·vîw	CST W/ 3MS SX	noun
וְאֶת־ אֵת	and (+ direct object marker) wə·ʾet-	--- W/ CONJ וְ	particle
אִמּוֹ אֵם	his mother ʾim·mô	CST W/ 3MS SX	noun

24c — וְדָבַק בְּאִשְׁתּוֹ

and clings to his wife,

וְדָבַק דבק	and he clings/will cling/ should cling/may cling wə·dā·vaq	QAL WEQATAL 3MS	verb
בְּאִשְׁתּוֹ אִשָּׁה	to his woman/wife bə·ʾiš·tô	CST W/ PREP בְּ + 3MS SX	noun

Based on v. 23, we might naturally assume that the woman would have to leave her mother and father to return to the man, from whose flesh she was taken. Rather, the story now swings in the other direction and indicates that it is the man who will leave (עזב) to cling (דבק) to his wife—suggesting both man and woman come from each other and seek each other and thus maintain an equal status.

24d — וְהָיוּ לְבָשָׂר אֶחָד׃

and they become one flesh.

וְהָיוּ היה	and they are/will be wə·hā·yû	QAL WEQATAL 3CP	verb
לְבָשָׂר בָּשָׂר	to/for/as flesh/meat lə·vā·śār	ABS W/ PREP לְ	noun

| אֶחָֽד׃ | one/single | ABS | cardinal |
| אֶחָד | ʾe·ḥād | | number |

The story now solidifies the union of man and woman by suggesting that marriage returns the pair to its primordial bond as literally one body, undifferentiated as "one flesh."

2:25

25a וַיִּהְיוּ שְׁנֵיהֶם עֲרוּמִּים
wayyihyû šənêhem ʿărûmmîm

And the both of them were naked,

25b הָאָדָם וְאִשְׁתּוֹ
hāʾādām wəʾištô

the man and his wife,

25c וְלֹא יִתְבֹּשָׁשׁוּ׃
wəlōʾ yitbōšāšû.

and they were not ashamed.

25a	וַיִּהְיוּ שְׁנֵיהֶם עֲרוּמִּים		
	And the both of them were naked,		
	וַיִּהְיוּ היה	and (they) were *way·yih·yû*	QAL WAYY 3MP	verb
	שְׁנֵיהֶם שְׁנַיִם	both of them *šə·nê·hem*	CST W/ 3MP SX	cardinal number
	עֲרוּמִּים עָרוֹם	naked/uncovered *ʿă·rûm·mîm*	MP PRED	adj

The fact that the story explicitly comments on their state of nudity and lack of shame serves to present the primal couple in a state of childlike innocence, while also gesturing forward to what is to come in the next chapter. The term for their nakedness, עֲרוּמִּים (singular עָרוֹם), is nearly the same (except for one vowel) as the term for the serpent's "craftiness" in 3:1 (עָרוּם), preparing us for the dramatic clash between the completely innocent people and the more experienced snake.

25b

הָאָדָם וְאִשְׁתּוֹ

the man and his wife,

הָאָדָם	the man/human	ABS	noun
אָדָם	hā·ʾā·dām	W/ DEF. ART.	
וְאִשְׁתּוֹ	and his wife	CST	noun
אִשָּׁה	wə·ʾiš·tô	W/ CONJ וְ + 3MS SX	

25c

וְלֹא יִתְבֹּשָׁשׁוּ׃

and they were not ashamed.

וְלֹא	and not	---	particle
לֹא	wə·lōʾ	W/ CONJ וְ	
יִתְבֹּשָׁשׁוּ׃	they were ashamed	HITHPOLEL IMPF 3MP	verb
בּוֹשׁ	yit·bō·šā·šû		

From Text to Sermon

*As you meditate on this passage and contemplate
how you might teach or preach it to others,
consider the following areas of emphasis.*

 Historical and Literary Context. Think about the two "panels" or "scenes" of creation in Gen 1 and 2. In ch. 2, the narrative prose style allows for a much more intimate take on the man and woman—matched by a longer and more intimate name for God, "the Lord [YHWH] God." Scripture thus already begins to offer a pattern, faint but distinct, for God to come out of abstraction and become embodied in the world in specific ways. That pattern will continue, in fits and starts, through the Old Testament and culminate in one of the central claims of the Christian theological tradition: that the Word becomes flesh in the person of Jesus Christ (John 1). Long before this, however, God gestures and moves toward this ultimate intimacy between the divine and material worlds. He crafts man and woman from earth and flesh (Gen 2:7, 21–22); he talks with Abraham and bargains with him (Gen 18); his presence takes material form in the tabernacle, moving along with Israel in the wilderness (Exod 25–26).

Our familiarity with these early chapters of Genesis can blind us to what is truly stunning and mysterious in the narrative that we read here. The God who creates the entire universe at the mere sound of his voice turns to search out a companion for the man . . . and initially fails? How are we to understand the cryptic phrase in 2:20, "but for the man no one could find a helper alongside him"? Could God not find that helper? If Gen 1 teaches us that humans, both male and female, are created in God's image, Gen 2 teaches us that true companionship is a process, involving drama, longing, unfulfilled searches, and further acts of creation. The God of Genesis thrives on drama—he flirts with vulnerability, engages in searching and finding, and takes emotional twists and turns that our theologies of an "immutable," "omniscient," "omnipotent" deity, however accurate they are, cannot always easily process. Perhaps it is best that we do not over-interpret or distort the text, but rather let it speak artistically and imaginatively to us. To help your listeners with this, you might consider asking them to visualize the scene. Imagine the man's naïveté and confusion. Consider the risk both for the Lord God and the man, as animal after animal comes to Adam and the helper is not found.

If as readers of Scripture we come away from Gen 2 awash with awe, wonder, and worship, then we have been faithful readers. We praise God for the men and women in our lives, and yet long for companionship and fulfillment. We seek a helper alongside us and feel the pain of relational failure. We feel the thrill of partnership when it arrives. And as we gaze upon the grandeur of the created order, we may ask, along with the psalmist, "What are humans that you are mindful of them, mortals that you care for them?" Yet, the psalm proclaims with worship and astonishment:

> You have made them a little lower than God and crowned them with glory and honor. You have given them dominion over the works of your hands; you have put all things under their feet. . . . O Lord, our Sovereign, how majestic is your name in all the earth!
>
> (Ps 8:4–10 [3–9] NRSVue, excerpts)

 Bridge to the Gospel. As a bridge to the preaching of the gospel in the New Testament, explore the central role our text at hand could play for thinking about gender. The vulnerable, dramatic process of creation pictured here culminates with woman, the "helper" whom God creates not beneath the man or over him but, tellingly, *alongside him*—an argument used by interpreters throughout Christian history to argue for Eve's equality with Adam and thus the equality of all women to all men. Indeed, in a famous passage where Jesus talks about men and women with a crowd of questioners, Jesus seems to go a step further: in the context of marriage, women and men are not simply "equals" with one another—they are "one" (Matt 19:3–9 // Mark 10:2–9, with some differences). When asked a question about divorce, Jesus appeals directly to Gen 2:24 and offers the following commentary regarding husband and wife: "So they are no longer two but one flesh. Therefore what God has joined together, let no one separate" (Mark 10:8–9 // Matt 19:6 NRSVue). Christians often invoke Jesus' words at weddings, and rightly so. It is also worth reading and rereading Gen 2 in the broader context of human relationships when thinking about creation and gender. How can we practice God's intended creation reality every day, acting with love and respect toward the women and men in our lives, appreciating and affirming their dignity and value as members of God's good creation?

GENESIS 3:1–7

MAN, WOMAN, AND SERPENT

Humans have their first antagonistic encounter in the world with a mysterious serpent—not named or identified in this passage or anywhere else in the Old or New Testaments, but interpreted as Satan in the Christian tradition. Where does the serpent come from? Why do the humans take the fruit? The text is as enigmatic as it is rich with pathos and possibility.

LARGER LITERARY CONTEXT ▸ 3:1–24

3:1–3

1a	וְהַנָּחָשׁ הָיָה עָרוּם *wəhannāḥāš hāyâ ʿārûm* **Now the serpent was craftier**
1b	מִכֹּל חַיַּת הַשָּׂדֶה *mikkōl ḥayyat haśśāde* **than any other wild animal of the field**
1c	אֲשֶׁר עָשָׂה יְהוָה אֱלֹהִים *ʾăšer ʿāśâ YHWH ʾĕlōhîm* **that the LORD God had made.**
1d	וַיֹּאמֶר אֶל־הָאִשָּׁה *wayyōʾmer ʾel-hāʾiššâ* **He said to the woman,**
1e	אַף כִּי־אָמַר אֱלֹהִים *ʾaf kî-ʾāmar ʾĕlōhîm* **"Did God really say**
1f	לֹא תֹאכְלוּ מִכֹּל עֵץ הַגָּן׃ *lōʾ tōʾkəlû mikkōl ʿēṣ haggān.* **that you should not eat from any tree of the garden?"**
2a	וַתֹּאמֶר הָאִשָּׁה אֶל־הַנָּחָשׁ *wattōʾmer hāʾiššâ ʾel-hannāḥāš* **The woman replied to the serpent,**
2b	מִפְּרִי עֵץ־הַגָּן נֹאכֵל׃ *mippərî ʿēṣ-haggān nōʾkēl.* **"From the fruit of the garden trees we may eat—**

3a

וּמִפְּרִי הָעֵץ אֲשֶׁר בְּתוֹךְ־הַגָּן אָמַר אֱלֹהִים

ûmippərî hā'ēṣ 'ăšer bətôk-haggān 'āmar 'ĕlōhîm

**but from the fruit of the tree that is
in the middle of the garden, God said,**

3b

לֹא תֹאכְלוּ מִמֶּנּוּ

lō' tō'kəlû mimmennû

'You may not eat from it,

3c

וְלֹא תִגְּעוּ בּוֹ

wəlō' tiggə'û bô

nor may you touch it,

3d

פֶּן־תְּמֻתוּן׃

pen-təmūtûn.

or else you will die.'"

1a

וְהַנָּחָשׁ הָיָה עָרוּם
Now the serpent was craftier

וְהַנָּחָשׁ נָחָשׁ	and/now the serpent/snake *wə·han·nā·ḥāš*	ABS W/ CONJ וְ + DEF. ART.		noun
הָיָה היה	(he) was *hā·yâ*	QAL PF 3MS		verb
עָרוּם עָרוּם	crafty *'ā·rûm*	MS PRED		adj

The double entendre that begins this scene is stark and strange. The humans are *naked* and the serpent is *crafty*, both indicated by the same consonantal word but with a different vowel (עָרוּם for "crafty," עָרוֹם for "naked"). Perhaps the most obvious connection is that we must be prepared for the craftiness of the serpent to clash with the nakedness (naïveté) of the humans.

Early Christian readers connected—and most Christians today connect—the serpent here with Satan, though nowhere in the Bible is this connection explicit. Texts such as Ezek 27–28 cryptically refer to a "king of Tyre" in "Eden." But we know Tyre was a Phoenician city, and the context of the passage makes reasonably clear that its (earthly) king and his people are being satirized for their excessive pride and wealth. In a taunt against the king of Babylon, Isa 14 proclaims, "How you are fallen from heaven, O Morning Star [הֵילֵל], son of Dawn!" (NRSVue); some have taken this as a reference to Satan (despite the clear context regarding a human king), given the fact that the King James Version translates this phrase as "How art thou fallen from heaven, O Lucifer . . ." The obscure Hebrew term הֵילֵל, "shining one," was translated by the influential Latin Vulgate as *lucifer*, which literally means "shining one," so the transformation of this term into "Lucifer" as a proper name for the devil is not appropriate. Revelation 12 and 20 depict Satan using serpent imagery (without mentioning Eden), but no wording here in Gen 3 could straightforwardly be adduced to make the Satan-serpent connection.

In the New Testament, demons can possess both humans and animals (Mark 5), but the Jesus of the Gospels never discusses the serpent in the garden. Moreover, when writing specifically about Adam and Eve and their sin, the apostle Paul never mentions Satan or any demonic presence (Rom 5; 1 Cor 13).

Milton's *Paradise Lost*, written in the 1660s–1670s, gave epic literary form to the storyline that Satan once dwelled with God in heaven as an angel but, as punishment for excessive pride, was expelled down to earth, where he took serpentine form and deceived humans. But Milton's origin story of Satan appears nowhere in Scripture (unless by symbolic leap from Ezek 27–28 and Isa 14:12).

1b	מִכֹּל חַיַּת הַשָּׂדֶה		
	than any other wild animal of the field		
מִכֹּל	from/than all/each/every	CST	noun
כֹּל	*mik·kōl*	W/ PREP מִ	
חַיַּת	living thing/creature/animal of	CST	noun
חַיָּה	*ḥay·yat*		
הַשָּׂדֶה	the field	ABS	noun
שָׂדֶה	*haś·śā·de*	W/ DEF. ART.	

On a straightforward reading, given the information we have here in the text (combined with the next clause), we would have every reason to think that the serpent is a "normal" animal, created by God, in the same way and at the same time as every other "animal of the field" (the phrase חַיַּת הַשָּׂדֶה appears in 2:19–20 to describe the animals God brings to the man in the search for a helper, and also appears many other times in the Old Testament to describe "wild animals" generally). The fact that this serpent is "craftier" than all other animals—marked by the use of the comparative מִן at the beginning of this phrase—does, however, alert us to the special status of this particular animal.

1c	אֲשֶׁר עָשָׂה יְהוָה אֱלֹהִים
	that the Lord God had made.

	אֲשֶׁר	that/which	---	relative pron
	אשׁר	'ă·šer		
	עָשָׂה	(he) made	QAL PF 3MS	verb
	עשה	'ā·śâ		
	יְהוָה	the Lord	ABS	noun
	יהוה	YHWH		
	אֱלֹהִים	God	ABS	noun
	אלהים	'ĕ·lō·hîm		

1d	וַיֹּאמֶר אֶל־הָאִשָּׁה
	He said to the woman,

	וַיֹּאמֶר	and he said/spoke	QAL WAYY 3MS	verb
	אמר	way·yō'·mer		
	אֶל־	to/toward	---	prep
	אל	'el-		
	הָאִשָּׁה	the woman	ABS W/ DEF. ART.	noun
	אשׁה	hā·'iš·šâ		

The animal speaks without any special narrative comment explaining why, exactly, he can speak or acknowledging the strangeness of a talking snake. The narrative simply assumes the serpent can talk. (The only other "natural" talking animal in the Bible is Balaam's donkey in Num 22.)

1e	אַף כִּי־אָמַר אֱלֹהִים
	"Did God really say

אַף כִּי־ אַף כִּי 'af kî-	sure/also/indeed for/since	---	adv
אָמַר אמר 'ā·mar	(he) said	QAL PF 3MS	verb
אֱלֹהִים אֱלֹהִים 'ĕ·lō·hîm	God	ABS	noun

The phrase אַף כִּי appears frequently in the Old Testament and indicates, most often, a rhetorical escalation by way of comparison ("how much more") or, less often, a de-escalation ("how much less"). Consider, for example, Prov 15:11 (NRSVue):

> Sheol and Abaddon lie open before the LORD;
> how much more [אַף כִּי] human hearts!

The exact sense of אַף כִּי here in Gen 3:1, however, is less clear. The phrase must indicate some rhetorical flourish, some indication of emphasis. Christian translators face the challenge of trying to match their translation of the phrase with its most common and later interpretation in the history of Christian thought, according to which the serpent is clearly the devil deceiving the woman in a malicious way. For example, one of the most popular English translations, the NIV, renders the clause here as, "Did God really say . . ." By contrast, the NRSVue takes a more neutral approach, omitting the phrase אַף כִּי in translation altogether: "Did God say . . ." Even if one chooses the approach taken by the NIV, as I have here, one may still puzzle at the tone: is the serpent questioning with true wonder, with cunning mock-naïveté, or with a malicious snarl?

1f	לֹא תֹאכְלוּ מִכֹּל עֵץ הַגָּן:
	that you should not eat from any tree of the garden?"

לֹא לֹא lō'	not	---	particle
תֹאכְלוּ אכל tō'·ḵa·lû	you shall/will/can eat	QAL IMPF 2MP	verb

מִכֹּל כֹּל	from any/all *mik·kōl*	CST W/ PREP מִן	noun
עֵץ עֵץ	(the) tree(s) of *ʿēṣ*	CST	noun
הַגָּן׃ גַּן	the garden *hag·gān*	ABS W/ DEF. ART.	noun

In 1:28–31, God gave humans "every green plant for food," with no exceptions. In 2:8–9, the Garden of Eden is created with the "tree of the knowledge of good and evil" within it. Finally, in 2:15–17, we get the full command, first repeating the permission to eat from any garden tree, but then offering the restriction: "of the tree of the knowledge of good and evil you shall not eat, for in the day that you eat of it you shall die."

2a	וַתֹּאמֶר הָאִשָּׁה אֶל־הַנָּחָשׁ
	The woman replied to the serpent,

וַתֹּאמֶר אמר	and (she) said/spoke/ replied *wat·tō'·mer*	QAL WAYY 3FS	verb
הָאִשָּׁה אִשָּׁה	the woman *hā·ʾiš·šâ*	ABS W/ DEF. ART.	noun
אֶל־ אֶל	to/toward *ʾel-*	---	prep
הַנָּחָשׁ נָחָשׁ	the serpent/snake *han·nā·ḥāš*	ABS W/ DEF. ART.	noun

The woman responds to the serpent with no hesitation, in what appears to be a completely casual tone.

2b	מִפְּרִי עֵץ־הַגָּן נֹאכֵל׃
	"From the fruit of the garden trees we may eat—

מִפְּרִי פְּרִי	from (the) fruit of *mip·pə·rî*	CST W/ PREP מִן	noun
עֵץ־ עֵץ	(the) tree(s) of *ʿēṣ-*	CST	noun

הַגָּן	the garden	ABS	noun
גַּן	hag·gān	W/ DEF. ART.	
נֹאכֵל׃	we shall/will/can eat	QAL IMPF 1CP	verb
אכל	nō'·kēl		

3a וּמִפְּרִי הָעֵץ אֲשֶׁר בְּתוֹךְ־הַגָּן אָמַר אֱלֹהִים

but from the fruit of the tree that is in the middle of the garden, God said,

וּמִפְּרִי	and/but from (the) fruit of	CST	noun
פְּרִי	û·mip·pə·rî	W/ CONJ וְ + PREP מִן	
הָעֵץ	the tree	ABS	noun
עֵץ	hā·'ēṣ	W/ DEF. ART.	
אֲשֶׁר	that/which	---	relative pron
אֲשֶׁר	'ă·šer		
בְּתוֹךְ־	in (the) midst/middle of	---	prep
בְּתוֹךְ	bə·tôk-		
הַגָּן	the garden	ABS	noun
גַּן	hag·gān	W/ DEF. ART.	
אָמַר	(he) said	QAL PF 3MS	verb
אמר	'ā·mar		
אֱלֹהִים	God	ABS	noun
אֱלֹהִים	'ĕ·lō·hîm		

3b לֹא תֹאכְלוּ מִמֶּנּוּ

'You may not eat from it,

לֹא	not	---	particle
לֹא	lō'		
תֹאכְלוּ	you shall/will/can eat	QAL IMPF 2MP	verb
אכל	tō'·kə·lû		
מִמֶּנּוּ	from it	---	prep
מִן	mim·men·nû	W/ 3MS SX	

3c	וְלֹא תִגְּעוּ בֹּו

	nor may you touch it,		
וְלֹא לֹא	and not wə·lōʾ	--- W/ CONJ וְ	particle
תִגְּעוּ נגע	you shall/will/can touch/approach tig·gə·ʿû	QAL IMPF 2MP	verb
בֹּו בְּ	in/to it bô	--- W/ 3MS SX	prep

This phrase, as readers have noticed throughout the centuries, is not part of the explicit command God gave regarding the tree in ch. 2. Is this a freewheeling addition by Eve? An implicit understanding? An unnarrated command God really gave? If they are not supposed to eat of the tree, why would they touch it? If, as interpreters sometimes claim, Eve's "addition" here is an example of overreaching legalism, how exactly would that make her more likely to blow past her own unnecessary boundary and take the fruit?

3d	פֶּן־תְּמֻתוּן:

	or else you will die.'"		
פֶּן־ פֶּן	lest pen-	---	conj
תְּמֻתוּן: מות	you shall/will/can die tə·mu·tûn	QAL IMPF 2MP W/ PARAGOGIC ן	verb

This element of Eve's recollection takes up the clause from 2:17: "for on the day you eat from it, you will surely die."

3:4–7

4a וַיֹּאמֶר הַנָּחָשׁ אֶל־הָאִשָּׁה
wayyōʾmer hannāḥāš ʾel-hāʾiššâ

But the serpent replied to the woman,

4b לֹא־מוֹת תְּמֻתוּן׃
lōʾ-môt təmūtûn.

"You will not surely die—

5a כִּי יֹדֵעַ אֱלֹהִים
kî yōdēaʿ ʾĕlōhîm

for God knows

5b כִּי בְּיוֹם אֲכָלְכֶם מִמֶּנּוּ
kî bəyôm ʾăkolkem mimmennû

that on the day you eat from it

5c וְנִפְקְחוּ עֵינֵיכֶם
wənifqəḥû ʿênêkem

your eyes will be opened

5d וִהְיִיתֶם כֵּאלֹהִים
wihyîtem kēʾlōhîm

and you will be like God,

5c יֹדְעֵי טוֹב וָרָע׃
yōdəʿê ṭôv wārāʿ.

knowers of good and evil."

6a וַתֵּרֶא הָאִשָּׁה כִּי טוֹב הָעֵץ לְמַאֲכָל
wattēreʾ hāʾiššâ kî ṭôv hāʿēṣ ləmaʾăkāl

The woman saw that the tree was good for food

6b	וְכִ֨י תַֽאֲוָה־ה֥וּא לָעֵינַ֙יִם֙
	wəkî taʾăwâ-hûʾ lāʿênayim

and that it was delightful to the eyes,

6c	וְנֶחְמָ֤ד הָעֵץ֙ לְהַשְׂכִּ֔יל
	wənehmād hāʿēṣ ləhaśkîl

and the tree was desirable for acquiring understanding,

6d	וַתִּקַּ֥ח מִפִּרְי֖וֹ
	wattiqqaḥ mippiryô

so she took of its fruit

6e	וַתֹּאכַ֑ל
	wattōʾkal

and she ate—

6f	וַתִּתֵּ֧ן גַּם־לְאִישָׁ֛הּ עִמָּ֖הּ
	wattittēn gam-ləʾîšāh ʿimmāh

and she also gave some to her husband, who was with her,

6g	וַיֹּאכַֽל׃
	wayyōʾkal.

and he ate.

7a	וַתִּפָּקַ֙חְנָה֙ עֵינֵ֣י שְׁנֵיהֶ֔ם
	wattippāqaḥnâ ʿênê šənêhem

Then the eyes of both of them were opened,

7b	וַיֵּ֣דְע֔וּ כִּ֥י עֵֽירֻמִּ֖ם הֵ֑ם
	wayyēdəʿû kî ʿêrummīm hēm

and they knew that they were naked.

7c	וַֽיִּתְפְּרוּ֙ עֲלֵ֣ה תְאֵנָ֔ה
	wayyitpərû ʿălē təʾēnâ

They sewed together fig leaves

MAN, WOMAN, AND SERPENT

7d

וַיַּעֲשׂוּ לָהֶם חֲגֹרֹת׃

wayyaʿăśû lāhem ḥăgōrōt.

and made loincloths for themselves.

4a

וַיֹּאמֶר הַנָּחָשׁ אֶל־הָאִשָּׁה

But the serpent replied to the woman,

וַיֹּאמֶר אמר	and (he) said *way·yō'·mer*	QAL WAYY 3MS	verb
הַנָּחָשׁ נחש	the snake/serpent *han·nā·ḥāš*	ABS W/ DEF. ART.	noun
אֶל־ אֶל	to/toward *'el-*	---	prep
הָאִשָּׁה אשה	the woman *hā·'iš·šâ*	ABS W/ DEF. ART.	noun

4b

לֹא־מוֹת תְּמֻתוּן׃

"You will not surely die—

לֹא־ לֹא	not *lō'-*	---	particle
מוֹת מות	to die/dying *môt*	QAL INF ABS	verb
תְּמֻתוּן׃ מות	you shall/will/can die *tə·mū·tûn*	QAL IMPF 2MP W/ PARAGOGIC ן	verb

Here the serpent's nefarious intention becomes clearer, as he directly contradicts the divine proclamation. However, we still do not have an explicit cue demanding that we interpret the serpent's words here as intentionally deceptive. Could the serpent truly believe the things he is saying to the woman? Later in the chapter, the woman claims that the serpent "tricked" her, but God's words to the serpent do not explicitly confirm this, only that the serpent has "done this." Why is the text ambiguous at all on this point, especially given the importance of this exchange between the woman and the serpent for Christian theology? Even if it makes us uncomfortable, we must acknowledge that Hebrew prose gains much of its power and charm from this kind of ambiguity. Perhaps our best approach here is to revel in that ambiguity for a moment, rather than smother it too quickly with clarity or "right answers." Such an approach does not automatically nullify our interpretive traditions or prevent us from seeking guidance elsewhere in Scripture for how to understand the serpent. Rather, this approach allows us to see beauty, strangeness, subtlety, and tragedy as part of the process by which God has given us the story of salvation.

5a	כִּי יֹדֵעַ אֱלֹהִים		
	for God knows		
כִּי כִּי	for/since kî	---	conj
יֹדֵעַ ידע	knows/knowing/ one who knows yō·dē·aʿ	QAL PTCP MS	verb
אֱלֹהִים אֱלֹהִים	God ʾĕ·lō·hîm	ABS	noun

The serpent here introduces the story's pivotal term: ידע, "to know." Who has the privilege to know things? What does God know? Why would God want to prevent the humans from knowing? We will continue to encounter this crucial term in Gen 3–4 (again later in this same verse, and also in 3:7, 22; 4:1, 9, 17, 25).

5b	כִּי בְּיוֹם אֲכָלְכֶם מִמֶּנּוּ		
	that on the day you eat from it		
כִּי כִּי	that kî	---	conj
בְּיוֹם יוֹם	on/in (the) day of bə·yôm	CST W/ PREP בְּ	noun

אֲכָלְכֶם	your eating	QAL INF CST W/ 2MP SX	verb
אכל	ʾă·ḵol·ḵem		
מִמֶּנּוּ	from it	--- W/ 3MS SX	prep
מִן	mim·men·nû		

The serpent quotes God's words from 2:17—changing, however, the second-person singular suffix of אֲכָלְךָ, "your [sg.] eating," from that verse to the plural, אֲכָלְכֶם, "your [pl.] eating." Whereas God had first addressed the man in the singular, as he was the only person to address at the time, the serpent now speaks as if he is speaking to both humans (a detail confirmed, we may presume, in 3:6).

5c	וְנִפְקְחוּ עֵינֵיכֶם
	your eyes will be opened

וְנִפְקְחוּ	(they) will be opened	NIPH WEQATAL 3CP	verb
פקח	wə·nip̄·qə·ḥû		
עֵינֵיכֶם	your eyes	CST W/ 2MP SX	noun
עַיִן	ʿê·nê·ḵem		

In what way are the humans' eyes "closed," that they need to be opened? The "eyes" are a leading image in this story, as the next verse repeats the concept of sight and eyes, alluding, it seems, both to the physical eyes that see but also to some deeper sense of seeing and knowing. A striking number of the total uses in the Old Testament of the verb פקח, "open," combined with the term "eyes," speak of eyes opening in terms of a visionary experience or divine guidance (Gen 21:19; 2 Kgs 6:17–20) or the healing of blindness (Isa 35:5; 42:7; Ps 146:8).

5d	וִהְיִיתֶם כֵּאלֹהִים
	and you will be like God,

וִהְיִיתֶם	and you will be	QAL WEQATAL 2MP	verb
היה	wih·yî·tem		
כֵּאלֹהִים	like God/gods	ABS W/ PREP כְּ	noun
אֱלֹהִים	kē(')·lō·hîm		

Three translation options present themselves here for כֵּאלֹהִים: "like God," "like gods," and "like (some other lesser) divine beings" (e.g., angels). Given the next phrase, as well as the serpent's claim above, "for God *knows* . . . ," it seems reasonable to think the serpent is comparing the potential for human knowledge to God's knowledge specifically.

5e	יֹדְעֵי טוֹב וָרָע:
	knowers of good and evil."

יֹדְעֵי ידע	knowers of/ones who know *yō·ḏə·'ê*	QAL (CST) PTCP MP	verb
טוֹב טוב	good *ṭôv*	ABS	noun
וָרָע: רע	and bad/evil *wā·rā'*	ABS W/ CONJ ן	noun

Does the "knowing" here refer to an intellectual understanding or some kind of lived experience? The conceptual overlap between knowing as an act of the mind and as a bodily act (a euphemism for sex; Gen 4:1, 17, 25) offers each as a possibility, or both simultaneously.

Used as a pair, טוֹב and רָע clearly indicate two extremes of experience or status: good and bad, right and wrong—compare with Deut 1:39, where children are referred to as those who do not yet know טוֹב וָרָע, "right from wrong." For the original ancient Israelite audience of Gen 3, רָע probably would not have indicated all we have come to think of as "evil" in a metaphysical sense or on a popular level, just as טוֹב may not have indicated all that later Christian authors in the Greek philosophical tradition would come to identify as "the Good." Rather, the phrase "good and evil" is a merism, a literary device used frequently in Hebrew that employs a pair of spatial or conceptual contrasts to indicate the whole of something. For example, the geographical phrase "from Dan to Beersheba" (e.g., Judg 20:1; 2 Sam 24:15) uses a city in the north of the country (Dan) and a city in the south of the country (Beersheba) as a way of saying "the whole country." Thus, Gen 3 invites us to wonder about the scope of what it would be to know "good and evil." Perhaps, by "good and evil," the serpent implies that the people would know *everything* if they ate the fruit. Alternatively, "the knowledge of good and evil" could be taken to refer to moral knowledge, such as the moment a young child grows up enough to consciously choose to rebel or obey (as opposed to merely crying out or misunderstanding what is at stake, as an infant or young toddler might do; see Deut 1:39). Regardless, the traditional rendering "good and evil" may still best convey for readers today the idea communicated by the merism טוֹב וָרָע in the Hebrew text.

6a	וַתֵּרֶא הָאִשָּׁה כִּי טוֹב הָעֵץ לְמַאֲכָל
	The woman saw that the tree was good for food,

וַתֵּרֶא	and/so (she) saw	QAL WAYY 3FS	verb
רָאָה	wat·tē·re'		
הָאִשָּׁה	the woman	ABS W/ DEF. ART.	noun
אִשָּׁה	hā·'iš·šâ		
כִּי	that	---	conj
כִּי	kî		
טוֹב	good	MS PRED	adj
טוֹב	ṭôv		
הָעֵץ	the tree	ABS W/ DEF. ART.	noun
עֵץ	hā·'ēṣ		
לְמַאֲכָל	for food	ABS W/ PREP לְ	noun
מַאֲכָל	lə·ma·'ă·kāl		

The phrases in the beginning of v. 6 offer the first glimpse into the workings of human desire—a desire intimately connected to the sensory experience of sight. The combination in this verse of seeing (ראה) and taking (לקח, in 6d below) is the first of two cases in Gen 1–11 that describe human transgression of a boundary—the second coming in Gen 6:2, when the "sons of God" *see* that the "daughters of man" are beautiful and *take* them in marriage (לקח is also an idiom in Hebrew for marriage). Much later in Israel's story, in 2 Sam 11:2–5, King David *sees* Bathsheba and *takes* her, a transgression for which he will be punished in various ways throughout the rest of 2 Samuel.

6b	וְכִי תַאֲוָה־הוּא לָעֵינַיִם
	and that it was delightful to the eyes,

וְכִי	and that	---	conj
כִּי	wə·kî	W/ CONJ וְ	

תַּאֲוָה־	desire/craving/longing/delight	ABS	noun
תַּאֲוָה	ta·'ă·wâ-		
הוּא	it	---	personal pron
הוּא	hû'		
לָעֵינַיִם	to the (two) eyes	ABS W/ PREP לְ + DEF. ART.	noun
עַיִן	lā·ê·nayim		

The expansion on the visual aspect of the tree elicits wonder—what exactly is this tree supposed to look like, that it arouses such delight and desire?

6c   וְנֶחְמָד הָעֵץ לְהַשְׂכִּיל

and the tree was desirable for acquiring understanding,

וְנֶחְמָד	and (it) was desirable	NIPH PTCP MS W/ CONJ וְ	verb
חמד	wə·neḥ·mād		
הָעֵץ	the tree	ABS W/ DEF. ART.	noun
עֵץ	hā·'ēṣ		
לְהַשְׂכִּיל	to make wise/discerning/understanding	HIPH INF CST W/ PREP לְ	verb
שׂכל	lə·haś·kîl		

The use of this term for "wisdom, understanding" (שׂכל) is the first of its many appearances, which resound throughout Israel's wisdom literature (in Proverbs, Job, and in many wisdom-oriented psalms). Clearly, "understanding" is desirable, as it is extolled throughout the Bible.

6d   וַתִּקַּח מִפִּרְיוֹ

so she took of its fruit

וַתִּקַּח	and/then she took	QAL WAYY 3FS	verb
לקח	wat·tiq·qaḥ		
מִפִּרְיוֹ	from its fruit	CST W/ PREP מִן + 3MS SX	noun
פְּרִי	mip·pir·yô		

See comment on v. 6a above.

MAN, WOMAN, AND SERPENT

6e

וַתֹּאכַל

and she ate—

וַתֹּאכַל אכל	and she ate wat·tōʾ·kal	QAL WAYY 3FS	verb

6f

וַתִּתֵּן גַּם־לְאִישָׁהּ עִמָּהּ

and she also gave some to her husband, who was with her,

וַתִּתֵּן נתן	and she gave wat·tit·tēn	QAL WAYY 3FS	verb
גַּם־ גַּם	also gam-	---	adv
לְאִישָׁהּ איש	to her husband/man lə·ʾî·šāh	CST W/ PREP לְ + 3FS SX	noun
עִמָּהּ עִם	with her ʿim·māh	--- W/ 3FS SX	prep

Through this subtle and often-missed reference, we learn that the man is with the woman, presumably throughout the exchange. Whether he is to be understood as passive, or somehow not as capable or informed as the woman, is left open to question. Does the man speak to the woman about the situation in the moment? Perhaps the phrase "with her" only implies "with her generally, in the garden," and he has no access to the conversation between the serpent and the woman. Here again we have occasion to notice that despite the concrete details these early chapters of Genesis provide, they are incredibly sparse and leave so much open to the imagination, concealing key details from us.

6g

וַיֹּאכַל׃

and he ate.

וַיֹּאכַל׃ אכל	and he ate way·yōʾ·kal	QAL WAYY 3MS	verb

The concepts of thoughtless eating (gluttony) and of eating in general as a metaphor for knowledge arise repeatedly in biblical wisdom literature (see Job 12:11; 20:14; 34:3; Ps 78:18; Prov 23:3, 19–21; 30:22). Compare the rash act of eating in which both the man and the woman engage here with the scene in Gen 25:29–34, where Esau sells his birthright to his brother, Jacob, for the price of bread and stew, which he eats quickly and thoughtlessly. In both of these passages, the one who eats in this manner suffers a dire consequence.

7a	וַתִּפָּקַחְנָה עֵינֵי שְׁנֵיהֶם		
	Then the eyes of both of them were opened,		
וַתִּפָּקַחְנָה פקח	and (they) were opened *wat·tip·pā·qaḥ·nâ*	NIPH WAYY 3FP	verb
עֵינֵי עַיִן	(the) eyes of *'ê·nê*	CST	noun
שְׁנֵיהֶם שְׁנַיִם	both of them *šə·nê·hem*	CST W/ 3MP SX	cardinal number

7b	וַיֵּדְעוּ כִּי עֵירֻמִּם הֵם		
	and they knew that they were naked.		
וַיֵּדְעוּ ידע	and they knew *way·yē·də·'û*	QAL WAYY 3MP	verb
כִּי כִּי	that *kî*	---	conj
עֵירֻמִּם עֵירֹם	naked *'ê·rum·mīm*	MP PRED	adj
הֵם הֵם	they *hēm*	---	personal pron

Nakedness now becomes a problem for the humans. With their eyes opened, they "see" their own body and the body of the other in a new way. They also seem to "see" deeper, spiritual realities: they are vulnerable and ashamed, and they instinctively know that what has been uncovered must now be covered up. Their instinct is appropriate to what they have done and the state in which they now find themselves, and God personally makes more durable clothes for them in 3:22.

7c	וַֽיִּתְפְּרוּ֙ עֲלֵ֣ה תְאֵנָ֔ה
	They sewed together fig leaves

	וַֽיִּתְפְּרוּ֙	and they sewed	QAL WAYY 3MP	verb
	תפר	way·yit·pə·rû		
	עֲלֵ֣ה	leaf/leaves of	CST	noun
	עָלֶה	ʿă·lē		
	תְאֵנָ֔ה	fig	ABS	noun
	תְּאֵנָה	tə·ʾē·nâ		

The reference to fig leaves in this verse may have given rise to the idea, found in popular imagination and art throughout the centuries, that the fruit they ate was a fig (though the story does not indicate this).

7d	וַיַּעֲשׂ֥וּ לָהֶ֖ם חֲגֹרֹֽת׃
	and made loincloths for themselves.

	וַיַּעֲשׂ֥וּ	and they made	QAL WAYY 3MP	verb
	עשׂה	way·ya·ʿă·śû		
	לָהֶ֖ם	for them/themselves	---	prep
	לְ	lā·hem	W/ 3MP SX	
	חֲגֹרֹֽת׃	loincloths/girdles/belts	ABS	noun
	חֲגוֹרָה	ḥă·gō·rōt		

This act is the first discernible human engagement in culture or creating a physical item of any kind. Although the clothing here is not decorative or expressive so much as functional, it does—in addition to its physical use—serve the symbolic function of covering their vulnerability and shame. (For comments on Satan, sin, and punishment, see the following section on 3:14–21 and its accompanying "From Text to Sermon" section.)

From Text to Sermon

*As you meditate on this passage and contemplate
how you might teach or preach it to others,
consider the following areas of emphasis.*

 Historical and Literary Context. When thinking about the broader historical and literary context, we discover that, oddly enough, the Old Testament authors almost never refer to Adam or Eve or the serpent anywhere outside of Gen 1–3. Why might this be?

 Bridge to the Gospel. When we move to the preaching of the gospel in the New Testament, however, we find a much richer context. This is primarily because the New Testament authors saw a direct line between the actions of the first humans narrated in Gen 3 (note that here they are not yet named "Adam" and "Eve," though they will be later) and the saving work of Jesus Christ. For example, in 1 Cor 15:20–22, Paul writes:

> But in fact Christ has been raised from the dead, the first fruits of those who have died. For since death came through a human, the resurrection of the dead has also come through a human, for as all die in Adam, so all will be made alive in Christ. (NRSVue)

And in Rom 5:12–15, Paul uses the word *typos*, "pattern, example," to describe Adam in relation to Christ:

> Therefore, just as sin came into the world through one man, and death came through sin, and so death spread to all because all have sinned ... death reigned from Adam to Moses, even over those who did not sin in the likeness of Adam, who is a pattern [*typos*] of the one who was to come. ... For if the many died through the one man's trespass, much more surely have the grace of God and the gift in the grace of the one man, Jesus Christ, abounded for the many. (NRSVue)

Inspired by texts such as these, Christians for centuries have engaged in a powerful method of interpretation called "typology" (a word derived from Greek *typos*) that offers the possibility of seeing symbolic and spiritual connections between different biblical characters, as well as between biblical characters and oneself.

For example, in addition to the typology between Adam and Christ, the comparison between Eve and Mary, the mother of Jesus, was a treasured typology in the early church. The comparison can cut two ways. On the one hand, Eve and Mary can be thought of as opposites: Eve fails to obey God, whereas in her own pivotal moment of decision Mary says, "Here am I, the servant of the Lord; let it be with me according to your word" (Luke 1:38 NRSVue). On the other hand, both Eve and Mary are open to new life through childbearing in strange circumstances, and both give birth to humanity in profound ways. How might you encourage your audience to compare and contrast these two women?

In the biblical vision, the first man and woman set a primal (typological) pattern for all humans. Thus, in light of what we learn about the characters Adam and Eve in what we have read, ask yourself and your audience to consider questions such as *Who are we?* and *What are we like?* The rise of personality tests of all kinds and hundreds of books on the psycho-spiritual possibilities of tools like the Enneagram, the Myers-Briggs Type Indicator, StrengthsFinder, and so on display our concern to understand ourselves. And while these materials can certainly help, those steeped in the Bible know that inspired Scripture offers us God's template for human identity, meaning, and belonging. Though the Bible is sometimes read for information or "tips and tricks" on how to have a better life or how to calm one's anxieties, this is not really how the Christian church has for centuries treasured the word of God. Rather, on the deepest level, we read the Bible to know our place in God's great divine drama. We read the text and listen to preaching on it because this story is our story. We are the characters. The God of Adam and Eve is our God, and our future is bound to their past. Engaging with Scripture in this way is not an easy task, however: One cannot skim through one of its chapters and find results like we would on a personality inventory. Reading is slow, and living is hard. We read and we live this story to know who we truly are.

Relevance for Today. As we think about how to consider the themes of Gen 3 in light of our own experience, we sometimes imagine that we would have been more obedient than the woman or the man if we were in the same situation. Just don't eat the fruit, and we'll all live in paradise forever! But our lived experience should teach us better—we are frail, we are curious; and not only would we do the same thing that they did, but we *do* do the same thing that they did, almost every day. Take time to meditate on the scene at hand and allow the story to come alive in your own life—with all of its promise and warning. Imagine your own first moments of exploration as a child. What were some of the earliest desires you can remember having? When did those desires cross the line into disobedience, shame, or an awareness of death? Recall your first encounter with someone who was devious, someone more sophisticated than you who did not have your best interests in mind—and then juxtapose that with the sweet innocence of childhood, the purity of discovery, of eyes lighting up. Parents can watch their children grow from being naked in public or taking baths with siblings to suddenly having some kind of awareness, some barrier to engaging the world in that way. The eyes are opened. All of that drama, and more, is packed into this enigmatic and powerful story.

GENESIS 3:14–21

CONSEQUENCES IN THE GARDEN

Humans do not live for long in the Garden of Eden without the pain and confusion that comes from lies, shame, and disobedience to God. This theologically rich poem establishes key themes that will resonate throughout Scripture—sin, suffering, and alienation from God, but also the hint of redemption and return.

LARGER LITERARY CONTEXT ▸ 3:1–24

3:14–15

14a	וַיֹּאמֶר יְהֹוָה אֱלֹהִים ׀ אֶל־הַנָּחָשׁ
	wayyōʾmer YHWH ʾĕlōhîm ʾel-hannāḥāš
	The Lord God said to the serpent,
14b	כִּי עָשִׂיתָ זֹּאת
	kî ʿāśîtā zōʾt
	"Because you have done this,
14c	אָרוּר אַתָּה
	ʾārûr ʾattâ
	cursed are you
14d	מִכָּל־הַבְּהֵמָה
	mikkol-habbəhēmâ
	more than any beast,
14e	וּמִכֹּל חַיַּת הַשָּׂדֶה
	ûmikkōl ḥayyat haśśāde
	more than any living thing of the field!
14f	עַל־גְּחֹנְךָ תֵלֵךְ
	ʿal-gəḥōnəkā tēlēk
	You will go about on your belly
14g	וְעָפָר תֹּאכַל
	wəʿāfār tōʾkal
	and lick the dust
14h	כָּל־יְמֵי חַיֶּיךָ׃
	kol-yəmê ḥayyêkā.
	all the days of your life.

15a	וְאֵיבָה ׀ אָשִׁית *wəʾêvâ ʾāšît* **Enmity I will set**	
15b	בֵּינְךָ *bênəkā* **between you**	
15c	וּבֵין הָאִשָּׁה *ûvên hāʾiššâ* **and the woman,**	
15d	וּבֵין זַרְעֲךָ *ûvên zarʿăkā* **between your seed**	
15e	וּבֵין זַרְעָהּ *ûvên zarʿāh* **and her seed;**	
15f	הוּא יְשׁוּפְךָ רֹאשׁ *hûʾ yəšûfəkā rōʾš* **he will strike your head,**	
15g	וְאַתָּה תְּשׁוּפֶנּוּ עָקֵב׃ *wəʾattâ təšûfennû ʿāqēv.* **and you will strike his heel."**	

14a	וַיֹּ֨אמֶר יְהֹוָ֧ה אֱלֹהִ֛ים ׀ אֶל־הַנָּחָשׁ֙

	The LORD God said to the serpent,		
וַיֹּ֨אמֶר אמר	and (he) said way·yō'·mer	QAL WAYY 3MS	verb
יְהֹוָ֧ה יהוה	the LORD YHWH	ABS	noun
אֱלֹהִ֛ים ׀ אֱלֹהִים	God 'ĕ·lō·hîm	ABS	noun
אֶל־ אֶל	to 'el-	---	prep
הַנָּחָשׁ֙ נָחָשׁ	the serpent/snake han·nā·ḥāš	ABS W/ DEF. ART.	noun

As discussed earlier, the narrator alternates between calling the deity "God" in ch. 1 and "the LORD God" in ch. 2. Following this, in the first dramatic act of ch. 3 (vv. 1–7), the serpent and the woman refer to "God" when quoting the deity's commands; but then, beginning at 3:8, the narrator changes back to "the LORD God," as the woman and the man are caught hiding in the garden and as the poem of punishment is delivered in vv. 14–19. The full title "the LORD God" may add some literary sense of God's full authority, as he proclaims the consequences that follow the forbidden eating.

14b	כִּ֣י עָשִׂ֣יתָ זֹּ֗את

	"Because you have done this,		
כִּ֣י כִּי	because/for/since kî	---	conj
עָשִׂ֣יתָ עשׂה	you did/have done 'ā·śî·tā	QAL PF 2MS	verb
זֹּ֗את זֹאת	this zō't	---	demonstr pron

Of theological importance here is the fact that the Lord first addresses the serpent—not the woman or the man—in the list of punishments, as if to suggest that the serpent is the first to blame. By contrast, notice that when the apostle Paul writes about sin in the garden story (Rom 5; 1 Cor

13), he mentions only the humans as the protagonists, with no reference to the serpent, Satan, or any other influence.

14c	אָר֥וּר אַתָּה֙		
	cursed are you		
	אָר֥וּר cursed ארר 'ā·rûr	QAL PASS PTCP MS	verb
	אַתָּה֙ you אַתָּה 'at·tâ	---	personal pron

Even though Christians often refer to the events and outcome of this chapter as "the curse of man," we should notice the exact wording of the text: as far as living beings are concerned, the specific language of being cursed (ארר) is applied only to the serpent. The passive form here for "cursed," אָרוּר, is also notable; clearly, God is doing the cursing, yet the passive grammar could lean into the notion that God is not so much personally "cursing" or "hexing" the serpent (or later, in v. 17, the earth) but rather that the actions result in certain natural consequences.

14d	מִכָּל־הַבְּהֵמָ֔ה		
	more than any beast,		
	מִכָּל־ from all/more than all כֹּל mik·kol-	CST W/ PREP מִן	noun
	הַבְּהֵמָ֔ה the beast(s)/animal(s) בְּהֵמָה hab·bə·hē·mâ	ABS W/ DEF. ART.	noun

14e	וּמִכֹּ֖ל חַיַּ֣ת הַשָּׂדֶ֑ה		
	more than any living thing of the field!		
	וּמִכֹּ֖ל and from/more than all כֹּל û·mik·kōl	CST W/ CONJ וְ + PREP מִן	noun
	חַיַּ֣ת (the) living thing(s) of חַיָּה ḥay·yat	CST	noun

CONSEQUENCES IN THE GARDEN

הַשָּׂדֶה	the field	ABS	noun
שָׂדֶה	haś·śā·de	W/ DEF. ART.	

14f — עַל־גְּחֹנְךָ תֵלֵךְ

You will go about on your belly

עַל־	on/upon	---	prep
עַל	'al-		
גְּחֹנְךָ	your belly/stomach	CST	noun
גָּחוֹן	gə·ḥō·nə·kā	W/ 2MS SX	
תֵלֵךְ	you will walk/go	QAL IMPF 2MS	verb
הלך	tē·lēk		

14g — וְעָפָר תֹּאכַל

and lick the dust

וְעָפָר	and dust	ABS	noun
עָפָר	wə·'ā·fār	W/ CONJ וְ	
תֹּאכַל	you will eat/consume	QAL IMPF 2MS	verb
אכל	tō'·kal		

This specified punishment would naturally lead to the assumption that the serpent was standing upon two legs or otherwise *not* crawling on his belly and licking the dust *before* this curse. How exactly we are to imagine that, or why the narrator doesn't give us more specific information, is not clear! In addition to its rich theological dimensions and symbolic connection to Satan in Christian tradition outside of the Bible (see comment above at 3:1), the story here is also etiological, i.e., a story of origins, one that explains the oddity of the snake among animals: it has no arms or legs and crawls about on its belly, occupying a low position upon the earth. The connection between the serpent's physical location on the ground thus connects with the curse on the "earth" (אֲדָמָה) in v. 17.

14h	כָּל־יְמֵי חַיֶּיךָ:
	all the days of your life.

	כָּל־ כֹּל *kol-*	all of	CST	noun
	יְמֵי יוֹם *yə·mê*	(the) days of	CST	noun
	חַיֶּיךָ: חַיִּים *ḥay·yê·kā*	your life	CST W/ 2MS SX	noun

15a	וְאֵיבָה ׀ אָשִׁית
	Enmity I will set

	וְאֵיבָה ׀ אֵיבָה *wə·ê·vâ*	and a state of being enemies/enmity	ABS W/ CONJ וְ	noun
	אָשִׁית שִׁית *'ā·šît*	I will set/place	QAL IMPF 1CS	verb

On the most basic, etiological level, we see the establishment of a primal human-animal relationship: almost all people have a natural fear of snakes, even those who have no negative experience with snakes or who have never even seen one in person. Controlled, professionally conducted psychological studies have shown that even infants have a clear reaction to snakes versus other animals. On a deeper level, God recognizes (or here institutes, for the first time?) a cosmic enemy relationship between what the snake represents (lies, being anti-God) and what the woman represents (innocence, being in relationship to God).

15b	בֵּינְךָ
	between you

	בֵּינְךָ בֵּין *bê·nə·kā*	between you	--- W/ 2MS SX	prep

CONSEQUENCES IN THE GARDEN

15c

וּבֵין הָאִשָּׁה

and the woman,

וּבֵין	and between	---	prep
bên	û·vên	W/ CONJ וְ	
הָאִשָּׁה	the woman	ABS	noun
אִשָּׁה	hā·ʾiš·šâ	W/ DEF. ART.	

15d

וּבֵין זַרְעֲךָ

between your seed

וּבֵין	and between	---	prep
בֵּין	û·vên	W/ CONJ וְ	
זַרְעֲךָ	your seed/offspring	CST	noun
זֶרַע	zar·ʿă·kā	W/ 2MS SX	

15e

וּבֵין זַרְעָהּ

and her seed;

וּבֵין	and between	---	prep
בֵּין	û·vên	W/ CONJ וְ	
זַרְעָהּ	her seed/offspring	CST	noun
זֶרַע	zar·ʿāh	W/ 3FS SX	

15f

הוּא יְשׁוּפְךָ רֹאשׁ

he will strike your head,

הוּא	it/he	---	personal pron
הוּא	hûʾ		
יְשׁוּפְךָ	(he) will bruise/strike you	QAL IMPF 3MS	verb
שׁוּף	yə·šû·fə·kā	W/ 2MS SX	
רֹאשׁ	head	ABS	noun
רֹאשׁ	rōʾš		

The poem offers us two rich levels of analysis—one directly from the words of the text and its basic concepts, accessible to any reader, but also a deeper reading within our Christian tradition. The basic antagonism between snake and human implies something serious and disastrous about the relationship between humans and nature in the new world humans must inhabit. The snake will bite, but the human will step on the snake; the same (rare) word, שׁוּף ("strike, crush"), is used in both phrases to describe what each will do to the other, without any clear sense that one is victorious. However, Christian theology transforms the cryptic phrase into something much bigger—Satan may bite at our heels, crucifying our Lord and inflicting what seem to be poisonous, mortal wounds upon all of humanity; but Jesus, the new Adam, will stomp on the head of the devil, rise from the dead, and deliver humanity from the curse. We see a glimpse of the end already in the beginning.

15g	וְאַתָּה תְּשׁוּפֶנּוּ עָקֵב׃		
	and you will strike his heel."		
	וְאַתָּה — and you	---	personal
	אַתָּה — wə·'at·tâ	W/ CONJ וְ	pron
	תְּשׁוּפֶנּוּ — (you) will bruise/strike it/him	QAL IMPF 2MS	verb
	שׁוּף — tə·šû·fen·nû	W/ 3MS SX	
	עָקֵב׃ — heel	ABS	noun
	עָקֵב — 'ā·qēv		

3:16

16a אֶל־הָאִשָּׁ֣ה אָמַ֔ר
’el-hā’iššâ ’āmar

To the woman he said,

16b הַרְבָּ֤ה אַרְבֶּה֙ עִצְּבוֹנֵ֣ךְ וְהֵֽרֹנֵ֔ךְ
harbâ ’arbe ’iṣṣəvônēk wəhērōnēk

"I will greatly increase your pregnancy pains—

16c בְּעֶ֖צֶב תֵּֽלְדִ֣י בָנִ֑ים
bə‘eṣev tēlədî vānîm

in pain you will bear children,

16d וְאֶל־אִישֵׁךְ֙ תְּשׁ֣וּקָתֵ֔ךְ
wə’el-’îšēk təšûqātēk

yet your desire will be for your husband,

16e וְה֖וּא יִמְשָׁל־בָּֽךְ׃
wəhû’ yimšol-bāk.

and he will rule over you."

16a	אֶל־הָאִשָּׁ֣ה אָמַ֔ר
	To the woman he said,

	אֶל־	to	---	prep
	אֶל	’el-		
	הָאִשָּׁה	the woman	ABS W/ DEF. ART.	noun
	אִשָּׁה	hā·’iš·šâ		
	אָמַ֔ר	he said	QAL PF 3MS	verb
	אמר	’ā·mar		

16b

הַרְבָּ֤ה אַרְבֶּה֙ עִצְּבוֹנֵ֣ךְ וְהֵֽרֹנֵ֔ךְ

"I will greatly increase your pregnancy pains—

הַרְבָּ֤ה רבה *har·bâ*	making great/many/ increasing	HIPH INF ABS	verb
אַרְבֶּה֙ רבה *'ar·be*	I will make great/many/ increase	HIPH IMPF 1CS	verb
עִצְּבוֹנֵ֣ךְ עִצָּבוֹן *'iṣ·ṣə·vô·nēḵ*	your pain/toil	CST W/ 2FS SX	noun
וְהֵֽרֹנֵ֔ךְ הֵרָיוֹן *wə·hē·rō·nēḵ*	and/by/in your conception of children	CST W/ CONJ וְ + 2FS SX	noun

On its own, the verb הרה (from which the noun הֵרָיוֹן here is derived) refers to conception, while the verb ילד (used in the next clause) refers to childbirth. The two terms are often used together to refer to the entire process of conception, pregnancy, and giving birth.

16c

בְּעֶ֖צֶב תֵּֽלְדִ֣י בָנִ֑ים

in pain you will bear children,

בְּעֶ֖צֶב עֶצֶב *bə·'e·ṣev*	in pain/toil	ABS W/ PREP בְּ	noun
תֵּֽלְדִ֣י ילד *tē·lə·dî*	you will bear	QAL IMPF 2FS	verb
בָנִ֑ים בֵּן *vā·nîm*	children/sons	ABS	noun

16d

וְאֶל־אִישֵׁךְ֙ תְּשׁ֣וּקָתֵ֔ךְ

yet your desire will be for your husband,

וְאֶל־ אֶל *wə·'el-*	and/but to/for	--- W/ CONJ וְ	prep

CONSEQUENCES IN THE GARDEN

אִישֵׁךְ	your husband/man	CST W/ 2FS SX	noun
אִישׁ	'î·šēḵ		
תְּשׁוּקָתֵךְ	your desire/longing	CST W/ 2FS SX	noun
תְּשׁוּקָה	tə·šû·qā·tēḵ		

The noun תְּשׁוּקָה, "desire, longing," occurs only three times in the Hebrew Bible. The second instance, like this one, is negative: in the story of Cain and Abel, we read about sin's "desire" to trap Cain as he festers with anger over the rejection of his sacrifice (4:7). Significantly, the third occurrence of תְּשׁוּקָה, found in Song 7:11 [10], appears to be a reversal of the curse found here in Gen 3:16—there, the female lover states, "I am my beloved's, and his desire [תְּשׁוּקָה] is for me." In the picture of love and intimacy painted in Song of Songs, female and male are restored to their primal state of unity and positive mutual longing.

16e	וְהוּא יִמְשָׁל־בָּךְ׃		
	and he will rule over you."		
וְהוּא	and/but he	--- W/ CONJ וְ	personal pron
הוּא	wə·hû'		
יִמְשָׁל־	(he) will rule	QAL IMPF 3MS	verb
מָשַׁל	yim·šol-		
בָּךְ׃	over/in you	--- W/ 2FS SX	prep
בְּ	bāḵ		

The connection between desire for the husband, pain in childbearing, and the hierarchical gender arrangement puts the woman in a truly difficult bind—though pregnancy and (presumably) the hierarchy will hurt her, she is doomed to desire the man anyway, thus perpetuating the cycle. The verb used here for "rule," מָשַׁל, also appears in the Cain and Abel story (4:7, on which see the previous comment), in God's admonition to Cain that he must "master" the desire of sin. The man and woman are now involved in a cycle of desire, sin, hierarchy, and mastery.

3:17–21

17a
וּלְאָדָ֣ם אָמַ֗ר
ûləʾādām ʾāmar

And to the man he said,

17b
כִּ֣י־שָׁמַ֘עְתָּ֮ לְק֣וֹל אִשְׁתֶּךָ֒
kî-šāmaʿtā ləqôl ʾištekā

"Because you listened to the voice of your wife

17c
וַתֹּ֙אכַל֙ מִן־הָעֵ֔ץ אֲשֶׁ֣ר צִוִּיתִ֣יךָ לֵאמֹ֔ר
wattōʾkal min-hāʿēṣ ʾăšer ṣiwwîtîkā lēʾmōr

and ate from the tree about which I commanded you, saying,

17d
לֹ֥א תֹאכַ֖ל מִמֶּ֑נּוּ
lōʾ tōʾkal mimmennû

'You shall not eat from it,'

17e
אֲרוּרָ֤ה הָֽאֲדָמָה֙ בַּֽעֲבוּרֶ֔ךָ
ʾărûrâ hāʾădāmâ baʿăvûrekā

cursed is the ground because of you!

17f
בְּעִצָּבוֹן֙ תֹּֽאכֲלֶ֔נָּה
bəʿiṣṣāvôn tōʾkălennâ

In pain you will eat from it

17g
כֹּ֖ל יְמֵ֥י חַיֶּֽיךָ׃
kōl yəmê ḥayyêkā.

all the days of your life;

18a
וְק֥וֹץ וְדַרְדַּ֖ר תַּצְמִ֣יחַֽ לָ֑ךְ
wəqôṣ wədardar taṣmîaḥ lāk

thorns and thistles will spring forth against you,

18b	וְאָכַלְתָּ֖ אֶת־עֵ֥שֶׂב הַשָּׂדֶֽה׃	
	wəʾāḵaltā ʾet-ʿēśev haśśāde.	

yet you will eat the green things of the field.

19a	בְּזֵעַ֤ת אַפֶּ֙יךָ֙ תֹּ֣אכַל לֶ֔חֶם	
	bəzēʿat ʾappêḵā tōʾḵal leḥem	

By the sweat of your face you will eat food,

19b	עַ֤ד שֽׁוּבְךָ֙ אֶל־הָ֣אֲדָמָ֔ה	
	ʿad šûvəḵā ʾel-hāʾăḏāmâ	

until you return to the ground—

19c	כִּ֥י מִמֶּ֖נָּה לֻקָּ֑חְתָּ	
	kî mimmennâ luqqāḥtā	

for from it you were taken.

19d	כִּֽי־עָפָ֣ר אַ֔תָּה	
	kî-ʿāfār ʾattâ	

For you are dust,

19e	וְאֶל־עָפָ֖ר תָּשֽׁוּב׃	
	wəʾel-ʿāfār tāšûv.	

and to dust you will return.

20a	וַיִּקְרָ֧א הָֽאָדָ֛ם שֵׁ֥ם אִשְׁתּ֖וֹ חַוָּ֑ה	
	wayyiqrāʾ hāʾāḏām šēm ʾištô ḥawwâ	

The man named his wife "Living"/Eve,

20b	כִּ֛י הִ֥וא הָֽיְתָ֖ה אֵ֥ם כָּל־חָֽי׃	
	kî hîʾ hāyətâ ʾēm kol-ḥāy.	

because she was the mother of all who are alive.

21a	וַיַּ֩עַשׂ֩ יְהוָ֨ה אֱלֹהִ֜ים לְאָדָ֧ם וּלְאִשְׁתּ֛וֹ	
	wayyaʿaś YHWH ʾĕlōhîm ləʾāḏām ûləʾištô	

The Lord God made for the man and his wife

21b	כָּתְנ֥וֹת ע֖וֹר
	kotnôt ʿôr
	clothes of skin,

21c	וַיַּלְבִּשֵֽׁם׃
	wayyalbīšēm.
	and he clothed them.

17a	וּלְאָדָ֣ם אָמַ֗ר
	And to the man he said,

וּלְאָדָ֣ם	and to Adam/man	ABS	noun
אָדָם	*û·lə ʾā·dām*	W/ CONJ וּ + PREP לְ	
אָמַ֗ר	he said	QAL PF 3MS	verb
אמר	*ʾā·mar*		

The lack of the definite article here offers the possibility of translating וּלְאָדָם as "and to Adam" (see also 2:20d for this same issue; in Hebrew, proper nouns as a rule cannot take the definite article). When Eve is named, however (three verses later, in 3:20), the narrator refers not to "Adam" but to "the man," as has been the narrator's convention throughout Gen 1–3 up to this point. Indeed, Adam has no naming ceremony parallel to Eve's; instead, beginning in 4:25, the narrator simply begins unambiguously referring to him as "Adam" (אָדָם) instead of "the man" (הָאָדָם).

17b	כִּֽי־שָׁמַ֘עְתָּ֮ לְק֣וֹל אִשְׁתֶּךָ֒
	"Because you listened to the voice of your wife

כִּֽי־	because/for/since	---	conj
כִּי	*kî-*		
שָׁמַ֘עְתָּ֮	you listened	QAL PF 2MS	verb
שמע	*šā·maʿ·tā*		

CONSEQUENCES IN THE GARDEN

לְקוֹל קוֹל	to (the) sound/voice of lə·qôl	CST W/ PREP לְ	noun
אִשְׁתֶּךָ אִשָּׁה	your woman/wife 'iš·te·kā	CST W/ 2MS SX	noun

17c — וַתֹּאכַל מִן־הָעֵץ אֲשֶׁר צִוִּיתִיךָ לֵאמֹר

and ate from the tree about which I commanded you, saying,

וַתֹּאכַל אכל	and you ate/consumed wat·tō'·kal	QAL WAYY 2MS	verb
מִן־ מִן	from min-	---	prep
הָעֵץ עֵץ	the tree hā·'ēṣ	ABS W/ DEF. ART.	noun
אֲשֶׁר אֲשֶׁר	that/which 'ă·šer	---	relative pron
צִוִּיתִיךָ צוה	I commanded you ṣiw·wî·tî·kā	PIEL PF 1CS W/ 2MS SX	verb
לֵאמֹר אמר	saying lē'·mōr	QAL INF CST W/ PREP לְ	verb

17d — לֹא תֹאכַל מִמֶּנּוּ

'You shall not eat from it,'

לֹא לֹא	not lō'	---	particle
תֹאכַל אכל	you will eat/consume tō'·kal	QAL IMPF 2MS	verb
מִמֶּנּוּ מִן	from it mim·men·nû	--- W/ 3MS SX	prep

17e	אֲרוּרָה הָאֲדָמָה בַּעֲבוּרֶךָ
	cursed is the ground because of you!

אֲרוּרָה ארר	cursed 'ā·rû·râ	QAL PASS PTCP FS	verb
הָאֲדָמָה אֲדָמָה	the ground hā·'ă·dā·**mâ**	ABS W/ DEF. ART.	noun
בַּעֲבוּרֶךָ בַּעֲבוּר	on your account/behalf ba·'ă·vû·**re**·kā	--- W/ 2MS SX	prep

Notice the wordplay between the terms for "man" (אָדָם) and "ground" (אֲדָמָה). In addition, the emphatic nature of this curse line is underscored by the repetition of a long "a" sound at the end of each word.

17f	בְּעִצָּבוֹן תֹּאכֲלֶנָּה
	In pain you will eat from it

בְּעִצָּבוֹן עִצָּבוֹן	in pain/toil bə·'iṣ·ṣā·**vôn**	ABS W/ PREP בְּ	noun
תֹּאכֲלֶנָּה אכל	you will eat/consume it tō'·ḵă·**len**·nâ	QAL IMPF 2MS W/ 3FS SX	verb

The term for "pain" (עִצָּבוֹן) here is the same word God uses in v. 16 when he tells Eve that he will greatly increase her pregnancy pains.

17g	כֹּל יְמֵי חַיֶּיךָ:
	all the days of your life;

כֹּל כֹּל	all of kōl	CST	noun
יְמֵי יוֹם	(the) days of yə·**mê**	CST	noun
חַיֶּיךָ: חַיִּים	your life ḥay·**yê**·kā	CST W/ 2MS SX	noun

CONSEQUENCES IN THE GARDEN

18a — וְק֥וֹץ וְדַרְדַּ֖ר תַּצְמִ֣יחַֽ לָ֑ךְ

thorns and thistles will spring forth against you,

Hebrew	Gloss	Parsing	POS
וְק֥וֹץ / קוֹץ / wə·qôṣ	and thorn(s)	ABS W/ CONJ ו	noun
וְדַרְדַּ֖ר / דַּרְדַּר / wə·dar·dar	and thistle(s)	ABS W/ CONJ ו	noun
תַּצְמִ֣יחַ / צמח / taṣ·mî·aḥ	(it) will sprout/spring forth/grow up	HIPH IMPF 3FS	verb
לָ֑ךְ / לְ / lāk	for you	W/ 2MS SX	prep

18b — וְאָכַלְתָּ֖ אֶת־עֵ֥שֶׂב הַשָּׂדֶֽה׃

yet you will eat the green things of the field.

Hebrew	Gloss	Parsing	POS
וְאָכַלְתָּ֖ / אכל / wə·'ā·kal·tā	and you will eat	QAL WEQATAL 2MS	verb
אֶת־ / אֵת / 'et-	(direct object marker)	---	particle
עֵ֥שֶׂב / עֵשֶׂב / 'ē·śev	(the) green things/plants of	CST	noun
הַשָּׂדֶֽה׃ / שָׂדֶה / haś·śā·de	the field	ABS W/ DEF. ART.	noun

Translating the initial ו here as "yet," as v. 16d is rendered above ("yet your desire will be for your husband"), demonstrates the symmetry of the punishment between man and woman. Whereas the woman was doomed to a paradoxical cycle of desire for her husband, which can lead to painful childbirth, the man is doomed to an earth that produces thorns and thistles but which he must nevertheless till in order to eat.

19a

בְּזֵעַת אַפֶּ֙יךָ֙ תֹּ֣אכַל לֶ֔חֶם

By the sweat of your face you will eat food,

Hebrew	Translation	Parsing	
בְּזֵעַת זֵעָה	by (the) sweat of bə·zēʿat	CST W/ PREP בְּ	noun
אַפֶּ֙יךָ֙ אַף	your nose/face ʾap·pê·ḵā	CST W/ 2MS SX	noun
תֹּ֣אכַל אכל	you will eat/consume tōʾ·ḵal	QAL IMPF 2MS	verb
לֶ֔חֶם לֶחֶם	bread/food le·ḥem	ABS	noun

19b

עַ֤ד שֽׁוּבְךָ֙ אֶל־הָ֣אֲדָמָ֔ה

until you return to the ground—

Hebrew	Translation	Parsing	
עַ֤ד עַד	until ʿad	---	prep
שֽׁוּבְךָ֙ שׁוּב	your returning/going back šû·və·ḵā	QAL INF CST W/ 2MS SX	verb
אֶל־ אֶל	to ʾel-	---	prep
הָאֲדָמָה אֲדָמָה	the earth/ground hā·ʾă·dā·mâ	ABS W/ DEF. ART.	noun

19c

כִּ֥י מִמֶּ֖נָּה לֻקָּ֑חְתָּ

for from it you were taken.

Hebrew	Translation	Parsing	
כִּ֥י כִּי	because/for/since kî	---	conj
מִמֶּ֖נָּה מִן	from it mim·men·nâ	--- W/ 3FS SX	prep
לֻקָּ֑חְתָּ לקח	you were taken luq·qāḥ·tā	PUAL PF 2MS	verb

CONSEQUENCES IN THE GARDEN

19d	כִּי־עָפָר אַתָּה		
	For you are dust,		
	כִּי־ because/for/since כִּי kî-	---	conj
	עָפָר dust עָפָר 'ā·fār	ABS	noun
	אָתָּה you אַתָּה 'at·tâ	---	personal pron

19e	וְאֶל־עָפָר תָּשׁוּב:		
	and to dust you will return.		
	וְאֶל־ and to אֶל wə·'el-	W/ CONJ וְ	prep
	עָפָר dust עָפָר 'ā·fār	ABS	noun
	תָּשׁוּב: you will return/go back שׁוּב tā·šûv	QAL IMPF 2.MS	verb

The culminating effect for the man is harsh indeed. What was at first celebrated as a joyful scene—God creating man from the dust of the earth like a careful potter—now turns full circle to a haunting end: the man will go back into the ground. Even though all humans—both men and women—die, the connection of the man's title (הָאָדָם) to the ground (אֲדָמָה) marks something mysterious and specific for the man in this poem: he will die. His grand work and "domination" over the earth and other people will come to dust. He will never be God.

20a	וַיִּקְרָא הָאָדָם שֵׁם אִשְׁתּוֹ חַוָּה		
	The man named his wife "Living"/Eve,		
	וַיִּקְרָא and (he) called/named קרא way·yiq·rā'	QAL WAYY 3MS	verb
	הָאָדָם the man אָדָם hā·'ā·dām	ABS W/ DEF. ART.	noun

שֵׁם šēm	(the) name of	CST	noun
אִשְׁתּוֹ ʾiš·tô	his wife	CST W/ 3MS SX	noun
חַוָּה ḥaw·wâ	Living/Havvah/Eve	ABS	noun

This naming ceremony follows somewhat incongruously upon the previous poem, but it does offer a note of hope and a turn toward life after what could have been a complete end for the humans. It also carries on with the themes of naming and creation that began in chs. 1–2. The name "Eve" transliterates the Hebrew word חַוָּה, as mediated through Latin (*Eva*). Since this Hebrew name comes from the root חיה/חוה, "live, be alive," one might translate it as "Living" or "The Living One," reflecting the statement found in the next clause.

20b   כִּי הִוא הָיְתָה אֵם כָּל־חָי׃

because she was the mother of all who are alive.

כִּי kî	because/for/since	---	conj
הִוא hîʾ	she	---	personal pron
הָיְתָה hā·yə·tâ	(she) was	QAL PF 3FS	verb
אֵם ʾēm	(the) mother of	CST	noun
כָּל־ kol-	each/every	CST	noun
חָי׃ ḥāy	living (one)	MS SUBST	adj

This is the Bible's first reference to motherhood, or to parenting of any kind.

CONSEQUENCES IN THE GARDEN

21a

	וַיַּעַשׂ יְהוָה אֱלֹהִים לְאָדָם וּלְאִשְׁתּוֹ		
	The LORD God made for the man and his wife		
וַיַּעַשׂ עשׂה	and (he) made way·yaʻaś	QAL WAYY 3MS	verb
יְהוָה יהוה	the LORD YHWH	ABS	noun
אֱלֹהִים אֱלֹהִים	God ʼĕ·lō·hîm	ABS	noun
לְאָדָם אָדָם	for Adam/man lə·ʼā·dām	ABS W/ PREP לְ	noun
וּלְאִשְׁתּוֹ אִשָּׁה	and for his wife/woman û·lə·ʼiš·tô	CST W/ CONJ וְ + PREP לְ + 3MS SX	noun

See the comments on the name "Adam" at 1:26 and 3:17.

21b

	כָּתְנוֹת עוֹר		
	clothes of skin,		
כָּתְנוֹת כֻּתֹּנֶת	clothes/tunics of kot·nôt	CST	noun
עוֹר עוֹר	skin/leather ʻôr	ABS	noun

21c

	וַיַּלְבִּשֵׁם׃		
	and he clothed them.		
וַיַּלְבִּשֵׁם׃ לבשׁ	and he clothed them way·yal·bi·šēm	HIPH WAYY 3MS W/ 3MP SX	verb

In another note of hope, perhaps even a surprising one, God now covers up the nakedness of the people that had caused them so much shame that they hid from each other and from God and attempted to create flimsy clothing for themselves out of leaves. These clothes of skin (or "leather") provide durability suitable for continued life.

From Text to Sermon

*As you meditate on this passage and contemplate
how you might teach or preach it to others,
consider the following areas of emphasis.*

 Theological Context. Consider the paradoxes that now come into view when reading the first three chapters of Genesis. We might define a "paradox" as a tension or contradiction that God has endorsed and made holy. Ask yourself or your audience to think about, for example, the incarnation in the person of Jesus Christ: God, who is wholly other and above and beyond and remote, became personal and clear and embodied. How can a being be both far and near at the same time? How can divinity and humanity, two very separate categories of existence, be reconciled in the same body? Other theological paradoxes force us to learn how to live in two ways at once: How can the church, which is called to be "holy," set apart from sin (Lev 19:2; 2 Cor 6:17; 1 Pet 1:15–17), also be "one," living in unity (John 17:21; Phil 2:2)? Holiness may ask us to step back, to set up boundaries; unity asks us to tear down boundaries and lean in. The opening three chapters of Genesis, culminating here in ch. 3, present us with one of the most primal of theological paradoxes, at the heart of what it means to be a human being: *We are created good, in the image of God, yet something is also horribly broken and painful in the human experience.*

As we seek to relate this story to others in the Old Testament, it can be helpful to meditate on other key moments of human choice gone wrong in the book of Genesis that nevertheless take a redemptive turn in God's graciousness toward humanity. Examples abound: Cain, Abraham and Sarah and Hagar, Jacob and Esau, Joseph and his brothers. This theme could be extended further in Scripture, to the life of David in 1–2 Samuel, for example, as well as to the painful central metaphor in the book of Hosea.

Given the broad familiarity many audiences have with Gen 3, you might find it effective to "defamiliarize" this text by reading it in a new translation, or to personalize it by asking your listeners to recall situations of lost innocence in their own lives. Sometimes a simple question such as *What does this poem teach us?* can be very effective. We can read it and simply affirm that the world is broken, pointing to its etiological function as a story of the origin of human suffering. The first man and woman did this, and now we suffer. Indeed, *we all do this*. Clearly the story sets the stage for what is to come in Gen 4–11, where the universal scope of human wickedness and hubris is on full display.

Although this poem and its aftermath can and should properly be read as a story of sin and its consequences, it is interesting to note that the word "sin" does not actually occur in this story (it first appears in Gen 4:7), nor are phrases like "the fall" or "the curse of man" present (as noted above, humans are not directly cursed in the story, only the serpent is). We might therefore also consider other (albeit related) prominent themes that allow additional spiritual dimensions of the story to open for us: *futility* and *forgiveness*.

The futility of human striving and our quest for some great wisdom through books and learning takes center stage in the book of Ecclesiastes, and we could profitably read Gen 3 alongside the dour words of the Preacher who proclaims, "Vanity of vanities! All is vanity" (Eccl 1:2 NRSVue). Adam and Eve seek esoteric knowledge, but the discovery to which this leads them is similar to the narrator of Ecclesiastes' lament that "much study is a weariness of the flesh" (Eccl 12:12 NRSVue). We desire knowledge, but it ends in pain. The man and woman seek to have their eyes opened, to cheat death, and to be like God; but they would have done well to heed Jesus' words in the Sermon on the Mount: "So do not worry about tomorrow, for tomorrow will bring worries of its own. Today's trouble is enough for today" (Matt 6:34 NRSVue).

But their alienation is not final. God provides a way out, a way back, through the provision of clothing. Their shame at their nakedness is surely part of their punishment, and yet God immediately seeks to help them reverse it. So too, for the horrible toil the man will experience when working, God provides the Sabbath, and our creativity as those created in "God's image" (Gen 1:26–27) means that we strive to make our work more effective and improve our use of technology. For the pain of childbearing, we draw upon our accumulated medical research and the wisdom of women who have gone before us to reduce pain and deliver children safely. For the sinful effects of sexism, we strive to reform our legal systems and cultural structures, and we also draw on the broader revelation of Scripture—ultimately in Jesus Christ—that affirms the nobility and equality of women alongside men. And in the end of the story in its broadest arc, as an act of incredible grace, God even offers the entire Garden of Eden back to us:

> Then the angel showed me the river of the water of life, bright as crystal, flowing from the throne of God and of the Lamb through the middle of the street of the city. On either side of the river is

the tree of life with its twelve kinds of fruit, producing its fruit each month, and the leaves of the tree are for the healing of the nations. Nothing accursed will be found there any more. But the throne of God and of the Lamb will be in it, and his servants will worship him; they will see his face, and his name will be on their foreheads. And there will be no more night; they need no light of lamp or sun, for the Lord God will be their light, and they will reign forever and ever.

(Rev 22:1–5 NRSVue)

GENESIS 4:1–16

BROTHER MURDERS BROTHER

The human drama deepens as brother rises up against brother, committing the first murder. Even so, following the pattern first presented in Gen 3 of the aftermath of rebellion against boundaries, God provides a way of redemption and new life, showing his proclivity to do so even in the worst cases.

LARGER LITERARY CONTEXT ▸ 4:1–26

4:1–2

1a

וְהָ֣אָדָ֔ם יָדַ֖ע אֶת־חַוָּ֣ה אִשְׁתּ֑וֹ

wəhā'ādām yāda' 'et-ḥawwâ 'ištô

Now the man knew Eve, his wife,

1b

וַתַּ֙הַר֙ וַתֵּ֣לֶד אֶת־קַ֔יִן

wattahar wattēled 'et-qayin

and she conceived and bore Cain.

1c

וַתֹּ֕אמֶר

wattō'mer

She said,

1d

קָנִ֥יתִי אִ֖ישׁ אֶת־יְהוָֽה׃

qānîtî 'îš 'et-YHWH.

"I have acquired a man with the Lord!"

2a

וַתֹּ֣סֶף לָלֶ֔דֶת אֶת־אָחִ֖יו אֶת־הָ֑בֶל

wattōsef lāledet 'et-'āḥîw 'et-hāvel

And she bore again—his brother, Abel.

2b

וַֽיְהִי־הֶ֙בֶל֙ רֹ֣עֵה צֹ֔אן

wayəhî-hevel rō'ē ṣō'n

Now Abel was a shepherd of sheep,

2c

וְקַ֕יִן הָיָ֖ה עֹבֵ֥ד אֲדָמָֽה׃

wəqayin hāyâ 'ōvēd 'ădāmâ.

and Cain was a worker of the ground.

1a

וְהָאָדָ֗ם יָדַ֖ע אֶת־חַוָּ֣ה אִשְׁתּ֑וֹ

Now the man knew Eve, his wife,

וְהָאָדָ֗ם אָדָם	and/now/then the man/human wə·hā·ʾā·dām	ABS W/ CONJ וְ + DEF. ART.	noun
יָדַ֖ע ידע	(he) knew yā·daʿ	QAL PF 3MS	verb
אֶת־ אֵת	(direct object marker) ʾet-	---	particle
חַוָּ֣ה חַוָּה	Eve ḥaw·wâ	ABS	proper noun
אִשְׁתּ֑וֹ אִשָּׁה	his wife ʾiš·tô	CST W/ 3MS SX	noun

The Hebrew term for "knowing" (ידע) is obviously used here, as it is elsewhere (e.g., Judg 11:39; 1 Sam 1:19), as a euphemism for sex (the verb שכב, "lie down," is also used this way; e.g., Gen 19:32; 1 Sam 2:22). There is probably no need here to endow the word with any particular or special meaning connecting knowledge and sex beyond the euphemism, though it is worth noticing the relationship among the concepts of knowledge, wisdom, sex, and childbirth in Gen 3.

1b

וַתַּ֙הַר֙ וַתֵּ֣לֶד אֶת־קַ֔יִן

and she conceived and bore Cain.

וַתַּ֙הַר֙ הרה	and she conceived wat·ta·har	QAL WAYY 3FS	verb
וַתֵּ֣לֶד ילד	and she bore/gave birth to wat·tē·led	QAL WAYY 3FS	verb
אֶת־ אֵת	(direct object marker) ʾet-	---	particle
קַ֔יִן קַיִן	Cain qayin	ABS	noun

1c	וַתֹּ֫אמֶר
	She said,

וַתֹּ֫אמֶר	and she said	QAL WAYY 3FS	verb
אמר	wat·tō'·mer		

1d	קָנִ֥יתִי אִ֖ישׁ אֶת־יְהוָֽה׃
	"I have acquired a man with the LORD!"

קָנִ֥יתִי	I acquired/purchased	QAL PF 1CS	verb
קנה	qā·nî·tî		
אִ֖ישׁ	man	ABS	noun
איש	'îš		
אֶת־	with	---	prep
אֶת	'et-		
יְהוָֽה׃	the LORD	ABS	noun
יהוה	YHWH		

Cain's name contains a wordplay connected to the action in the text (as, in fact, do most other names in these early chapters of Genesis): the verb קנה, "to purchase, acquire," echoes two of the consonants in Cain's name (קין). The final phrase here, אֶת־יְהוָה, is confusing. Should we understand it as "with *the help of* the LORD," as some translations have it? Or might it mean that Eve thinks she has done this "*just as well as* the LORD could have done," marking a rise in either human agency—or hubris?

2a	וַתֹּ֣סֶף לָלֶ֔דֶת אֶת־אָחִ֖יו אֶת־הָ֑בֶל
	And she bore again—his brother, Abel.

וַתֹּ֣סֶף	and she added/did again	HIPH WAYY 3FS	verb
יסף	wat·tō·sef		
לָלֶ֔דֶת	to bear/give birth to	QAL INF CST W/ PREP לְ	verb
ילד	lā·le·det		
אֶת־	(direct object marker)	---	particle
אֶת	'et-		

אָחִיו אָח	his brother 'ā·ḥiw	CST W/ 3MS SX	noun
אֶת־ אֵת	(direct object marker) 'et-	---	particle
הֶבֶל הֶבֶל	Abel hā·vel	ABS	noun

Here is another wordplay, which will come into focus shortly: Abel's name, הֶבֶל, also means "vanity, breath, futility, vapor." Indeed, it is the same term with which the book of Ecclesiastes famously proclaims, "Vanity of vanities! All is vanity [הֲבֵל הֲבָלִים הַכֹּל הָבֶל]" (Eccl 1:2 NRSVue). Abel's existence on earth will be little more than a passing shadow. Given the fact that he is the first to offer an acceptable sacrifice to the Lord, his short life and violent death take on an especially tragic dimension.

2b וַיְהִי־הֶבֶל רֹעֵה צֹאן

Now Abel was a shepherd of sheep,

וַיְהִי־ היה	and (he) was wa·yə·hî-	QAL WAYY 3MS	verb
הֶבֶל הֶבֶל	Abel he·vel	ABS	noun
רֹעֵה רעה	one who herds/shepherd of rō·'ē	QAL (CST) PTCP MS	verb
צֹאן צֹאן	sheep/small cattle ṣō'n	ABS	noun

2c וְקַיִן הָיָה עֹבֵד אֲדָמָה:

and Cain was a worker of the ground.

וְקַיִן קַיִן	and Cain wə·qayin	ABS W/ CONJ וְ	noun
הָיָה היה	(he) was hā·yâ	QAL PF 3MS	verb
עֹבֵד עבד	one who works/serves/slaves 'ō·vēd	QAL (CST) PTCP MS	verb

| אֲדָמָה: | earth/ground | ABS | noun |
| אֲדָמָה | ʾă·dā·**mâ** | | |

These two professions—shepherd and farmer—echo two major ways of life in the ancient world, thus setting up a primal, existential contrast between the brothers.

4:3–7

3a
וַיְהִי מִקֵּץ יָמִים
wayəhî miqqēṣ yāmîm

Now it happened after some time

3b
וַיָּבֵא קַיִן מִפְּרִי הָאֲדָמָה מִנְחָה לַיהוָה:
wayyāvē' qayin mippərî hā'ădāmâ minḥâ laYHWH.

that Cain brought from the produce of the ground an offering to the LORD,

4a
וְהֶבֶל הֵבִיא גַם־הוּא מִבְּכֹרוֹת צֹאנוֹ וּמֵחֶלְבֵהֶן
wəhevel hēvî' gam-hû' mibbəḵōrôt ṣō'nô ûmēḥelvēhen

and Abel also brought from the firstfruits of his flock, and from their fat portions.

4b
וַיִּשַׁע יְהוָה אֶל־הֶבֶל וְאֶל־מִנְחָתוֹ:
wayyiša' YHWH 'el-hevel wə'el-minḥātô.

The LORD regarded Abel and his offering,

5a
וְאֶל־קַיִן וְאֶל־מִנְחָתוֹ לֹא שָׁעָה
wə'el-qayin wə'el-minḥātô lō' šā'â

but Cain and his offering he did not regard.

5b
וַיִּחַר לְקַיִן מְאֹד
wayyiḥar ləqayin mə'ōd

Cain burned greatly with anger,

5c
וַיִּפְּלוּ פָּנָיו:
wayyippəlû pānāyw.

and his face fell.

6a
וַיֹּאמֶר יְהוָה אֶל־קָיִן
wayyō'mer YHWH 'el-qāyin

The LORD said to Cain,

6b	לָ֥מָּה חָ֣רָה לָ֔ךְ	
	lāmmâ ḥārâ lāk	
	"Why are you angry?	

6c	וְלָ֖מָּה נָפְל֥וּ פָנֶֽיךָ׃	
	wəlāmmâ nāfəlû fānêkā.	
	Why has your face fallen?	

7a	הֲל֤וֹא אִם־תֵּיטִיב֙	
	hălô' 'im-têṭîv	
	Is it not the case that if you do right	

7b	שְׂאֵ֔ת	
	śə'ēt	
	you will be lifted up?	

7c	וְאִם֙ לֹ֣א תֵיטִ֔יב	
	wə'im lō' têṭîv	
	But if you do not do what is right,	

7d	לַפֶּ֖תַח חַטָּ֣את רֹבֵ֑ץ	
	lappetaḥ ḥaṭṭā't rōvēṣ	
	sin is crouching at the door.	

7e	וְאֵלֶ֙יךָ֙ תְּשׁ֣וּקָת֔וֹ	
	wə'ēlêkā təšûqātô	
	Its desire will be for you,	

7f	וְאַתָּ֖ה תִּמְשָׁל־בּֽוֹ׃	
	wə'attâ timšol-bô.	
	yet you should rule over it."	

3a

וַיְהִי מִקֵּץ יָמִים

Now it happened after some time

וַיְהִי היה	and/now/then it was *wa·yə·hî-*	QAL WAYY 3MS	verb
מִקֵּץ קֵץ	from/at end/course of *miq·qēṣ*	CST W/ PREP מִן	noun
יָמִים יוֹם	days *yā·mîm*	ABS	noun

The action here and in the phrases that follow represents the terse, laconic style of Gen 1–11 in ways that are simultaneously frustrating and mysteriously inviting. How much time? Why did they decide to bring these offerings? Does God require them? Why does God accept one and not the other?

3b

וַיָּבֵא קַיִן מִפְּרִי הָאֲדָמָה מִנְחָה לַיהוָה:

that Cain brought from the produce of the ground an offering to the LORD,

וַיָּבֵא בוא	and (he) brought *way·yā·vē'*	HIPH WAYY 3MS	verb
קַיִן קַיִן	Cain *qayin*	ABS	noun
מִפְּרִי פְּרִי	from (the) fruit/produce of *mip·pə·rî*	CST W/ PREP מִן	noun
הָאֲדָמָה אֲדָמָה	the earth/ground *hā·'ă·dā·mâ*	ABS W/ DEF. ART.	noun
מִנְחָה מִנְחָה	offering *min·ḥâ*	ABS	noun
לַיהוָה: יהוה	to the LORD *la·YHWH*	ABS W/ PREP לְ	noun

BROTHER MURDERS BROTHER

4a	וְהֶ֨בֶל הֵבִ֥יא גַם־ה֛וּא מִבְּכֹר֥וֹת צֹאנ֖וֹ וּמֵֽחֶלְבֵהֶ֑ן
	and Abel also brought from the firstfruits of his flock, and from their fat portions.

וְהֶ֨בֶל הֶ֨בֶל	and Abel wə·**he**·vel	ABS W/ CONJ וְ	noun
הֵבִ֥יא בוא	(he) brought hē·**vî**'	HIPH PF 3MS	verb
גַם־ גַּם	also gam-	---	adv
ה֛וּא הוּא	he hû'	---	personal pron
מִבְּכֹר֥וֹת בְּכוֹר	from (the) firstborn of mib·bə·ḵō·**rôt**	CST W/ PREP מִן	noun
צֹאנ֖וֹ צֹאן	his flock/sheep ṣō'·**nô**	CST W/ 3MS SX	noun
וּמֵֽחֶלְבֵהֶ֑ן חֵלֶב	and from their fat portions û·mē·ḥel·vē·**hen**	CST W/ CONJ וְ + PREP מִן +3FP SX	noun

Later in the story of Israel, at Mount Sinai, God not only indicates that he will accept plant offerings but actually commands them (e.g., in the form of grain) for certain purposes (Lev 2:1–16; 6:7–11 [14–18]). "Firstfruits" (בִּכּוּרִים) offerings of agricultural products are likewise commanded in many texts (e.g., Exod 23:16–19; Neh 10:36 [35]). Of course, at this point in the narrative, no command has been given for any kind of offering.

4b	וַיִּ֣שַׁע יְהוָ֔ה אֶל־הֶ֖בֶל וְאֶל־מִנְחָתֽוֹ׃
	The LORD regarded Abel and his offering,

וַיִּ֣שַׁע שׁעה	and (he) regarded/gazed/looked upon way·yi·šaʿ	QAL WAYY 3MS	verb
יְהוָ֔ה יהוה	the LORD YHWH	ABS	noun
אֶל־ אֶל	to/toward 'el-	---	prep

הֶ֫בֶל *he·vel*	Abel	ABS	noun
וְאֶל־ *wə·'el-*	and to/toward	--- W/ CONJ וְ	prep
מִנְחָתֽוֹ׃ *min·ḥā·tô*	his offering	CST W/ 3MS SX	noun

The verb שעה appears far more infrequently than other terms for "looking" or "seeing," such as ראה. It may not have any particular or special meaning beyond that of ראה.

5a וְאֶל־קַ֫יִן וְאֶל־מִנְחָתוֹ לֹא שָׁעָה

but Cain and his offering he did not regard.

וְאֶל־ *wə·'el-*	and/but to/toward	--- W/ CONJ וְ	prep
קַ֫יִן *qayin*	Cain	ABS	noun
וְאֶל־ *wə·'el-*	and to	--- W/ CONJ וְ	prep
מִנְחָתוֹ *min·ḥā·tô*	his offering	CST W/ 3MS SX	noun
לֹא *lō'*	not	---	particle
שָׁעָה *šā·'â*	he regarded/gazed/ looked upon	QAL PF 3MS	verb

Common interpretations of God's preference for Abel's offering are that (1) Cain is clearly holding something back (in distinction to Abel, who is explicitly described in the next phrase offering "firstfruits"); (2) God favors animal sacrifice; (3) God favors the younger son over the older (a pattern repeated in Genesis with Isaac and Ishmael, Jacob and Esau, Joseph and his brothers, and Ephraim and Manasseh—and then, later, with David and his brothers).

5b

	וַיִּ֣חַר לְקַ֖יִן מְאֹ֑ד		
	Cain burned greatly with anger,		
וַיִּ֣חַר חרה	and it burned/grew angry way·yi·ḥar	QAL WAYY 3M.S	verb
לְקַ֖יִן קין	to/for Cain lə·qayin	ABS W/ PREP לְ	noun
מְאֹ֑ד מאד	very much mə·'ōd	---	adv

5c

	וַֽיִּפְּל֖וּ פָּנָֽיו׃		
	and his face fell.		
וַֽיִּפְּל֖וּ נפל	and they fell way·yip·pə·lû	QAL WAYY 3M.P	verb
פָּנָֽיו׃ פָּנֶה	his face pā·nāyw	CST W/ 3MS SX	noun

Notice that in Hebrew, the term for "face," פָּנֶה, always occurs in the plural, lit., "faces" (פָּנִים)—the idea apparently being that each half of the face (on either side of the nose) is a "face." This story repeatedly uses the idiomatic language of faces falling and being lifted up to talk about the emotional struggle of acceptance and failure. (Compare the similar language in the story of Jacob and Esau in Gen 32:21 [20].)

6a

	וַיֹּ֥אמֶר יְהוָ֖ה אֶל־קָ֑יִן		
	The LORD said to Cain,		
וַיֹּ֥אמֶר אמר	and (he) said way·yō'·mer	QAL WAYY 3MS	verb
יְהוָ֖ה יהוה	the LORD YHWH	ABS	noun
אֶל־ אֶל	to/toward 'el-	---	prep
קָ֑יִן קין	Cain qāyin	ABS	noun

6b — לָ֥מָּה חָ֖רָה לָ֑ךְ

"Why are you angry?"

לָ֥מָּה	why	---	adv
לָ֫מָּה	lām·mâ		
חָ֖רָה	it burns/grows angry	QAL PF 3MS	verb
חרה	ḥā·râ		
לָ֑ךְ	to/for you	---	prep
לְ	lāḵ	W/ 2MS SX	

6c — וְלָ֖מָּה נָפְל֥וּ פָנֶֽיךָ׃

Why has your face fallen?

וְלָ֖מָּה	and why	---	adv
לָ֫מָּה	wə·lām·mâ	W/ CONJ וְ	
נָפְל֥וּ	(they) fall [i.e., (it) falls]	QAL PF 3CP	verb
נפל	nā·p̄ə·lû		
פָנֶֽיךָ׃	your face	CST	noun
פָּנֶה	p̄ā·nê·ḵā	W/ 2MS SX	

7a — הֲל֤וֹא אִם־תֵּיטִיב֙

Is it not the case that if you do right

הֲל֤וֹא	is it not	---	particle
לֹא	hă·lô'	W/ INTERR הֲ	
אִם־	if	---	conj
אִם	'im-		
תֵּיטִיב֙	you will do good/right	HIPH IMPF 2MS	verb
יטב	tê·ṭîv		

7b	שְׂאֵת		
	you will be lifted up?		
שְׂאֵת	lifting	ABS	noun
שְׂאֵת	śə·'ēt		

Here the language of "you will be" is implied but not stated in Hebrew. A more "literal" translation of v. 7 up to this point might be: "If you do right, will there not be lifting?"

7c	וְאִם לֹא תֵיטִיב		
	But if you do not do what is right,		
וְאִם	and/but if	--- W/ CONJ וְ	conj
אִם	wə·'im		
לֹא	not	---	particle
לֹא	lō'		
תֵיטִיב	you will do good/right	HIPH IMPF 2MS	verb
יטב	tê·ṭîv		

7d	לַפֶּתַח חַטָּאת רֹבֵץ		
	sin is crouching at the door.		
לַפֶּתַח	at the doorway/opening	ABS W/ PREP לְ + DEF. ART.	noun
פֶּתַח	lap·**pe**·taḥ		
חַטָּאת	sin	ABS	noun
חַטָּאת	ḥaṭ·ṭā't		
רֹבֵץ	crouching/lying down	QAL PTCP MS	verb
רבץ	rō·vēṣ		

The term רבץ is often used of animals (e.g., Gen 49:9; Isa 13:20–21; Ezek 19:2); thus, sin here is personified as an animal presence waiting to pounce upon Cain. Many commentators point to a cognate term in another Semitic language, Akkadian, which describes a demonic creature called a *rābiṣum* ("crouching one") who threateningly crouches around doorways (see Speiser 1964:33).

7e	וְאֵלֶ֙יךָ֙ תְּשׁ֣וּקָת֔וֹ
	Its desire will be for you,

	וְאֵלֶ֙יךָ֙ אֶל	and to/for you wə·'ē·le·ḵā	--- W/ CONJ ו + 2MS SX	prep
	תְּשׁ֣וּקָת֔וֹ תְּשׁוּקָה	its desire tə·šū·qā·tô	CST W/ 3MS SX	noun

7f	וְאַתָּ֖ה תִּמְשָׁל־בּֽוֹ׃
	yet you should rule over it."

	וְאַתָּ֖ה אַתָּה	but/and you wə·'at·tâ	--- W/ CONJ ו	personal pron
	תִּמְשָׁל־ מָשַׁל	(you) will/could/should/must rule over tim·šol-	QAL IMPF 2MS	verb
	בּֽוֹ׃ בְּ	it bô	--- W/ 3MS SX	prep

The Hebrew imperfect (or prefix conjugation) form in this phrase (תִּמְשָׁל־) is an apt reminder that Hebrew does not function strictly on a tense system in terms of past, present, and future. Rather, this type of verbal form can indicate what in English we might call "modal verbs," which communicate ideas such as "might, could, should, would, may, can," etc. (Hebrew has no distinct or single word for these modal concepts outside of its main verbal system and syntax.) To translate תִּמְשָׁל־ here as "you will overcome" or "you will rule over" would be odd, since in fact Cain does not master the sin that seeks to overcome him. We are thus left to interpret the phrase in light of these modal possibilities.

BROTHER MURDERS BROTHER

4:8

8a וַיֹּ֥אמֶר קַ֖יִן אֶל־הֶ֣בֶל אָחִ֑יו
wayyōʾmer qayin ʾel-hevel ʾāḥîw

Cain said to his brother, Abel, . . .

8b וַֽיְהִי֙ בִּהְיוֹתָ֣ם בַּשָּׂדֶ֔ה
wayəhî bihyôtām baśśāde

When they were in the field,

8c וַיָּ֥קָם קַ֛יִן אֶל־הֶ֥בֶל אָחִ֖יו
wayyāqom qayin ʾel-hevel ʾāḥîw

Cain rose up against his brother, Abel,

8d וַיַּהַרְגֵֽהוּ׃
wayyahargēhû.

and killed him.

8a	וַיֹּ֥אמֶר קַ֖יִן אֶל־הֶ֣בֶל אָחִ֑יו		
	Cain said to his brother, Abel, . . .		
וַיֹּ֥אמֶר	and/so/now/then (he) said/spoke	QAL WAYY 3MS	verb
אמר	*way·yō'·mer*		
קַ֖יִן	Cain	ABS	noun
קַיִן	*qayin*		
אֶל־	to/toward	---	prep
אֶל	*ʾel-*		
הֶ֣בֶל	Abel	ABS	noun
הֶבֶל	*he·vel*		

אָחִיו	his brother	CST	noun
אָח	ʾā·ḥîw	W/ 3MS SX	

The ellipsis (". . .") in the translation here marks the fact that something is lost—or that we are to assume or imagine a conversation that the narrator does not provide. In the Bible, the introductory phrase וַיֹּאמֶר, "and he said," almost always introduces the content of what the speaker says, but in this case no material follows. We could avoid this by translating as "Cain spoke to his brother, Abel, and when they were in the field . . . ," though it is not entirely clear that וַיֹּאמֶר can be translated this way (i.e., without the content of what is said). Many translations supply an extra phrase here, reflecting content that does appear in some manuscript traditions (such as early Greek and Latin texts): "Cain said to his brother Abel, *'Let us go out into the field,'* and when they were in the field . . ." The earliest Hebrew traditions we possess, however, do not have this phrase. Such a case reminds us that readers of the original languages of Scripture must still occasionally recognize parts of the text that may need to be "repaired" through careful study of language, archaeology, and related subjects. It is still possible, however, that the text was intended to be read as is, with a haunting gap intended to make us wonder what Cain might have said to his brother right before the murder.

8b	וַיְהִי בִּהְיוֹתָם בַּשָּׂדֶה		
	When they were in the field,		
וַיְהִי	and it happened/came about	QAL WAYY 3MS	verb
היה	wa·yə·hî		
בִּהְיוֹתָם	in their being	QAL INF CST	verb
היה	bih·yô·tām	W/ PREP בְּ + 3MP SX	
בַּשָּׂדֶה	in the field	ABS	noun
שָׂדֶה	baś·śā·de	W/ PREP בְּ + DEF. ART.	

8c	וַיָּקָם קַיִן אֶל־הֶבֶל אָחִיו		
	Cain rose up against his brother, Abel,		
וַיָּקָם	(he) rose up	QAL WAYY 3MS	verb
קום	way·yā·qom		

BROTHER MURDERS BROTHER

קַ֫יִן *qayin*	Cain	ABS	noun
אֶל־ *'el-*	to/toward/against	---	prep
הֶ֫בֶל *he·vel*	Abel	ABS	noun
אָחִיו *'ā·ḥîw*	his brother	CST W/ 3MS SX	noun

8d — וַיַּהַרְגֵהוּ׃

and killed him.

וַיַּהַרְגֵהוּ׃ *way·ya·har·gē·hû* הרג	and he killed him	QAL WAYY 3MS W/ 3MS SX	verb

4:9–15

9a

וַיֹּ֤אמֶר יְהוָה֙ אֶל־קַ֔יִן

wayyō'mer YHWH 'el-qayin

The Lord said to Cain,

9b

אֵ֖י הֶ֣בֶל אָחִ֑יךָ

'ê hevel 'āḥîḵā

"Where is your brother, Abel?"

9c

וַיֹּ֖אמֶר

wayyō'mer

He said,

9d

לֹ֣א יָדַ֔עְתִּי

lō' yāda'tî

"I don't know.

9e

הֲשֹׁמֵ֥ר אָחִ֖י אָנֹֽכִי׃

hăšōmēr 'āḥî 'ānōḵî.

Am I the guardian of my brother?"

10a

וַיֹּ֖אמֶר

wayyō'mer

He said,

10b

מֶ֣ה עָשִׂ֑יתָ

me 'āśîtā

"What have you done?

10c

ק֚וֹל דְּמֵ֣י אָחִ֔יךָ צֹעֲקִ֥ים אֵלַ֖י מִן־הָאֲדָמָֽה׃

qôl dəmê 'āḥîḵā ṣō'ăqîm 'ēlay min-hā'ădāmâ.

The sound of your brother's blood screams out to me from the ground!

11a	וְעַתָּ֖ה אָר֣וּר אָ֑תָּה	
	wəʿattâ ʾārûr ʾāttâ	
	Now—cursed are you	

11b	מִן־הָאֲדָמָה֙	
	min-hāʾădāmâ	
	from the ground	

11c	אֲשֶׁ֣ר פָּצְתָ֣ה אֶת־פִּ֔יהָ	
	ʾăšer pāṣətâ ʾet-pîhā	
	that opened up its mouth	

11d	לָקַ֛חַת אֶת־דְּמֵ֥י אָחִ֖יךָ מִיָּדֶֽךָ׃	
	lāqaḥat ʾet-dəmê ʾāḥîkā miyyādekā.	
	to take the blood of your brother from your hand.	

12a	כִּ֤י תַֽעֲבֹד֙ אֶת־הָ֣אֲדָמָ֔ה	
	kî taʿăvōd ʾet-hāʾădāmâ	
	When you work the ground,	

12b	לֹֽא־תֹסֵ֥ף תֵּת־כֹּחָ֖הּ לָ֑ךְ	
	lōʾ-tōsēf tēt-kōḥāh lāk	
	it will no longer give its strength to you.	

12c	נָ֥ע וָנָ֖ד תִּֽהְיֶ֥ה בָאָֽרֶץ׃	
	nāʿ wānād tihye vāʾāreṣ.	
	You'll be a wanderer and a fugitive on the earth."	

13a	וַיֹּ֥אמֶר קַ֖יִן אֶל־יְהוָ֑ה	
	wayyōʾmer qayin ʾel-YHWH	
	Cain said to the Lord,	

13b	גָּד֥וֹל עֲוֺנִ֖י מִנְּשֹֽׂא׃	
	gādôl ʿăwōnî minnəśōʾ.	
	"My iniquity is too great to bear!	

14a	הֵן גֵּרַשְׁתָּ אֹתִי הַיּוֹם	
	hēn gēraštā 'ōtî hayyôm	
	You have driven me out today	
14b	מֵעַל פְּנֵי הָאֲדָמָה	
	mē'al pənê hā'ădāmâ	
	from upon the face of the ground,	
14c	וּמִפָּנֶיךָ אֶסָּתֵר	
	ûmippānêkā 'essātēr	
	and from your face I will be hidden.	
14d	וְהָיִיתִי נָע וָנָד בָּאָרֶץ	
	wəhāyîtî nā' wānād bā'āreṣ	
	I will be a wanderer and fugitive upon the earth,	
14e	וְהָיָה כָל־מֹצְאִי יַהַרְגֵנִי׃	
	wəhāyâ kol-mōṣə'î yahargēnî	
	and anyone who finds me will kill me."	
15a	וַיֹּאמֶר לוֹ יְהוָה	
	wayyō'mer lô YHWH	
	The Lord said to him,	
15b	לָכֵן כָּל־הֹרֵג קַיִן	
	lākēn kol-hōrēg qayin	
	"Therefore: anyone who kills Cain	
15c	שִׁבְעָתַיִם יֻקָּם	
	šiv'ātayim yuqqām	
	will suffer sevenfold vengeance."	
15d	וַיָּשֶׂם יְהוָה לְקַיִן אוֹת	
	wayyāśem YHWH ləqayin 'ôt	
	And the Lord set a sign upon Cain	

15e	לְבִלְתִּי הַכּוֹת־אֹתוֹ כָּל־מֹצְאוֹ׃
	ləviltî hakkôt-'ōtô kol-mōṣə'ô.
	to stop anyone who found him from striking him down.

9a	וַיֹּאמֶר יְהוָה אֶל־קַיִן
	The Lord said to Cain,

וַיֹּאמֶר	and/then (he) said	QAL WAYY 3MS	verb
אמר	way·yō'·mer		
יְהוָה	the Lord	ABS	noun
יהוה	YHWH		
אֶל־	to/toward	---	prep
אֶל	'el-		
קַיִן	Cain	ABS	noun
קַיִן	qayin		

9b	אֵי הֶבֶל אָחִיךָ
	"Where is your brother, Abel?"

אֵי	where	---	interr pron
אֵי	'ê		
הֶבֶל	Abel	ABS	noun
הֶבֶל	he·vel		
אָחִיךָ	your brother	CST W/ 2MS SX	noun
אח	'ā·ḥî·kā		

The constant repetition of the qualifier "your brother" continually draws Cain's (and our) attention to the familial bond that he has ruptured by murdering Abel. Compare the important repetition of a similar term of relationship, "my son," in the story of Abraham and Isaac in Gen 22.

9c

וַיֹּאמֶר

He said,

| וַיֹּאמֶר | and/then he said | QAL WAYY 3MS | verb |
| אמר | way·yōʾ·mer | | |

9d

לֹא יָדַעְתִּי

"I don't know.

לֹא	not	---	particle
לֹא	lōʾ		
יָדַעְתִּי	I know	QAL PF 1CS	verb
ידע	yā·daʿ·tî		

9e

הֲשֹׁמֵר אָחִי אָנֹכִי:

Am I the guardian of my brother?"

הֲשֹׁמֵר	is it (the case that) guard/ keeper of/one who guards/ keeps	QAL (CST) PTCP MS W/ INTERR הֲ	verb
שמר	hă·šō·mēr		
אָחִי	my brother	CST W/ 1CS SX	noun
אח	ʾā·ḥî		
אָנֹכִי:	I	---	personal pron
אָנֹכִי	ʾā·nō·ḵî		

10a

וַיֹּאמֶר

He said,

| וַיֹּאמֶר | and/then he said | QAL WAYY 3MS | verb |
| אמר | way·yōʾ·mer | | |

BROTHER MURDERS BROTHER

10b	מֶה עָשִׂיתָ
	"What have you done?"

מֶה	what	---	interr pron
מָה	*me*		
עָשִׂיתָ	you did/have done	QAL PF 2MS	verb
עשׂה	*'ā·śî·tā*		

This echoes God's question to the woman in 3:13.

10c	קוֹל דְּמֵי אָחִיךָ צֹעֲקִים אֵלַי מִן־הָאֲדָמָה:
	The sound of your brother's blood screams out to me from the ground!

קוֹל	voice/sound of	CST	noun
קוֹל	*qôl*		
דְּמֵי	(the) blood(s) of	CST	noun
דָּם	*də·mê*		
אָחִיךָ	your brother	CST W/ 2MS SX	noun
אָח	*'ā·ḥî·kā*		
צֹעֲקִים	crying out	QAL PTCP MP	verb
צעק	*ṣō·'ă·qîm*		
אֵלַי	to/toward me	W/ 1CS SX	prep
אֶל	*'ē·lay*		
מִן־	from	---	prep
מִן	*min-*		
הָאֲדָמָה:	the ground	ABS W/ DEF. ART.	noun
אֲדָמָה	*hā·'ă·dā·mâ*		

In the plural, "bloods" (i.e., דָּמִים) can also mean "bloodguilt" or "shed blood."

11a

וְעַתָּה אָרוּר אָתָּה

Now—cursed are you

וְעַתָּה עַתָּה	and/so now wəʿattâ	--- W/ CONJ וְ	adv
אָרוּר ארר	cursed ʾārûr	QAL PASS PTCP MS	verb
אָתָּה אַתָּה	you ʾattâ	---	personal pron

This echoes God's curse against the serpent in 3:14. This same language (אָרוּר אַתָּה, "cursed are you") also reappears in the covenant curses in Deut 28:16, 19.

11b

מִן־הָאֲדָמָה

from the ground

מִן־ מִן	from min-	---	prep
הָאֲדָמָה אֲדָמָה	the ground hāʾădāmâ	ABS W/ DEF. ART.	noun

The attention the text draws to the "ground" (אֲדָמָה) in this passage reminds us of the name "Adam" and of what transpired in Gen 3, and how the ground was the focus of the curse there (3:17). The translation "from the ground" here, following the straightforward meaning of מִן "from," may indicate alienation *between* Cain and the ground, along the lines of what his father Adam experienced. Alternatively, we might understand this phrase to mean "*by* the ground," indicating that the ground now joins God in condemning the murderer.

11c

אֲשֶׁר פָּצְתָה אֶת־פִּיהָ

that opened up its mouth

אֲשֶׁר אֲשֶׁר	that/which ʾăšer	---	relative pron

BROTHER MURDERS BROTHER

פָּצְתָה פצה	opened up pā·ṣə·tâ	QAL PF 3FS	verb
אֶת־ אֵת	(direct object marker) 'et-	---	particle
פִּיהָ פֶּה	its/her mouth pî·hā	CST W/ 3FS SX	noun

The imagery of the earth opening up its personified mouth to drink human blood is striking indeed. Is the "cursed" earth pictured here as an enemy who is thirsty for human blood? Or has it calmly received, with sadness (as it were), the spilled blood? Interestingly, Num 16:30, the only other place in the Old Testament that features this same cluster of key words (פֶּה, אֲדָמָה, and פצה), also speaks of human wrongdoing and divine punishment.

11d	לָקַחַת אֶת־דְּמֵי אָחִיךָ מִיָּדֶךָ׃		
	to take the blood of your brother from your hand.		
לָקַחַת לקח	to take/receive lā·qa·ḥat	QAL INF CST W/ PREP לְ	verb
אֶת־ אֵת	(direct object marker) 'et-	---	particle
דְּמֵי דָּם	(the) blood(s) of də·mê	CST	noun
אָחִיךָ אָח	your brother 'ā·ḥî·ḵā	CST W/ 2MS SX	noun
מִיָּדֶךָ׃ יָד	from your hand miy·yā·de·ḵā	CST W/ PREP מִן + 2MS SX	noun

12a	כִּי תַעֲבֹד אֶת־הָאֲדָמָה		
	When you work the ground,		
כִּי כִּי	for/because/since/when kî	---	conj
תַעֲבֹד עבד	you will till/work/slave over ta·'ă·vōd	QAL IMPF 2MS	verb

אֶת־ אֵת 'et-	(direct object marker)	---	particle
הָאֲדָמָה אֲדָמָה hā·ʼă·dā·mâ	the ground	ABS W/ DEF. ART.	noun

---

12b — לֹא־תֹסֵף תֵּת־כֹּחָהּ לָךְ

it will no longer give its strength to you.

לֹא־ לֹא lō'-	not	---	particle
תֹסֵף יסף tō·sēf	it will continue/do again	HIPH JUSS 3FS	verb
תֵּת־ נתן tēt-	to give/put	QAL INF CST	verb
כֹּחָהּ כֹּחַ kō·ḥāh	its strength/produce	CST W/ 3FS SX	noun
לָךְ לְ lāḵ	to you	W/ 2MS SX	prep

The word "strength" (כֹּחַ) here likely refers to the agricultural produce of the land. The covenant curse language in Lev 26:20 offers a similar idea for the one who does not obey the Lord's commandments: "Your strength [כֹּחַ] shall be spent to no purpose: your land shall not yield its produce, and the trees of the land shall not yield their fruit" (NRSVue).

12c — נָע וָנָד תִּהְיֶה בָאָרֶץ׃

You'll be a wanderer and a fugitive on the earth."

נָע נוע nāʻ	wanderer/one who wanders/shakes	QAL PTCP MS	verb
וָנָד נוד wā·nād	and vagrant/wanderer/ one who moves/wanders	QAL PTCP MS W/ CONJ ו	verb
תִּהְיֶה היה tih·ye	you will be/become	QAL IMPF 2MS	verb

BROTHER MURDERS BROTHER

בָּאָֽרֶץ׃	in/on the earth	ABS	noun
אֶרֶץ	vā·'ā·reṣ	W/ PREP בְּ + DEF. ART.	

The imagery of wandering on the earth here foreshadows the aftermath of the Tower of Babel incident in ch. 11. In the Bible, to wander or live as a fugitive is generally viewed as a negative state of being (see Isa 24:19–20, which employs this same verbal pair of נוע and נוד in a scene involving guilt and judgment).

13a — וַיֹּאמֶר קַיִן אֶל־יְהוָה

Cain said to the LORD,

וַיֹּאמֶר	then/so/and (he) said	QAL WAYY 3MS	verb
אמר	way·yō'·mer		
קַיִן	Cain	ABS	noun
קַיִן	qayin		
אֶל־	to/toward	---	prep
אֶל	'el-		
יְהוָה	the LORD	ABS	noun
יהוה	YHWH		

13b — גָּדוֹל עֲוֺנִי מִנְּשֹׂא׃

"My iniquity is too great to bear!"

גָּדוֹל	great/large	MS PRED	adj
גָּדוֹל	gā·dôl		
עֲוֺנִי	my iniquity/punishment	CST	noun
עָוֺן	'ă·wō·nî	W/ 1CS SX	
מִנְּשֹׂא׃	from/than bearing/carrying	QAL INF CST	verb
נשׂא	min·nə·śō'	W/ PREP מִן	

עָוֺן here can be translated as either "iniquity" or "punishment." Does Cain's response here indicate remorse? Does he feel that God has treated him unfairly? If we translate עָוֺן as "punishment," then he would be more easily understood as protesting God's actions. Even so, if we translate "iniquity," as I have here, we can understand his words in the next verse, combined with God's concession to protect him, as moving God to accommodate his new situation.

14a	הֵן גֵּרַ֨שְׁתָּ אֹתִ֤י הַיּ֣וֹם		
	You have driven me out today		
הֵ֣ן	see/look/behold	---	particle
הֵן	hēn		
גֵּרַ֨שְׁתָּ	you drove/banished/ have driven/banished	PIEL PF 2MS	verb
גרשׁ	gē·raš·tā		
אֹתִ֤י	(direct object marker +) me	---	particle
אֵת	'ō·tî	W/ 1CS SX	
הַיּ֣וֹם	today/this day	ABS W/ DEF. ART.	noun
יוֹם	hay·yôm		

הֵן is a byform of הִנֵּה, "behold, look" (see comment at 1:31b).

Significantly, the verb גרשׁ has appeared already, in Gen 3:24, to describe God's banishment of Adam and Eve from Eden.

14b	מֵעַ֖ל פְּנֵ֣י הָֽאֲדָמָ֑ה		
	from upon the face of the ground,		
מֵעַ֖ל	from on/upon	---	prep
עַל	mē·'al	W/ PREP מִן	
פְּנֵ֣י	(the) face/surface of	CST	noun
פָּנֶה	pə·nê		
הָֽאֲדָמָ֑ה	the ground	ABS W/ DEF. ART.	noun
אֲדָמָה	hā·'ă·dā·mâ		

The phrase "upon the face of the ground" occurs twelve other times in the Old Testament, in addition to this instance. It always occurs in a negative or destructive context, akin to how the English phrase "to wipe off the face of the earth" is used (see, e.g., Exod 32:12; Deut 6:15; 2 Sam 14:7). In Genesis, this phrase has particular weight in the flood narrative (Gen 6:7; 7:4, 23), offering us a haunting connection: the entire earth and all humans now bound to it follow in Cain's murderous footsteps.

14c	וּמִפָּנֶיךָ אֶסָּתֵר
	and from your face I will be hidden.

	וּמִפָּנֶיךָ פָּנֶה	and from your face/presence û·mip·pā·**nê**·ḵā	CST W/ CONJ וְ + PREP מִן + 2MS SX	noun
	אֶסָּתֵר סתר	I will be hidden/lost 'es·sā·**tēr**	NIPH IMPF 1CS	verb

In Old Testament terms, to hide one's face from someone is a distressing sign of distance and shame; see, e.g., Pss 22:25 [24]; 27:9; 102:3 [2].

14d	וְהָיִיתִי נָע וָנָד בָּאָרֶץ
	I will be a wanderer and fugitive upon the earth,

	וְהָיִיתִי היה	and I will be wə·hā·**yî**·tî	QAL WEQATAL 1CS	verb
	נָע נוע	wanderer/one who wanders/shakes nā'	QAL PTCP MS	verb
	וָנָד נוד	and vagrant/wanderer/ one who moves/wanders wā·**nād**	QAL PTCP MS W/ CONJ וְ	verb
	בָּאָרֶץ אֶרֶץ	in/on the earth bā·'ā·reṣ	ABS W/ PREP בְּ + DEF. ART.	noun

14e	וְהָיָה כָל־מֹצְאִי יַהַרְגֵנִי׃
	and anyone who finds me will kill me."

	וְהָיָה היה	and it will be wə·hā·**yâ**	QAL WEQATAL 3MS	verb
	כָל־ כֹּל	all/each/every/any ḵol-	CST	noun
	מֹצְאִי מצא	one who finds me mō·ṣə·'**î**	QAL PTCP MS W/ 1CS SX	verb

	יַהַרְגֵֽנִי׃	(he) will kill me	QAL IMPF 3MS W/ 1CS SX	verb
	הרג	*ya·har·gē·nî*		

As with questions that arise about the origin and identity of Cain's wife in v. 17, readers here may wonder who these others are on earth who would kill Cain if they found him wandering abroad. Perhaps we are to assume the earth is populated and that the narrative simply focuses on the actions of one family. Or perhaps Cain's fear is an emotional outburst as he imagines the possibility of a world filled with the same kind of violence he enacted.

15a	וַיֹּאמֶר לוֹ יְהוָה
	The LORD said to him,

	וַיֹּאמֶר	then/so/and (he) said	QAL WAYY 3MS	verb
	אמר	*way·yō'·mer*		
	לוֹ	to him	---	prep
	ל	*lô*	W/ 3MS SX	
	יְהוָה	the LORD	ABS	noun
	יהוה	*YHWH*		

15b	לָכֵן כָּל־הֹרֵג קַיִן
	"Therefore: anyone who kills Cain

	לָכֵן	therefore/thus	---	adv
	לכן	*lā·kēn*		
	כָּל־	all/each/every/any	CST	noun
	כל	*kol-*		
	הֹרֵג	killer of/one who kills	QAL (CST) PTCP MS	verb
	הרג	*hō·rēg*		
	קַיִן	Cain	ABS	noun
	קין	*qayin*		

15c	שִׁבְעָתַיִם יֻקָּם
	will suffer sevenfold vengeance."

שִׁבְעָתַיִם שִׁבְעָתַיִם	seven/sevenfold/seven times šiv·ʿā·tayim	ABS	cardinal number
יֻקָּם נקם	(he) will suffer vengeance/ be avenged yuq·qām	HOPHAL IMPF 3MS	verb

Later (in Gen 4:23–24), an individual named Lamech will refer to this sevenfold vengeance for killing Cain by escalating the stakes of violence, claiming that any act of aggression toward him should be met with seventy-sevenfold retribution. Cain's act thus reverberates outward generationally, offering precedent for future murders and threats.

15d	וַיָּשֶׂם יְהוָה לְקַיִן אוֹת
	And the Lord set a sign upon Cain

וַיָּשֶׂם שׂים	and (he) set/placed way·yā·śem	QAL WAYY 3MS	verb
יְהוָה יהוה	the Lord YHWH	ABS	noun
לְקַיִן קַיִן	to/for/upon Cain lə·qayin	ABS W/ PREP לְ	noun
אוֹת אוֹת	mark/sign ʾôt	ABS	noun

The nature of this "sign" (אוֹת) is ultimately unexplained. The language of a "sign" almost always refers to some physical action or mark, though in this case it would be difficult to guess what kind of mark would, in and of itself, indicate that Cain is not to be killed. Alternatively, we could translate the phrase as "And he gave a sign to Cain," noting that Jer 32:20 uses the same idiom to refers to God "making" or "giving" signs, not to placing a sign on someone as a physical mark.

15e לְבִלְתִּי הַכּוֹת־אֹתוֹ כָּל־מֹצְאוֹ׃

to stop anyone who found him from striking him down.

לְבִלְתִּי בִּלְתִּי	so as not lə·vil·tî	--- W/ PREP לְ	adv
הַכּוֹת־ נכה	to strike/strike down/smite hak·kôt-	HIPH INF CST	verb
אֹתוֹ אֵת	(direct object marker +) him 'ō·tô	--- W/ 3MS SX	particle
כָּל־ כֹּל	all/each/every/any kol-	CST	noun
מֹצְאוֹ׃ מצא	one who finds him mō·ṣə·'ô	QAL PTCP MS W/ 3MS SX	verb

4:16

16a וַיֵּצֵא קַיִן מִלִּפְנֵי יְהוָה
wayyēṣēʾ qayin millifnê YHWH

So Cain went out from before the face of the Lord,

16b וַיֵּשֶׁב בְּאֶרֶץ־נוֹד קִדְמַת־עֵדֶן׃
wayyēšev bəʾereṣ-nôd qidmat-ʿēden.

and he settled in the land of Wandering, east of Eden.

16a וַיֵּצֵא קַיִן מִלִּפְנֵי יְהוָה

So Cain went out from before the face of the Lord,

וַיֵּצֵא יצא	and (he) went out *way·yē·ṣē*	QAL WAYY 3MS	verb
קַיִן קין	Cain *qayin*	ABS	noun
מִלִּפְנֵי לִפְנֵי	from before/to (the) face/ presence of *mil·lif·nê*	--- W/ PREP מִן	prep
יְהוָה יהוה	the Lord *YHWH*	ABS	noun

The phrase מִלִּפְנֵי יְהוָה is here translated "from before the face of the Lord" rather than "from the presence of the Lord," as it might more idiomatically be rendered, to emphasize the repeated term "face" in this text. Keeping the language attached to parts of the body, as it was in Hebrew, draws us back into the bodily world of reference the text has in its original language.

16b

וַיֵּשֶׁב בְּאֶרֶץ־נוֹד קִדְמַת־עֵדֶן׃

and he settled in the land of Wandering, east of Eden.

Hebrew	Translation	Parsing	Type
וַיֵּשֶׁב *way·yē·šev*	and/then he dwelled/sat	QAL WAYY 3MS	verb
בְּאֶרֶץ־ *bə·'e·reṣ-*	in (the) land of	CST W/ PREP בְּ	noun
נוֹד *nôd*	Wandering/Nod	ABS	noun
קִדְמַת־ *qid·mat-*	east of	CST	noun
עֵדֶן׃ *'ē·den*	Eden	ABS	noun

The juxtaposition of "settling" and "wandering" conveys the uneasiness of Cain's new position, and indeed something of humanity's hard situation: there are curses and wandering and a deep sense of uprootedness, but also a need to settle and continue living. The paradox here echoes that of the opening chapters of Genesis as a whole: humans are created good, in God's image, but they are broken and have gone astray.

From Text to Sermon

*As you meditate on this passage and contemplate
how you might teach or preach it to others,
consider the following areas of emphasis.*

 Historical and Literary Context. Take time to study other acts of familial violence in the Bible. In what contexts do these kinds of things occur? Is there a chance for forgiveness or redemption? Scripture does not record many murders of the type that Cain commits against Abel—i.e., where there is no prior act or broader military or political context that might be invoked to justify the killing. The murder of the Levite's concubine in Judg 19 might be considered alongside this story as comparable in terms of the innocence of the victim, as might be the murder of Naboth in 1 Kgs 21. And we can gain further insight into the dynamics of violence between brothers by reading 2 Sam 13–14, where Absalom kills his brother Amnon and then, in light of this, a woman from Tekoa tells a parable that contains echoes of the Cain and Abel story.

 Bridge to the Gospel. One fruitful avenue to pursue here would be a reading of the Sermon on the Mount—particularly Jesus' words about murder in Matt 5:21–24:

> You have heard that it was said to those of ancient times, "You shall not murder, and "whoever murders shall be liable to judgment." But I say to you that if you are angry with a brother or sister, you will be liable to judgment, and if you insult a brother or sister, you will be liable to the council, and if you say, "You fool," you will be liable to the hell of fire. (NRSVue)

Most of us would recognize a massive and consequential difference between experiencing feelings of anger, or saying a dismissive thing toward someone or even hating them, and literally committing a murder. However, consider how Jesus challenges his listeners to examine their lives in a manner congruent with how God asks Cain to master the sin that crouches at the door of his own emotions.

 Illustrations. As we think about how to illustrate the themes of Gen 4, consider the profound meditation on this story's concept of fate and choice found in John Steinbeck's 1952 novel *East of Eden*. As a focal point for the core dramatic tension in his own story, Steinbeck evokes the Hebrew word תִּמְשָׁל־—translated above as "you should rule over"—from this very passage in Genesis (4:7–8; note that Steinbeck transliterates the word with an *e*-vowel, *timshel*, instead of with the expected *o*-vowel, *timšol*). One crucial passage in the novel—in which the characters Lee and Adam are talking about guilt, salvation, and human choice—reads as follows:

> Lee's hand shook as he filled the delicate cups. He drank his down in one gulp. "Don't you see?" he cried. "The American Standard translation orders men to triumph over sin, and you can call sin ignorance. The King James translation makes a promise in 'Thou shalt,' meaning that men will surely triumph over sin. But the Hebrew word, the word *timshel*—'Thou mayest'—that gives a choice. It might be the most important word in the world. That says the way is open. That throws it right back on a man. For if 'Thou mayest'—it is also true that 'Thou mayest not.' Don't you see?"
>
> "Yes, I see. I do see. But you do not believe this is divine law. Why do you feel its importance?"
>
> "Ah!" said Lee. "I've wanted to tell you this for a long time. I even anticipated your questions and I am well prepared. Any writing which has influenced the thinking and the lives of innumerable people is important. Now, there are many millions in their sects and churches who feel the order, 'Do thou,' and throw their weight into obedience. And there are millions more who feel predestination in 'Thou shalt.' Nothing they may do can interfere with what will be. But 'Thou mayest'! Why, that makes a man great, that gives him stature with the gods, for in his weakness and his filth and his murder of his brother he has still the great choice. He can choose his course and fight it through and win."
>
> (John Steinbeck, *East of Eden*
> [New York: Penguin, 2002; orig. 1952], 301)

GENESIS 6:1–22

GOD DECIDES TO FLOOD THE EARTH

The human misadventure continues with a strange and striking instance of crossing a divine boundary—a transgression that apparently involves sexual relations between humans and divine beings. In response to the state of corruption on earth, God decides to destroy every breathing thing, saving only Noah, his family, and a select group of animals on a huge boat.

LARGER LITERARY CONTEXT › 6:1–22

6:1–10

1a
וַיְהִי֙ כִּֽי־הֵחֵ֣ל הָֽאָדָ֔ם
wayəhî kî-hēḥēl hā'ādām

Now it happened that when humans began

1b
לָרֹ֖ב עַל־פְּנֵ֣י הָֽאֲדָמָ֑ה
lārōv 'al-pənê hā'ădāmâ

to proliferate upon the face of the ground

1c
וּבָנ֖וֹת יֻלְּד֥וּ לָהֶֽם׃
ûvānôt yullədû lāhem.

that daughters were born to them.

2a
וַיִּרְא֤וּ בְנֵי־הָֽאֱלֹהִים֙ אֶת־בְּנ֣וֹת הָֽאָדָ֔ם
wayyir'û vənê-hā'ĕlōhîm 'et-bənôt hā'ādām

When the sons of God saw the daughters of man,

2b
כִּ֥י טֹבֹ֖ת הֵ֑נָּה
kî ṭōvōt hēnnâ

that they were pleasing,

2c
וַיִּקְח֤וּ לָהֶם֙ נָשִׁ֔ים
wayyiqḥû lāhem nāšîm

they took wives for themselves

2d
מִכֹּ֖ל אֲשֶׁ֥ר בָּחָֽרוּ׃
mikkōl 'ăšer bāḥārû.

from any that they chose.

3a
וַיֹּ֣אמֶר יְהוָ֗ה
wayyō'mer YHWH

The LORD said,

| 3b | לֹא־יָד֨וֹן רוּחִ֤י בָֽאָדָם֙ לְעֹלָ֔ם |

lōʾ-yādôn rûḥî vāʾādām ləʿōlām

"My breath shall not remain with humans forever—

| 3c | בְּשַׁגַּ֖ם ה֣וּא בָשָׂ֑ר |

bəšaggam hûʾ vāśār

they are merely flesh.

| 3d | וְהָי֣וּ יָמָ֔יו מֵאָ֥ה וְעֶשְׂרִ֖ים שָׁנָֽה׃ |

wəhāyû yāmāyw mēʾâ wəʿeśrîm šānâ

Their days will be one hundred and twenty years."

| 4a | הַנְּפִלִ֞ים הָי֣וּ בָאָרֶץ֮ בַּיָּמִ֣ים הָהֵם֒ |

hannəfīlîm hāyû vāʾāreṣ bayyāmîm hāhēm

The Nephilim—they were on the earth in those days,

| 4b | וְגַ֣ם אַֽחֲרֵי־כֵ֗ן |

wəgam ʾaḥărê-kēn

and also afterward,

| 4c | אֲשֶׁ֨ר יָבֹ֜אוּ בְּנֵ֤י הָֽאֱלֹהִים֙ אֶל־בְּנ֣וֹת הָֽאָדָ֔ם |

ʾăšer yāvōʾû bənê hāʾĕlōhîm ʾel-bənôt hāʾādām

when the sons of God entered into the daughters of man

| 4d | וְיָלְד֖וּ לָהֶ֑ם |

wəyālədû lāhem

and they bore children to them.

| 4e | הֵ֧מָּה הַגִּבֹּרִ֛ים אֲשֶׁ֥ר מֵעוֹלָ֖ם |

hēmmâ haggibbōrîm ʾăšer mēʿôlām

They were the ancient Heroes,

| 4f | אַנְשֵׁ֥י הַשֵּֽׁם׃ |

ʾanšê haššēm

famous men.

| 5–10 | [SUMMARIZED BELOW] |

GOD DECIDES TO FLOOD THE EARTH

1a	וַיְהִי כִּי־הֵחֵל הָאָדָם
	Now it happened that when humans began

	וַיְהִי	and/now it came to pass/ happened	QAL WAYY 3MS	verb
	היה	wa·yə·hî		
	כִּי־	that/for/since/because/when	---	conj
	כי	kî-		
	הֵחֵל	(he) began	HIPH PF 3MS	verb
	חלל	hē·ḥēl		
	הָאָדָם	the man/humankind	ABS W/ DEF. ART.	noun
	אדם	hā·'ā·dām		

Similarly to the way the narrator introduces the Cain and Abel drama in 4:3 (וַיְהִי מִקֵּץ יָמִים, "Now it happened after some time . . ."), the introductory structure here (וַיְהִי כִּי, "Now it happened that . . .") does not specify how much time has elapsed between the preceding material (the genealogy in ch. 5) and what now occurs. At any rate, the multiplication of the human population seems connected to the rise of conflict. Intriguingly, the verb חלל, which in the Hiphil means "to begin," also (in fact, more commonly) means "profane," in the Piel. The use of this verb here perhaps injects a hint of the problem to come.

1b	לָרֹב עַל־פְּנֵי הָאֲדָמָה
	to proliferate upon the face of the ground

	לָרֹב	to increase/proliferate	QAL INF CST W/ PREP לְ	verb
	רבב	lā·rōv		
	עַל־	on/upon	---	prep
	על	'al-		
	פְּנֵי	(the) face/surface of	CST	noun
	פנה	pə·nê		
	הָאֲדָמָה	the ground	ABS W/ DEF. ART.	noun
	אדמה	hā·'ă·dā·mâ		

The reference here to the "ground" (אֲדָמָה) raises the specter of the cursing of the ground in 3:17 and also echoes Cain's status as a tiller (or, in light of the curse, perhaps a "servant" or "slave") of the ground in 4:2, 12.

1c	וּבָנוֹת יֻלְּדוּ לָהֶם׃		
	that daughters were born to them.		
	וּבָנוֹת and daughters בַּת *û·vā·nôt*	ABS W/ CONJ וּ	noun
	יֻלְּדוּ (they) were born יָלַד *yul·lə·dû*	PUAL PF 3CP	verb
	לָהֶם׃ to them לְ *lā·hem*	--- W/ 3MP SX	prep

2a	וַיִּרְאוּ בְנֵי־הָאֱלֹהִים אֶת־בְּנוֹת הָאָדָם		
	When the sons of God saw the daughters of man,		
	וַיִּרְאוּ and (they) saw/observed רָאָה *way·yir·'û*	QAL WAYY 3MP	verb
	בְנֵי־ (the) sons/members of בֵּן *və·nê-*	CST	noun
	הָאֱלֹהִים the gods/divine beings/God אֱלֹהִים *hā·'ĕ·lō·hîm*	ABS W/ DEF. ART.	noun
	אֶת־ (direct object marker) אֵת *'et-*	---	particle
	בְּנוֹת (the) daughters of בַּת *bə·nôt*	CST	noun
	הָאָדָם the man/humankind אָדָם *hā·'ā·dām*	ABS W/ DEF. ART.	noun

The phrase בְּנֵי־הָאֱלֹהִים appears only in Gen 6 (here in v. 2 and in v. 4 below) and in the opening to the book of Job (1:6; 2:1; see also variations in Job 38:7; Pss 29:1; 82:6; 89:7 [6]; and in Deut 32:8, as attested in the Dead Sea Scrolls [see, e.g., NRSVue]). The translation could vary; because of the plural form of אֱלֹהִים, grammatically possible options include "the sons of God," "the sons of the gods," and—more periphrastically—"the divine beings" (of some indeterminate type). Given the largely monotheistic thrust of the Old Testament, there would seem to be little possibility that בְּנֵי־הָאֱלֹהִים describes deities of equal status to the biblical God. Indeed, in the examples from Job, it is reasonably clear that the beings described by this title constitute a divine court that sits in a heavenly council with (and beneath) God. Although the phrase is sometimes translated or interpreted as "angels," the Old Testament does have another common term for what readers have typically understood as angels, i.e., מַלְאָךְ ("messenger"). The translation "sons of God" here is meant to preserve the genuine ambiguity of the phrase.

As for בְּנוֹת הָאָדָם, translators have had less trouble rendering this as "daughters of man" or "human women." However, wishing to avoid the unseemly suggestion that divine beings mated with human women under God's watch, some seek to interpret the "sons of God" and "daughters of man" in purely human categories—one example sees the first group as the offspring of the murderer Cain and the second as the offspring of Seth, the son who is born in place of the murdered Abel and whose line leads through Noah to Abraham and David and beyond. The most obvious problems with this interpretation are that: *(a)* in every other case in which בְּנֵי הָאֱלֹהִים or parallel phrases are used, they clearly refer to divine beings of some kind, not humans; *(b)* there is no grammatical or thematic justification in the context of Gen 6 for interpreting them as humans; and *(c)* the text itself indicates that the result of this sexual encounter is something extraordinary (not merely human).

2b	כִּי טֹבֹת הֵנָּה		
	that they were pleasing,		
	כִּי that/for/since/because כִּי *kî*	---	conj
	טֹבֹת good/beautiful/pleasing טוֹב *ṭō·vōt*	FP PRED	adj
	הֵנָּה they הֵנָּה *hēn·nâ*	---	personal pron

2c	וַיִּקְח֤וּ לָהֶם֙ נָשִׁ֔ים		
	they took wives for themselves		
וַיִּקְח֤וּ לקח	and/so they took way·yiq·ḥû	QAL WAYY 3MP	verb
לָהֶם֙ ל	to/for them/themselves lā·hem	--- W/ 3MP SX	prep
נָשִׁ֔ים אשה	women/wives nā·šîm	ABS	noun

The combination of the verbs for seeing (ראה, in v. 2a) and taking (לקח, here in v. 2c), combined with the theme of desire and physical attraction (signaled by טוב, "pleasing, beautiful," in v. 2b), echoes the words and theme of Gen 3:6—there, Eve "sees" (ראה) that the fruit is "good" (טוב) for food (as well as "delightful" and "desirable") and "takes" (לקח) it to eat. This allusion to the garden incident could suggest a broad thematic connection between this story and that one, since both deal with transgression against divine boundaries.

2d	מִכֹּ֖ל אֲשֶׁ֥ר בָּחָֽרוּ׃		
	from any that they chose.		
מִכֹּ֖ל כל	from all/each/every/any mik·kōl	ABS W/ PREP מִן	noun
אֲשֶׁ֥ר אשר	that/which 'ă·šer	---	relative pron
בָּחָֽרוּ׃ בחר	they chose/selected bā·ḥā·rû	QAL PF 3CP	verb

3a	וַיֹּ֣אמֶר יְהוָ֗ה		
	The Lord said,		
וַיֹּ֣אמֶר אמר	and/so/then (he) said way·yō'·mer	QAL WAYY 3MS	verb
יְהוָ֗ה יהוה	the Lord YHWH	ABS	noun

GOD DECIDES TO FLOOD THE EARTH

3b

לֹא־יָד֨וֹן רוּחִ֤י בָֽאָדָם֙ לְעֹלָ֔ם

"My breath shall not remain with humans forever—

לֹא־ לֹא	not *lō-*	---	particle
יָד֨וֹן דוֹן	(he/it) will stay/remain *yā·dôn*	QAL IMPF 3MS	verb
רוּחִ֤י רוּחַ	my spirit/breath *rû·ḥî*	CST W/ 1CS SX	noun
בָֽאָדָם֙ אָדָם	with/in man/humankind *vā·ʾā·dām*	ABS W/ PREP בְּ + DEF. ART.	noun
לְעֹלָ֔ם עוֹלָם	forever/in perpetuity *lə·ʿō·lām*	ABS W/ PREP לְ	noun

As in Gen 1, I have translated the word רוּחַ here as "breath." Many render the term as "spirit," which is also possible, though "breath" is the more literal, physical meaning. Here in 6:3, the "breath" implies a life force that sustains humanity, like the air that flows through our lungs; and in Gen 1, the physical context of the action implies windiness. However, other notions of a "spirit" could be understood within the image of (particularly) God's "breath."

Generations of translators have struggled with the term יָדוֹן, which may be a *hapax legomenon* (i.e., "a thing said once," a term appearing only here in the Bible) and which I have translated here as "remain." The other main option would be to translate as "contend against" (i.e., taking it to be a form of the verb דִין, "judge").

3c

בְּשַׁגַּ֖ם ה֣וּא בָשָׂ֑ר

they are merely flesh.

בְּשַׁגַּ֖ם גַּם	in which/that also/insofar as (?) *bə·šag·gam*	W/ PREP בְּ + RELATIVE PRON שֶׁ	adv
ה֣וּא הוּא	he/it *hû'*	---	personal pron
בָשָׂ֑ר בָּשָׂר	flesh *vā·śār*	ABS	noun

The opening phrase here, בְּשַׁגַּם, has long been a problem for translators, as it seems to combine the preposition בְּ and the relative pronoun שֶׁ ("that, which") with the particle גַּם, resulting in a single, otherwise unprecedented word.

3d	וְהָיוּ יָמָיו מֵאָה וְעֶשְׂרִים שָׁנָה:
	Their days will be one hundred and twenty years."

וְהָיוּ היה	and/so (they) will be/become wə·hā·yû	QAL WEQATAL 3CP	verb
יָמָיו יוֹם	their [lit., his] days yā·māyw	CST W/ 3MS SX	noun
מֵאָה מֵאָה	one hundred mē·'â	ABS	cardinal number
וְעֶשְׂרִים עֶשְׂרִים	and twenty wə·'eś·rîm	ABS W/ CONJ וְ	cardinal number
שָׁנָה: שָׁנָה	year(s) šā·nâ	ABS	noun

Interpretations of what "Their days will be one hundred and twenty years" means here have varied. I take this to refer to a limit on individual human lifespans, though one might also consider it a description of the time that will elapse between this incident and the onset of the flood. The round number 120 appears several times in the Old Testament, with reference to rituals and gifts (e.g., Num 7:86; 1 Kgs 9:14; 10:10; 2 Chr 3:4; 5:12) and also as the age of two prominent people at the time of their death—Sarah (Gen 23:1) and Moses (Deut 34:7). Why, exactly, human life would be limited to 120 years following this incident is unclear. Moreover, interpreters have struggled to understand why, in fact, human life is not in fact limited to 120 immediately after this event (e.g., Noah lives to be 950 [Gen 9:28–29]). In addition, it should be observed that the text does not actually state that life will be limited to this age, but rather that humans will "be" (or "become") this age, which does not account for people in or outside the Bible who live either longer or far less than 120 years.

Nevertheless, the narrative in Genesis does record a gradual diminishing of lifespans, from nearly a millennium for individuals like Adam, Seth, Noah, and others in chs. 1–9 down to the three-to-four-hundred-year range in ch. 11. And later in the book, Abraham dies at the age of 175

(25:7–8), Isaac at 180 (Gen 35:28), Jacob at 147 (Gen 47:28; 49:33), and Joseph at 110 (Gen 50:22). At its uppermost limits today, human lifespan does, interestingly, peak around 120, with only one (verified) example of someone living beyond this mark—to 122—and the next 99 oldest documented people living to between 114 and 119.

4a	הַנְּפִלִ֞ים הָי֣וּ בָאָרֶץ֮ בַּיָּמִ֣ים הָהֵם֒
	The Nephilim—they were on the earth in those days,

הַנְּפִלִים נְפִלִים	the Nephilim han·nə·fī·lîm	ABS W/ DEF. ART.	noun
הָיוּ היה	(they) were hā·yû	QAL PF 3CP	verb
בָאָרֶץ אֶרֶץ	in/on the earth vā·'ā·reṣ	ABS W/ PREP בְּ + DEF. ART.	noun
בַּיָּמִים יוֹם	in (the) days bay·yā·mîm	ABS W/ PREP בְּ + DEF. ART.	noun
הָהֵם הֵם	those hā·hēm	--- W/ DEF. ART.	demonstr pron

Most interpreters have presumed that the odd term נְפִלִים is based on the root נפל, "to fall." Even if this etymology is accurate—and it is the simplest option—we still do not learn what or where these beings are fallen from, or why they would have fallen. Christians wishing to import an understanding here of "fallen angels" (i.e., demons) could find some purchase in this reference, and an early Jewish writing produced around the fourth–second century BCE called 1 Enoch (esp. chs. 1–36 of that book) takes Gen 6:4 as its point of departure to describe fallen angelic beings ("Watchers") who give birth to giant and monstrous beings (i.e., these "Nephilim"). With very limited exceptions, Christians have not considered the Enochic material to be Scripture (nor do Jewish audiences in any ongoing or organized manner today), so it is not clear, from a Christian perspective, what credence one is to give to ancient non-canonical portrayals of fallen heavenly beings and their relationship to these Nephilim.

Moreover, the text here does not explicitly tell us what the relationship is between these Nephilim and the activity that has just been narrated in Gen 6:1–2. We are only left to infer that the Nephilim might be the offspring of the sons of God and the daughters of man. If one asserts that the intention of Scripture here is to teach us that this event was the birth of "demons" or a reference to fallen satanic beings, one would have to explain why the text does not simply say that—and why, moreover, the New Testament does not clearly refer to this event or clarify what would seem to be (in this interpretation) such an important story.

Further complicating matters is the fact that the subsequent account of the flood (Gen 6:5–9:29) narrates the death of all living things, human and animal and otherwise, on earth—and yet in Num 13:33, Israelite spies who have been sent into the land of Canaan explicitly report seeing the "Nephilim" there (with an added narrative comment clarifying that the sons of Anak, or Anakites, are descended "from the Nephilim"). Some early Jewish sources creatively solved this problem by positing that Noah himself (or one of his family members) was a member of the Nephilim, or that some Nephilim mysteriously survived the flood.

4b	וְגַ֖ם אַחֲרֵי־כֵ֗ן		
	and also afterward,		
	וְגַ֖ם — and also — *wə·gam*	--- W/ CONJ וְ	adv
	אַחֲרֵי־כֵ֗ן — afterward — *'a·ḥă·rê-kēn*	---	adv

Like so many other things in this passage, the meaning of this phrase is obscure. Perhaps it refers to the tradition that the Nephilim were living in the land of Canaan during a later period, as stated in Num 13:33.

4c	אֲשֶׁ֨ר יָבֹ֜אוּ בְּנֵ֤י הָֽאֱלֹהִים֙ אֶל־בְּנ֣וֹת הָֽאָדָ֔ם		
	when the sons of God entered into the daughters of man		
	אֲשֶׁ֨ר — that/which — *'ă·šer*	---	relative pron
	יָבֹ֜אוּ — (they) came/entered — *yā·vō·'û*	QAL IMPF 3MP	verb
	בְּנֵ֤י — (the) sons/members of — *bə·nê*	CST	noun

GOD DECIDES TO FLOOD THE EARTH 181

הָאֱלֹהִים֙ hā·ʾĕ·lō·hîm	the gods/divine beings/God	ABS W/ DEF. ART.	noun
אֶל־ ʾel-	to/toward/into	---	prep
בְּנוֹת bə·nôt	(the) daughters of	CST	noun
הָֽאָדָ֔ם hā·ʾā·dām	the man/humankind	ABS W/ DEF. ART.	noun

Translating אֲשֶׁר as "when" in this context, or even with the connotation of "the result of which was," which is grammatically permissible, allows for the potential of connecting the origins of the Nephilim with the activity described in Gen 6:1–2. Although not certain, this is a possible (if not the most natural) interpretation.

4d — וְיָלְדוּ לָהֶם

and they bore children to them.

וְיָלְדוּ wə·yā·lə·dû	and/so they bore/gave birth	QAL PF 3CP W/ CONJ וְ	verb
לָהֶ֑ם lā·hem	to/for them	--- W/ 3MP SX	prep

4e — הֵמָּה הַגִּבֹּרִים אֲשֶׁר מֵעוֹלָם

They were the ancient Heroes,

הֵ֧מָּה hēm·mâ	they	---	personal pron
הַגִּבֹּרִ֛ים hag·gib·bō·rîm	the heroes/valiant ones/ warriors/Gibborim	MP SUBST W/ DEF. ART.	adj
אֲשֶׁ֥ר ʾă·šer	that/which/who	---	relative pron
מֵעוֹלָ֖ם mē·ʿô·lām	from antiquity/of old	ABS W/ PREP מִן	noun

In ordinary usage, the term גִּבּוֹר refers to a "mighty man" or a "hero" (usually in a military context), though in one instance (Isa 9:5 [6]) it appears in a divine title, "Mighty God" (אֵל גִּבּוֹר). Here we capitalize "Heroes" to signal that in this context there is something unusual about the term's referent and about the resultant divine-human offspring (the nature of which is ambiguous, however).

4f	אַנְשֵׁי הַשֵּׁם:		
	famous men.		
	אַנְשֵׁי (the) men of אִישׁ ʾan·šê	CST	noun
	הַשֵּׁם: name/fame/renown שֵׁם haš·šēm	ABS W/ DEF. ART.	noun

The phrase אַנְשֵׁי הַשֵּׁם literally means "men of name." Somewhat ironically, however, these ancient and famous heroic figures are not named and remain quite mysterious. One possibility is that the text here is making oblique reference to the whole of ancient Near Eastern and Mediterranean mythology, which recounted the exploits of divine-human figures like Gilgamesh, the Greek heroes, and so on. On this interpretation, the brief, passing reference to these types of figures here simultaneously accounts for and dismisses them as the result of a primeval rebellion against divine boundaries.

5–10	**SUMMARY**

In Gen 6:5–10, the Lord considers the utter wickedness of humankind to be so egregious that he decides to blot out all humans on earth. Noah, however, stands out as righteous, and the text gives a brief genealogy of Noah's sons: Shem, Ham, and Japheth.

6:11–12

11a וַתִּשָּׁחֵת הָאָרֶץ לִפְנֵי הָאֱלֹהִים
wattiššāḥēt hā'āreṣ lifnê hā'ĕlōhîm

Now the earth was ruined before God,

11b וַתִּמָּלֵא הָאָרֶץ חָמָס׃
wattimmālē' hā'āreṣ ḥāmās.

because the earth was filled with violence.

12a וַיַּרְא אֱלֹהִים אֶת־הָאָרֶץ
wayyar' 'ĕlōhîm 'et-hā'āreṣ

God saw the earth—

12b וְהִנֵּה נִשְׁחָתָה
wəhinnē nišḥātâ

and it was truly ruined,

12c כִּי־הִשְׁחִית כָּל־בָּשָׂר אֶת־דַּרְכּוֹ עַל־הָאָרֶץ׃
kî-hišḥît kol-bāśār 'et-darkô 'al-hā'āreṣ.

because all flesh had ruined its way upon the earth.

11a	וַתִּשָּׁחֵת הָאָרֶץ לִפְנֵי הָאֱלֹהִים		
	Now the earth was ruined before God,		
וַתִּשָּׁחֵת	and/now (it) was corrupted/ destroyed/ruined/spoiled	NIPH WAYY 3FS	verb
שחת	wat·tiš·šā·ḥēt		
הָאָרֶץ	the earth	ABS W/ DEF. ART.	noun
אֶרֶץ	hā·'ā·reṣ		

לִפְנֵי	to (the) face of/ in (the) presence of	---	prep
לִפְנֵי	lif·nê		
הָאֱלֹהִים	(the) God	ABS W/ DEF. ART.	noun
אֱלֹהִים	hā·ʾĕ·lō·hîm		

11b — וַתִּמָּלֵא הָאָרֶץ חָמָס׃

because the earth was filled with violence.

וַתִּמָּלֵא	and (it) was full/filled	NIPH WAYY 3FS	verb
מלא	wat tim·mā·lē		
הָאָרֶץ	the earth	ABS W/ DEF. ART.	noun
אֶרֶץ	hā·ʾā·reṣ		
חָמָס׃	violence	ABS	noun
חָמָס	ḥā·mās		

The exact nature of the ruination and violence mentioned here is left open to the imagination. Given the relationship of this passage with the preceding material in 6:1–4, and the declaration of humankind's total wickedness in 6:5–9, one might assume that the problem has to do with the transgressive acts narrated there. Whatever the problem, by using the verb שחת in this verse and repeating it twice in the next verse, the narrator emphasizes that the situation is completely hopeless and thus presents as justified an act as extreme as the complete annihilation of all living things.

12a — וַיַּרְא אֱלֹהִים אֶת־הָאָרֶץ

God saw the earth—

וַיַּרְא	and (he) saw	QAL WAYY 3MS	verb
ראה	way·yarʾ		
אֱלֹהִים	God	ABS	noun
אֱלֹהִים	ʾĕ·lō·hîm		
אֶת־	(direct object marker)	---	particle
אֶת	ʾet-		
הָאָרֶץ	the earth	ABS W/ DEF. ART.	noun
אֶרֶץ	hā·ʾā·reṣ		

When God "sees," God acts. Whereas in Gen 1, God "saw" creation and pronounced it "good," here it is the opposite: God saw the earth . . . and it was ruined. Recall the curse against the ground in Gen 3 and the reiteration of that curse in Gen 4 after Cain kills Abel.

12b	וְהִנֵּה נִשְׁחָתָה
	and it was truly ruined,

	וְהִנֵּה	and behold/look	---	particle
	הִנֵּה	wə·hin·nē	W/ CONJ וְ	
	נִשְׁחָתָה	it was corrupted/destroyed/ruined/spoiled	NIPH PF 3FS	verb
	שׁחת	niš·ḥā·tâ		

12c	כִּי־הִשְׁחִית כָּל־בָּשָׂר אֶת־דַּרְכּוֹ עַל־הָאָרֶץ׃
	because all flesh had ruined its way upon the earth.

	כִּי־	for/since/because	---	conj
	כִּי	kî-		
	הִשְׁחִית	(he/it) made corrupt/destroyed/ruined/spoiled	HIPH PF 3MS	verb
	שׁחת	hiš·ḥît		
	כָּל־	all/each/every	CST	noun
	כֹּל	kol-		
	בָּשָׂר	flesh	ABS	noun
	בָּשָׂר	bā·śār		
	אֶת־	(direct object marker)	---	particle
	אֵת	'et-		
	דַּרְכּוֹ	his/its way/path	CST W/ 3MS SX	noun
	דֶּרֶךְ	dar·kô		
	עַל־	on/upon/against	---	prep
	עַל	'al-		
	הָאָרֶץ׃	the earth	ABS W/ DEF. ART.	noun
	אֶרֶץ	hā·'ā·reṣ		

This is the first of twelve occurrences of the phrase כָּל־בָּשָׂר, "all flesh," in Gen 6–9 (and in Genesis it is only in these chapters that this phrase appears). Here God determines to make an end of "all flesh," but after the flood he makes his covenant with "all flesh" (Gen 9:11, 15–17). Thus, after destruction, God re-creates and offers a way forward for "all flesh."

6:13–16

13a
וַיֹּ֤אמֶר אֱלֹהִים֙ לְנֹ֔חַ
wayyōʾmer ʾĕlōhîm lənōaḥ

So God said to Noah,

13b
קֵ֤ץ כָּל־בָּשָׂר֙ בָּ֣א לְפָנַ֔י
qēṣ kol-bāśār bāʾ ləfānay

"The end of all flesh has come before me,

13c
כִּֽי־מָלְאָ֥ה הָאָ֛רֶץ חָמָ֖ס מִפְּנֵיהֶ֑ם
kî-mālə'â hā'āreṣ ḥāmās mippənêhem

because the earth is filled with violence from their presence—

13d
וְהִנְנִ֥י מַשְׁחִיתָ֖ם אֶת־הָאָֽרֶץ׃
wəhinənî mašḥîtām ʾet-hā'āreṣ.

so I am about to wipe them out, along with the earth.

14a
עֲשֵׂ֤ה לְךָ֙ תֵּבַ֣ת עֲצֵי־גֹ֔פֶר
'ăśē ləkā tēvat 'ăṣê-gōfer

Make for yourself a vessel of gopher wood.

14b
קִנִּ֖ים תַּֽעֲשֶׂ֣ה אֶת־הַתֵּבָ֑ה
qinnîm taʿăśe ʾet-hattēvâ

Make rooms for the vessel,

14c
וְכָפַרְתָּ֥ אֹתָ֛הּ מִבַּ֥יִת וּמִח֖וּץ בַּכֹּֽפֶר׃
wəkāfartā ʾōtāh mibbayit ûmiḥûṣ bakkōfer.

and cover it inside and outside with pitch.

15a
וְזֶ֕ה אֲשֶׁ֥ר תַּעֲשֶׂ֖ה אֹתָ֑הּ
wəze ʾăšer taʿăśe ʾōtāh

This is how you should make it:

15b	שְׁלֹשׁ מֵאוֹת אַמָּה אֹרֶךְ הַתֵּבָה	
	šəlōš mē'ôt 'ammâ 'ōreḵ hattēvâ	

The vessel should be three hundred cubits long,

15c	חֲמִשִּׁים אַמָּה רָחְבָּהּ	
	ḥămiššîm 'ammâ roḥbāh	

fifty cubits wide,

15d	וּשְׁלֹשִׁים אַמָּה קוֹמָתָהּ:	
	ûšəlōšîm 'ammâ qômātāh.	

and thirty cubits high.

16a	צֹהַר ׀ תַּעֲשֶׂה לַתֵּבָה	
	ṣōhar ta'áśe lattēvâ	

Make a roof for the vessel,

16b	וְאֶל־אַמָּה תְּכַלֶנָּה מִלְמַעְלָה	
	wə'el-'ammâ təḵalennâ milma'lâ	

and to a cubit above finish it.

16c	וּפֶתַח הַתֵּבָה בְּצִדָּהּ תָּשִׂים	
	ûfetaḥ hattēvâ bəṣiddāh tāśîm	

Place the opening of the vessel in its side.

16d	תַּחְתִּיִּם שְׁנִיִּם וּשְׁלִשִׁים תַּעֲשֶׂהָ:	
	taḥtiyyim šəniyyîm ûšəlišîm ta'áśehā.	

Make lower, second, and third levels.

13a	וַיֹּאמֶר אֱלֹהִים לְנֹחַ
	So God said to Noah,

	וַיֹּאמֶר אמר	and/so/then (he) said *way·yōʾ·mer*	QAL WAYY 3MS	verb
	אֱלֹהִים אלהים	God *ʾĕ·lō·hîm*	ABS	noun
	לְנֹחַ נֹחַ	to Noah *lə·nō·aḥ*	ABS W/ PREP לְ	noun

Noah's birth is recorded earlier, in 5:28–29, where he is named נֹחַ as a wordplay on a term meaning "to comfort, bring relief," נחם, with the explanation that Noah will relieve humanity: "Out of the ground that the LORD has cursed this one shall bring us relief from our work and from the toil of our hands" (5:29 NRSVue). The nature of this relief is not immediately clear; it could be related to Noah's role in cultivating grapes for wine (9:20).

In 6:8–9, the narrator emphasizes Noah's complete moral excellence as one who finds "favor" (חֵן) with the Lord and who is "righteous" (צַדִּיק) and "blameless" (תָּמִים). This contrasts with other ancient flood stories from the Bible's broader Mesopotamian context, such as the one found in the famous Epic of Gilgamesh. In that story, the survivor of the flood, Utnapishtim (or Uta-napishtim), is chosen for survival by the deities for no obvious moral reason but rather because he seems to be a favorite of a particular god. Moreover, the reason for the flood that kills all humanity in the epic is murky—the deities simply decide to do it. Thus, we see the Bible injecting a strong endorsement of upright moral behavior into the flood story, as well as making a strong statement on the consequence of immoral behavior (6:5–8, 11–13), which clarifies that the human response to God—for good or for ill—is decisive. In the Bible's moral universe, human behavior matters; sin and obedience matter.

13b	קֵץ כָּל־בָּשָׂר בָּא לְפָנַי
	"The end of all flesh has come before me,

	קֵץ קֵץ	end/limit of *qēṣ*	CST	noun
	כָּל־ כֹּל	all/each/every *kol-*	CST	noun

בָּשָׂר֙ בָּשָׂר	flesh bā·śār	ABS	noun
בָּ֣א בוא	(it) comes/has come bā'	QAL PF 3MS	verb
לְפָנַ֔י לְפָנַי	before/in front of/to my face lə·fā·**nay**	--- W/ 1CS SX	prep

For related language in the context of judgment, see Ezek 7:2–3, 5–7.

13c	כִּי־מָלְאָ֥ה הָאָ֛רֶץ חָמָ֖ס מִפְּנֵיהֶ֑ם
	because the earth is filled with violence from their presence—

כִּי־ כִּי	for/since/because kî-	---	conj
מָלְאָ֥ה מלא	(it) is filled mā·lə·'â	QAL PF 3FS	verb
הָאָ֛רֶץ אֶרֶץ	the earth hā·'ā·reṣ	ABS W/ DEF. ART.	noun
חָמָ֖ס חָמָס	violence/wickedness/wrong ḥā·mās	ABS	noun
מִפְּנֵיהֶ֑ם מִפְּנֵי	from their face/presence mip·pə·nê·**hem**	--- W/ 3MP SX	prep

The Hebrew word translated here as "from their presence," מִפְּנֵיהֶם, uses the keyword "face" (literally, מִפְּנֵיהֶם means "from their *faces*," i.e., "on account of them"), which, as we have seen, is so crucial in the exchange between God and Cain in Gen 4.

13d	וְהִנְנִ֥י מַשְׁחִיתָ֖ם אֶת־הָאָֽרֶץ׃
	so I am about to wipe them out, along with the earth.

וְהִנְנִ֥י הִנֵּה	and look I/I am about to wə·hi·nə·**nî**	--- W/ CONJ וְ + 1CS SX	particle

GOD DECIDES TO FLOOD THE EARTH

מַשְׁחִיתָם	destroying them/ wiping them out/ erasing them	HIPH PTCP MS W/ 3MP SX	verb
שחת	maš·ḥî·tām		
אֶת־	with	---	prep
אֵת	ʾet-		
הָאָֽרֶץ:	the earth	ABS W/ DEF. ART.	noun
אֶרֶץ	hā·ʾā·reṣ		

The two preceding verses (6:11–12) use this same verb שחת (translated "to wipe out" here in v. 13) three times to describe how humans have "ruined" the earth. Humanity has destroyed the earth, and therefore God will destroy them. This type of measure-for-measure punishment appears at various points in the Bible (e.g., in the "eye for an eye" principle expressed in Exod 21:24).

14a — עֲשֵׂה לְךָ תֵּבַת עֲצֵי־גֹפֶר

Make for yourself a vessel of gopher wood.

עֲשֵׂה	make	QAL IMPV MS	verb
עשׂה	ʿă·śē		
לְךָ	for you/yourself	--- W/ 2MS SX	prep
לְ	lə·ḵā		
תֵּבַת	vessel/ark/boat/basket of	CST	noun
תֵּבָה	tē·vat		
עֲצֵי־	tree(s)/wood of	CST	noun
עֵץ	ʿă·ṣê-		
גֹפֶר	gopher (type of wood)	ABS	noun
גֹּפֶר	gō·fer		

The term here for "vessel" (תֵּבָה), most commonly translated "ark" (i.e., chest, box, vessel), is rare and not related to any of the more common Hebrew terms for "boat" (though boats generally do not play a major role in Old Testament spirituality and geography). (Note also that, somewhat confusingly, the term rendered "ark" in the phrase "ark of the covenant" is an altogether different Hebrew word, אָרוֹן, another term meaning "chest, box.") Outside of the flood story in Gen 6–9, the only other use of the term תֵּבָה in the Bible occurs in Exod 2:3, 5, where the phrase תֵּבַת גֹּמֶא,

"papyrus vessel," refers to the little basket Moses' mother places him in to survive the slaughter of the infants in Egypt. The sense of a תֵּבָה being a cocoon of survival for a limited person or group passing through water applies in both cases.

Rather than trying to identify this exact type of wood (e.g., by calling it "cypress," for which a different Hebrew word exists that is not used here), leaving the term roughly transliterated from Hebrew as "gopher"—a term used only here in the Hebrew Bible—allows the reader to imagine some type of exotic wood. Alternatively, as various commentators have noted, the presence of a similar word later in the verse, כֹּפֶר ("pitch"), could prompt us to wonder whether the initial ג in גֹפֶר should be a כ; in this case, one could translate the phrase (עֲצֵי כֹפֶר) as "wood covered in pitch" or "pitch-covered wood."

14b	קִנִּים תַּעֲשֶׂה אֶת־הַתֵּבָה
	Make rooms for the vessel,

קִנִּים קֵן	nests/rooms qin·nîm	ABS	noun
תַּעֲשֶׂה עשׂה	you will make ta·ʿă·śe	QAL IMPF 2MS	verb
אֶת־ אֵת	(direct object marker) 'et-	---	particle
הַתֵּבָה תֵּבָה	the vessel/ark/boat/basket hat·tē·vâ	ABS W/ DEF. ART.	noun

The term here translated "rooms" (קֵן) can also mean "nest"—perhaps reinforcing the idea that Noah is to survive in a protected, cocoon-like environment.

14c	וְכָפַרְתָּ אֹתָהּ מִבַּיִת וּמִחוּץ בַּכֹּפֶר׃
	and cover it inside and outside with pitch.

וְכָפַרְתָּ כפר	and you will cover wə·kā·far·tā	QAL WEQATAL 2MS	verb
אֹתָהּ אֵת	(direct object marker +) it ʾō·tāh	--- W/ 3FS SX	particle

GOD DECIDES TO FLOOD THE EARTH

מִבַּ֫יִת bayit · mib בַּ֫יִת	from house/inside	ABS W/ PREP מִן	noun
וּמִח֖וּץ û · mi · ḥûṣ ח֖וּץ	and from outside	ABS W/ CONJ וְ + PREP מִן	noun
בַּכֹּֽפֶר׃ bak · kō · fer כֹּ֫פֶר	with/in the pitch	ABS W/ PREP בְּ + DEF. ART.	noun

The verb used here for "cover" and the term for "pitch" are from the same root, כפר.

The phrase translated here as "inside" is literally "from (the) house" (מִבַּ֫יִת). In combination with the following phrase (וּמִח֖וּץ, "and from outside"), the smoothest English rendering seems to be "inside and outside."

15a		וְזֶ֕ה אֲשֶׁ֥ר תַּעֲשֶׂ֖ה אֹתָ֑הּ	
	This is how you should make it:		
וְזֶ֕ה wə · ze זֶה	and this	--- W/ CONJ וְ	demonstr pron
אֲשֶׁ֥ר 'ă · šer אֲשֶׁר	that/which	---	relative pron
תַּעֲשֶׂ֖ה ta · 'ă · śe עשׂה	you will make	QAL IMPF 2MS	verb
אֹתָ֑הּ 'ō · tāh אֵת	(direct object marker +) it	--- W/ 3FS SX	particle

---

15b		שְׁלֹ֧שׁ מֵא֣וֹת אַמָּ֗ה אֹ֚רֶךְ הַתֵּבָ֔ה	
	The vessel should be three hundred cubits long,		
שְׁלֹ֧שׁ šə · lōš שָׁלֹשׁ	three	CST	cardinal number
מֵא֣וֹת mē · 'ôt מֵאָה	hundreds	ABS	cardinal number
אַמָּ֗ה 'am · mâ אַמָּה	cubit	ABS	noun

אֹ֫רֶךְ֙ ’ō·rek	length of	CST	noun
הַתֵּבָ֔ה hat·tē·vâ	the vessel/ark/boat/basket	ABS W/ DEF. ART.	noun

15c

חֲמִשִּׁ֥ים אַמָּ֖ה רָחְבָּ֑הּ
fifty cubits wide,

חֲמִשִּׁ֥ים ḥă·miš·šîm	fifty	ABS	cardinal number
אַמָּ֖ה ’am·mâ	cubit	ABS	noun
רָחְבָּ֑הּ roḥ·bāh	its width/thickness	CST W/ 3FS SX	noun

15d

וּשְׁלֹשִׁ֥ים אַמָּ֖ה קוֹמָתָֽהּ׃
and thirty cubits high.

וּשְׁלֹשִׁ֥ים û·šə·lō·šîm	and thirty	ABS W/ CONJ וְ	cardinal number
אַמָּ֖ה ’am·mâ	cubit	ABS	noun
קוֹמָתָֽהּ׃ qô·mā·tāh	its height	CST W/ 3FS SX	noun

Some wishing to see the scale of this boat have created life-sized replicas. The traditional understanding of a cubit as the distance from a human elbow to the fingertips would yield a vessel roughly twice the length of a jetliner. As far as the shape is concerned, those who would like to imagine this vessel should be thinking of a form much more like a giant, slender, floating submarine—ten times as long as it is high, and six times as long as it is wide—rather than the "boxy"-looking boat of popular imagination.

16a

צֹהַר ׀ תַּעֲשֶׂה לַתֵּבָה

Make a roof for the vessel,

צֹהַר ׀ צֹהַר	roof ṣō·har	ABS	noun
תַּעֲשֶׂה עשׂה	you will make ta·ʿă·śe	QAL IMPF 2MS	verb
לַתֵּבָה תֵּבָה	for the vessel/ark/boat/basket lat·tē·vâ	ABS W/ PREP לְ + DEF. ART.	noun

The meaning of צֹהַר, rendered here as "roof," is not clear, since this term is a *hapax legomenon* in the Old Testament and is not clearly related to any known term in a cognate (i.e., related) language. Other translation possibilities include "window," "opening," and "vent."

16b

וְאֶל־אַמָּה תְּכַלֶנָּה מִלְמַעְלָה

and to a cubit above finish it.

וְאֶל־ אֶל	and to/toward wə·ʾel-	--- W/ CONJ וְ	prep
אַמָּה אַמָּה	cubit ʾam·mâ	ABS	noun
תְּכַלֶנָּה כלה	you will finish/complete it tə·ḵa·**len**·nâ	PIEL IMPF 2MS W/ 3FS SX	verb
מִלְמַעְלָה מַעַל	from to height [i.e., above] mil·**maʿ**·lâ	--- W/ PREP מִן + PREP לְ + LOCATIVE ה	noun

The individual words in this phrase are all clear (the compound word מִלְמַעְלָה is in fact a common term for "above" in the Bible), but making sense of them together is difficult. Is the "roof" (צֹהַר) to be a cubit higher than the top of the vessel?

16c

וּפֶ֥תַח הַתֵּבָ֖ה בְּצִדָּ֣הּ תָּשִׂ֑ים

Place the opening of the vessel in its side.

וּפֶ֥תַח û·fe·taḥ	and (the) door of	CST W/ CONJ וּ	noun
הַתֵּבָ֖ה hat·tē·vâ	the vessel/ark/boat/basket	ABS W/ DEF. ART.	noun
בְּצִדָּ֣הּ bə·ṣid·dāh	in its side	CST W/ PREP בְּ + 3FS SX	noun
תָּשִׂ֑ים tā·śîm	you will place/set	QAL IMPF 2MS	verb

16d

תַּחְתִּיִּ֛ם שְׁנִיִּ֥ם וּשְׁלִשִׁ֖ים תַּֽעֲשֶֽׂהָ׃

Make lower, second, and third levels for it.

תַּחְתִּיִּ֛ם taḥ·tiy·yim	lower (ones)	MP SUBST	adj
שְׁנִיִּ֥ם šə·niy·yīm	second (ones)	---	ordinal number
וּשְׁלִשִׁ֖ים û·šə·lī·šîm	and third (ones)	--- W/ CONJ וּ	ordinal number
תַּֽעֲשֶֽׂהָ׃ ta·'ă·śe·hā	you will make it	QAL IMPF 2MS W/ 3FS SX	verb

Though no word appears for "levels" (or "decks" or "parts"?), most assume the terms for lower, second, and third must be describing levels.

6:17–18

17a וַאֲנִ֗י הִנְנִי֩ מֵבִ֨יא אֶת־הַמַּבּ֥וּל
wa'ănî hinənî mēvî' 'et-hammabbûl
I am about to bring the flood—

17b מַ֙יִם֙ עַל־הָאָ֔רֶץ
mayim 'al-hā'āreṣ
waters upon the earth—

17c לְשַׁחֵ֣ת כָּל־בָּשָׂ֗ר
ləšaḥēt kol-bāśār
to wipe out all flesh

17d אֲשֶׁר־בּוֹ֙ ר֣וּחַ חַיִּ֔ים
'ăšer-bô rûaḥ ḥayyîm
that has the breath of life in it

17e מִתַּ֖חַת הַשָּׁמָ֑יִם
mittaḥat haššāmāyim
from under the heavens.

17f כֹּ֥ל אֲשֶׁר־בָּאָ֖רֶץ יִגְוָֽע׃
kōl 'ăšer-bā'āreṣ yigwā'
Everyone on earth will die—

18a וַהֲקִמֹתִ֥י אֶת־בְּרִיתִ֖י אִתָּ֑ךְ
wahăqīmōtî 'et-bərîtî 'ittāk
but I will raise up my covenant with you,

18b וּבָאתָ֙ אֶל־הַתֵּבָ֔ה
ûvā'tā 'el-hattēvâ
and you will enter the vessel,

18c	אַתָּה וּבָנֶיךָ
	'attâ ûvānêkā
	you and your sons

18d	וְאִשְׁתְּךָ וּנְשֵׁי־בָנֶיךָ אִתָּךְ׃
	wəʾištəkā ûnəšê-vānêkā 'ittāk.
	and your wife and the wives of your sons with you.

17a	וַאֲנִי הִנְנִי מֵבִיא אֶת־הַמַּבּוּל
	I am about to bring the flood—

וַאֲנִי	and/but I	---	personal
אֲנִי	wa·ʾă·nî	W/ CONJ ו	pron
הִנְנִי	look I/I am about to	---	particle
הִנֵּה	hi·nə·nî	W/ 1CS SX	
מֵבִיא	bringing/causing to come	HIPH PTCP MS	verb
בוא	mē·vîʾ		
אֶת־	(direct object marker)	---	particle
אֵת	ʾet-		
הַמַּבּוּל	the flood	ABS	noun
מַבּוּל	ham·mab·bûl	W/ DEF. ART.	

Parallel to the way the term ברא is used only to describe special acts of divine creation (as in Gen 1) and never common acts of making (for which other verbs, such as עשה, are used), so the term מַבּוּל appears only to describe this cosmic flood. One possible exception (the only place the word occurs outside of Genesis) is found in Ps 29:10, "The Lord sits enthroned over the מַבּוּל"—though the poet here may be referring to this same flood. At any rate, מַבּוּל is never used to describe normal rising waters or common floods (see other terminology in, e.g., 2 Sam 5:20; Job 22:11; Nah 1:8).

17b

מַ֫יִם עַל־הָאָ֫רֶץ

waters up on the earth—

מַ֫יִם / mayim	water(s)	ABS	noun
עַל־ / ʿal-	on/upon/against	---	prep
הָאָ֫רֶץ / hā·ʾā·reṣ	the earth	ABS W/ DEF. ART.	noun

17c

לְשַׁחֵת כָּל־בָּשָׂר

to wipe out all flesh

לְשַׁחֵת / lə·ša·ḥēt	to destroy/wipe out	PIEL INF CST W/ PREP לְ	verb
כָּל־ / kol-	all/each/every	CST	noun
בָּשָׂר / bā·śār	flesh	ABS	noun

See comment at 6:13d.

17d

אֲשֶׁר־בּוֹ ר֣וּחַ חַיִּים

that has the breath of life in it

אֲשֶׁר־ / ʾă·šer-	that/which	---	relative pron
בּוֹ / bô	in it	W/ 3MS SX	prep
ר֣וּחַ / rû·aḥ	wind/spirit/breath of	CST	noun
חַיִּים / ḥay·yîm	life	ABS	noun

17e — מִתַּחַת הַשָּׁמָיִם

from under the heavens.

מִתַּחַת תַּחַת	from beneath/below mit·ta·ḥat	--- W/ PREP מִן	prep
הַשָּׁמַיִם שָׁמַיִם	the heavens/skies/air above haš·šā·mayim	ABS W/ DEF. ART.	noun

With the exception of the use of this phrase in Gen 1:9, every instance of מִתַּחַת הַשָּׁמָיִם in the Bible portends extreme judgment. (Compare with the use of the phrase "upon the face of the ground" in Gen 4:14b.)

17f — כֹּל אֲשֶׁר־בָּאָרֶץ יִגְוָע׃

Everything on earth will die—

כֹּל כֹּל	all/each/everything kōl	ABS	noun
אֲשֶׁר־ אֲשֶׁר	that/which 'ă·šer-	---	relative pron
בָּאָרֶץ אֶרֶץ	in/on/upon the earth bā·'ā·reṣ	ABS W/ PREP בְּ + DEF. ART.	noun
יִגְוָע׃ גוע	(it) will die/perish yig·wā'	QAL IMPF 3MS	verb

The term here for "die" (גוע), while common enough in the Hebrew Bible, is not nearly as common as the verb מות, which has the same semantic range.

18a — וַהֲקִמֹתִי אֶת־בְּרִיתִי אִתָּךְ

but I will raise up my covenant with you,

וַהֲקִמֹתִי קום	but/and/then I will raise up/establish wa·hă·qī·mō·tî	HIPH WEQATAL 1CS	verb
אֶת־ אֵת	(direct object marker) 'et-	---	particle

GOD DECIDES TO FLOOD THE EARTH

בְּרִיתִי בְּרִית	my covenant bə·rî·tî	CST W/ 1CS SX	noun
אִתָּךְ אֵת	with you 'it·tāḵ	--- W/ 2MS SX	prep

This is the first appearance of one of the most important theological concepts in the Old Testament: "covenant" (בְּרִית). In its ancient Near Eastern context, the terminology of covenant held important political and legal connotations—covenants described the bond between two parties, such as nations or kings, clarifying their relationship with one another and often stipulating consequences for both obedience and disobedience to the arrangement. The use of בְּרִית language features heavily later in the flood story (ch. 9) and then in the stories of Abraham (e.g., Gen 15 and 17) and the book of Exodus. The book of Deuteronomy utilizes a formal structure that has often been analyzed in terms of its similarity to ancient Near Eastern treaties (i.e., with a prologue or historical review, terms of the agreement, and consequences). This covenant language is then echoed throughout Israel's entry into the land in the book of Joshua, and it culminates in the promise to David and the relationship that God enters into with Israel and that Israel enters into with the nations around it in Samuel–Kings. The Prophets and the Psalms also resound with the language of covenant.

The verbal idiom used here for establishing or (more literally) "raising up" (Hiphil of קוּם) a covenant may find its origin in some physical act in which covenant partners would engage, such as erecting a written monument in stone or even a pile of stones (e.g., Gen 31:51–54).

18b	וּבָאתָ אֶל־הַתֵּבָה		
	and you will enter the vessel,		
וּבָאתָ בּוֹא	and you will come/enter û·vā·tā	QAL WEQATAL 2MS	verb
אֶל־ אֶל	to/toward 'el-	---	prep
הַתֵּבָה תֵּבָה	the vessel/ark/boat/basket hat·tē·vâ	ABS W/ DEF. ART.	noun

18c

אַתָּ֖ה וּבָנֶ֥יךָ

you and your sons

אַתָּ֖ה	you	---	personal pron
אַתָּה	'at·tâ		
וּבָנֶ֥יךָ	and your sons	CST W/ CONJ ו + 2MS SX	noun
בֵּן	û·vā·nê·ḵā		

18d

וְאִשְׁתְּךָ֛ וּנְשֵֽׁי־בָנֶ֥יךָ אִתָּֽךְ׃

and your wife and the wives of your sons with you.

וְאִשְׁתְּךָ֛	and your wife	CST W/ CONJ ו + 2MS SX	noun
אִשָּׁה	wə·'iš·tə·ḵā		
וּנְשֵֽׁי־	and (the) wives of	CST W/ CONJ ו	noun
אִשָּׁה	û·nə·šê-		
בָנֶ֥יךָ	your sons	CST W/ 2MS SX	noun
בֵּן	vā·nê·ḵā		
אִתָּֽךְ׃	with you	W/ 2MS SX	prep
אֵת	'it·tāḵ		

Here we get a glimpse of the distinctive way human identity was conceived of in ancient Israel: Noah himself is singled out for his righteousness (6:8–9), yet his entire family and even his daughters-in-law are saved. We thus find an interplay between individual choice and group identity, wherein the socio-theological assumption is that in certain cases a righteous individual can (at least temporarily) save others around him. Though Christians who have been reared in settings where the reigning assumption is that an individual alone is responsible before God may find such an idea troubling (and see also Scripture to this effect, e.g., Ezek 14:12–20), we could also consider a model like this to be a helpful means of preparing humanity for the revelation of Jesus Christ, who saves others through his unique righteousness. Similar biblical models could include Job (42:7–9), whom God instructs to pray on behalf of his friends for their forgiveness, and God's offer that the presence of even a small number of righteous individuals in Sodom would allow him to spare that whole city (Gen 18:22–33). Communal punishment can work the same way in the Old Testament, with families dying for the sins of their father—see the story of Achan, whose children are executed along with him for his actions (Josh 7:16–26; and note Exod 20:5–6 and Jer 32:18). In the New Testament, see 1 Cor 12:12–14 for a communal image of salvation with exodus and baptismal imagery. None of this, of course, negates the crucial importance of an individual's response to God. But it does offer insight into a broader picture of the meaning of the group and family in the spirituality of the biblical world.

6:19–21

19a וּמִכָּל־הָחַי מִכָּל־בָּשָׂר
ûmikkol-hāḥay mikkol-bāśār

From every living being, from all flesh,

19b שְׁנַיִם מִכֹּל תָּבִיא אֶל־הַתֵּבָה
šənayim mikkōl tāvî' 'el-hattēvâ

you will bring two of each into the vessel

19c לְהַחֲיֹת אִתָּךְ
ləhaḥăyōt 'ittāk

to keep them alive with you.

19d זָכָר וּנְקֵבָה יִהְיוּ׃
zākār ûnəqēvâ yihyû.

Male and female they will be:

20a מֵהָעוֹף לְמִינֵהוּ
mēhā'ôf ləmînēhû

from birds according to their kind,

20b וּמִן־הַבְּהֵמָה לְמִינָהּ
ûmin-habbəhēmâ ləmînāh

and from beasts according to their kind,

20c מִכֹּל רֶמֶשׂ הָאֲדָמָה לְמִינֵהוּ
mikkōl remeś hā'ădāmâ ləmînēhû

from all things that creep upon the earth according to their kind—

20d שְׁנַיִם מִכֹּל יָבֹאוּ אֵלֶיךָ
šənayim mikkōl yāvō'û 'ēlêkā

two from each will come to you

20e	לְהַחֲיֽוֹת׃
	ləhaḥăyôt.

to keep them alive.

21a	וְאַתָּ֣ה
	wəʾattâ

And as for you:

21b	קַֽח־לְךָ֗ מִכָּל־מַֽאֲכָל֙
	qaḥ-ləkā mikkol-maʾăkāl

take for yourself from all food

21c	אֲשֶׁ֣ר יֵֽאָכֵ֔ל
	ʾăšer yēʾākēl

that can be eaten,

21d	וְאָסַפְתָּ֖ אֵלֶ֑יךָ
	wəʾāsaftā ʾēlêkā

and gather it up for yourself

21e	וְהָיָ֥ה לְךָ֛ וְלָהֶ֖ם לְאָכְלָֽה׃
	wəhāyâ ləkā wəlāhem ləʾoklâ.

so that it can be food for you and for them.

19a	וּמִכָּל־הָחַ֤י מִכָּל־בָּשָׂר֙
	From every living being, from all flesh,

וּמִכָּל־	and from all/each/every	CST	noun
û·mik·kol-		W/ CONJ וְ + PREP מִן	
הָחַ֤י	the living	MS SUBST	adj
hā·ḥay		W/ DEF. ART.	

מִכָּל־	from all/each/every	CST W/ PREP מִן	noun
כֹּל	mik·kol-		
בָּשָׂר	flesh	ABS	noun
בָּשָׂר	bā·śār		

19b — שְׁנַיִם מִכֹּל תָּבִיא אֶל־הַתֵּבָה

you will bring two of each into the vessel

שְׁנַיִם	two	ABS	cardinal number
שְׁנַיִם	šə·nayim		
מִכֹּל	from all/each/everything	ABS W/ PREP מִן	noun
כֹּל	mik·kōl		
תָּבִיא	you will bring/ cause to come	HIPH IMPF 2MS	verb
בוא	tā·vi'		
אֶל־	to/toward	---	prep
אֶל	'el-		
הַתֵּבָה	the vessel/ark/boat/basket	ABS W/ DEF. ART.	noun
תֵּבָה	hat·tē·vâ		

19c — לְהַחֲיֹת אִתָּךְ

to keep them alive with you.

לְהַחֲיֹת	to cause to live	HIPH INF CST W/ PREP לְ	verb
חיה	lə·ha·ḥă·yōt		
אִתָּךְ	with you	--- W/ 2MS SX	prep
אֵת	'it·tāk		

In light of the comment above at v. 18d about one person's positive character and actions saving a group, we might also consider Gen 45:7 and 50:20, both of which use חיה in the Hiphil to describe Joseph preserving the lives of many through his actions. In 2 Kgs 8:5, the Hiphil of this verb literally refers to resurrecting someone from the dead.

19d

	זָכָר וּנְקֵבָה יִהְיוּ׃
	Male and female they will be:

זָכָר	male	ABS	noun
זָכָר	zā·**ḵār**		
וּנְקֵבָה	and female	ABS	noun
נְקֵבָה	û·nə·qē·**vâ**	W/ CONJ וְ	
יִהְיוּ׃	they will be	QAL IMPF 3MP	verb
היה	yih·**yû**		

Notice here the resumption of the language for "male and female" that previously appeared in Gen 1:27 and 5:2. This is one of many instances of the flood story echoing and in some sense reenacting the creation story.

20a

	מֵהָעוֹף לְמִינֵהוּ
	from birds according to their kind,

מֵהָעוֹף	from the bird(s)	ABS	noun
עוֹף	mē·hā·**ʿôf**	W/ PREP מִן + DEF. ART.	
לְמִינֵהוּ	to/after its kind/type	CST	noun
מִין	lə·mî·**nē**·hû	W/ PREP לְ + 3MS SX	

20b

	וּמִן־הַבְּהֵמָה לְמִינָהּ
	and from beasts according to their kind,

וּמִן־	and from	---	prep
מִן	û·min-	W/ CONJ וְ	
הַבְּהֵמָה	the beast(s)/animal(s)	ABS	noun
בְּהֵמָה	hab·bə·hē·**mâ**	W/ DEF. ART	
לְמִינָהּ	to/after its kind/type	CST	noun
מִין	lə·mî·**nāh**	W/ PREP לְ + 3FS SX	

20c

	מִכֹּל רֶמֶשׂ הָאֲדָמָה לְמִינֵהוּ		
	from all things that creep upon the earth according to their kind—		
מִכֹּל כֹּל *mik·kōl*	from all/each/every	CST W/ PREP מִן	noun
רֶמֶשׂ רֶמֶשׂ *re·meś*	(the) creeping thing of	CST	noun
הָאֲדָמָה אֲדָמָה *hā·ʾă·dā·mâ*	the ground	ABS W/ DEF. ART.	noun
לְמִינֵהוּ מִין *lə·mî·nē·hû*	to/after its kind/type	CST W/ PREP לְ + 3MS SX	noun

20d

	שְׁנַיִם מִכֹּל יָבֹאוּ אֵלֶיךָ		
	two from each will come to you		
שְׁנַיִם שְׁנַיִם *šə·nayim*	two	ABS	cardinal number
מִכֹּל כֹּל *mik·kōl*	from all/each/every	ABS W/ PREP מִן	noun
יָבֹאוּ בוֹא *yā·vō·ʾû*	(they) will come	QAL IMPF 3MP	verb
אֵלֶיךָ אֶל *ʾē·le·kā*	to/toward you	--- W/ 2MS SX	prep

20e

	לְהַחֲיוֹת:		
	to keep them alive.		
לְהַחֲיוֹת: חיה *lə·ha·ḥă·yôt*	to cause to live	HIPH INF CST W/ PREP לְ	verb

The specification of animal categories adds literary detail and dramatic buildup to the story, and calls to mind these same categories of animals in the creation story of Gen 1: God is now prepared to un-create and re-create the world.

21a — וְאַתָּה

And as for you:

וְאַתָּה	and you	---	personal
אַתָּה	wə·'at·tâ	W/ CONJ וְ	pron

21b — קַח־לְךָ מִכָּל־מַאֲכָל

take for yourself from all food

קַח־	take	QAL IMPV MS	verb
לקח	qaḥ-		
לְךָ	for you/yourself	---	prep
לְ	lə·kā	W/ 2MS SX	
מִכָּל־	from all/each/every	CST	noun
מִן	mik·kol-	W/ PREP מִן	
מַאֲכָל	food	ABS	noun
מַאֲכָל	ma·'ă·kāl		

21c — אֲשֶׁר יֵאָכֵל

that can be eaten,

אֲשֶׁר	that/which	---	relative
אֲשֶׁר	'ă·šer		pron
יֵאָכֵל	(it) is eaten	NIPH IMPF 3MS	verb
אכל	yē·'ā·kēl		

21d — וְאָסַפְתָּ אֵלֶיךָ

and gather it up for yourself

וְאָסַפְתָּ	and you will gather	QAL WEQATAL 2MS	verb
אסף	wə·'ā·saf·tā		
אֵלֶיךָ	to/for you/yourself	---	prep
אֶל	'ē·le·kā	W/ 2MS SX	

21e	וְהָיָ֥ה לְךָ֛ וְלָהֶ֖ם לְאָכְלָֽה׃
	so that it can be food for you and for them.

וְהָיָ֥ה	and it will be	QAL WEQATAL 3MS	verb
היה	wə·hā·yâ		
לְךָ֛	to/for you/yourself	---	prep
ל	lə·kā	W/ 2MS SX	
וְלָהֶ֖ם	and tc/for them	---	prep
ל	wə·lā·hem	W/ CONJ וְ + 3MP SX	
לְאָכְלָֽה׃	for food	ABS	noun
אָכְלָה	lə·'ok̲·lâ	W/ PREP לְ	

This statement, as well as v. 21b above, harks back to language directed to the first man in Gen 1:29 and 2:16. Indeed, Noah becomes something of a "second Adam" in this text, as God starts over and re-creates humanity through Noah and his family.

6:22

22a וַיַּ֖עַשׂ נֹ֑חַ
wayyaʿaś nōaḥ
Noah did

22b כְּ֠כֹל אֲשֶׁ֨ר צִוָּ֥ה אֹת֛וֹ אֱלֹהִ֖ים
kəḵōl ʾăšer ṣiwwâ ʾōtô ʾĕlōhîm
all that God commanded him.

22c כֵּ֥ן עָשָֽׂה׃
kēn ʿāśâ.
That is what he did.

22a	וַיַּ֖עַשׂ נֹ֑חַ		
	Noah did		
וַיַּ֖עַשׂ עשׂה	and/so/then (he) did *way·yaʿaś*	QAL WAYY 3MS	verb
נֹ֑חַ נֹחַ	Noah *nō·aḥ*	ABS	noun

22b	כְּ֠כֹל אֲשֶׁ֨ר צִוָּ֥ה אֹת֛וֹ אֱלֹהִ֖ים		
	all that God commanded him.		
כְּכֹל כֹּל	like/as/according to all/each/every *kə·ḵōl*	ABS W/ PREP כְּ	noun
אֲשֶׁר אֲשֶׁר	that/which *ʾă·šer*	---	relative pron

צִוָּה צוה	(he) commanded/ordered ṣiw·wâ	PIEL PF 3MS	verb
אֹתוֹ אֵת	*(direct object marker +)* him ʾō·tô	--- W/ 3MS SX	particle
אֱלֹהִים אֱלֹהִים	God ʾĕ·lō·hîm	ABS	noun

The specific vocabulary of a divine "command" (צִוָּה) has come up three times so far in Genesis, always in reference to the command that the Lord God gave Adam and Eve in the garden to not eat from the fruit of the tree of the knowledge of good and evil (2:16; 3:11, 17). Significantly, the statement here that Noah did all that God had commanded him immediately follows the description (in 6:21) of God's positive provision of food for Noah, his family, and the animals for their voyage in the ark.

Exodus, Leviticus, Numbers, and Deuteronomy employ the vocabulary of command very frequently (over two hundred times); it is formal language, and Noah's prompt, wordless obedience to God (which is repeated almost verbatim in Gen 7:5) makes him the first in a righteous tradition of immediate compliance that will be carried on most prominently in Genesis with Abraham in ch. 12 (when God commands him to leave his homeland) and ch. 22 (when God commands him to offer up Isaac). It may also be significant that in Exodus, when God is once again preparing to bring his people safely through a threatening body of water (the Red Sea), we find a statement about Moses' and Aaron's obedience to God's command that is almost identical to the present verse (Gen 6:22).

22c	כֵּן עָשָׂה:		
	That is what he did.		
	כֵּן כֵּן	thus/so kēn	---	adv
	עָשָׂה: עשה	he did/made ʿā·śâ	QAL PF 3MS	verb

GOD DECIDES TO FLOOD THE EARTH

From Text to Sermon

*As you meditate on this passage and contemplate
how you might teach or preach it to others,
consider the following areas of emphasis.*

 Historical and Literary Context. You may wish to consult the Epic of Gilgamesh (available in many commercial translations and online) to get a sense for how some audiences among ancient Israel's neighbors thought about divine violence and a specific story of a catastrophic flood. When reading the epic, consider, for example, the divine attitude toward humans, the reasons for the flood, and other details that can be compared and contrasted with the biblical flood narrative.

It is also fascinating to notice that the story of the flood is referred to very infrequently in the Old Testament outside of Gen 6–9, and the bizarre tale of the "sons of God" and the "daughters of man" seems not to be mentioned again at all. One reference to the flood is found in Isa 54:9, which mentions the flood not in order to focus on God's wrath and destruction (a major theme in the Genesis story), but rather (by alluding to Gen 9:11, 15) to emphasize *forgiveness* in the context of Israel's exile in Babylon: "This is like the days of Noah to me: Just as I swore that the waters of Noah would never again go over the earth, so I have sworn that I will not be angry with you and will not rebuke you" (NRSVue). Another reference is found in Ezek 14 (vv. 14, 20), where the prophet invokes the name of Noah in a discussion of salvation and individual responsibility, emphasizing the personal nature of sin and repentance. Although the story of the "sons of God" and the "daughters of man" does not appear again in the Old Testament outside Gen 6:1–4, it takes on a detailed life in the so-called intertestamental literature of the early Jewish period, such as in the book of 1 Enoch, whose authors explore the detailed names and deeds of fallen angelic creatures. Similar stories reflecting on giants, angels, and demons related to the events of Gen 6:1–4 have also been found among the fragments of the Dead Sea Scrolls.

Readers interested in the darker ethical implications of God's wiping out all of humanity in such a stark way could compare the flood story with the story of the conquest of Canaan anticipated in the book of Deuteronomy (7:2, 26; 13:13–19 [12–18]; 20:17) and then carried out in the book of Joshua (chs. 6–12). Believers and scholars throughout history have wrestled with, and continue to wrestle with, the theological and ethical implications of texts like these.

🌱 ***Bridge to the Gospel.*** Consider how the flood story prepares our hearts to think of key spiritual themes that resonate with the saving work of Jesus, such as divine judgment, righteousness before God, and salvation from harm. On the theme of judgment, Jesus refers to the "days of Noah" as a time when people were carrying on with their lives without considering disaster that could befall them (Matt 24:37; Luke 17:26). There is a "suddenness" to the arrival of the flood that Jesus recognized as similar to his own appearance. And the themes of both judgment and salvation appear in 1 Pet 3:20 and 2 Pet 2:5, where Noah's name is also invoked. Noah's unquestioning obedience to God and righteous faith in what God had promised qualify him for inclusion in the famous roll call of heroes from the Old Testament in Heb 11—as he built a massive boat before any rain had fallen, he acted as a model of faith, which is the "assurance of things hoped for, the conviction of things not seen" (Heb 11:1 NRSVue).

🌱 ***Illustrations.*** As we think about how to illustrate the themes of Gen 6 in our contemporary world, we might compare two very different film adaptations of the flood story: *Noah's Ark* (1999), a TV miniseries produced by Hallmark, and *Noah* (2014), a feature film by the acclaimed director Darren Aronofsky. In each example, viewers will find places where the screenwriters took liberties with the plot and characters, all by way of trying (with varying degrees of success) to provide life and flesh around what in the Bible is a mysterious story that lacks the kinds of detail we might like to find. For example, what was happening on earth that had so corrupted it? What was Noah like as a person, and with what attitude did he receive the divine command? What was life like on the boat with his family and all the animals? Readers who treasure the biblical story may well revel in these ambiguities and find fault with filmmakers who alter the story for commercial ends; yet audiences from the biblical world until today have found a need to hear continued re-dramatizations of drastic situations and epic material, of which the flood story remains a prime example.

GENESIS 8:20–9:7

GOD RESTORES THE EARTH AFTER THE FLOOD

As Noah exits the boat after the flood and offers a sacrifice, God responds by promising never to flood the earth again and by reaffirming his bond with the earth and human beings.

LARGER LITERARY CONTEXT ▸ 8:5–9:17

8:20–22

8:20a

וַיִּ֥בֶן נֹ֛חַ מִזְבֵּ֖חַ לַיהוָ֑ה

wayyiven nōaḥ mizbēaḥ laYHWH

Noah built an altar to the Lord

8:20b

וַיִּקַּ֣ח מִכֹּ֣ל ׀ הַבְּהֵמָ֣ה הַטְּהוֹרָ֗ה

wayyiqqaḥ mikkōl habbəhēmâ haṭṭəhôrâ

and took from every clean beast

8:20c

וּמִכֹּל֙ הָע֣וֹף הַטָּה֔וֹר

ûmikkōl hā'ôf haṭṭāhōr

and from every clean bird

8:20d

וַיַּ֥עַל עֹלֹ֖ת בַּמִּזְבֵּֽחַ׃

wayya'al 'ōlōt bammizbēaḥ.

and offered up burnt offerings upon the altar.

8:21a

וַיָּ֣רַח יְהוָה֮ אֶת־רֵ֣יחַ הַנִּיחֹחַ֒

wayyāraḥ YHWH 'et-rêaḥ hannîḥōaḥ

The Lord smelled the pleasing smell,

8:21b

וַיֹּ֨אמֶר יְהוָ֜ה אֶל־לִבּ֗וֹ

wayyō'mer YHWH 'el-libbô

and the Lord said in his heart,

8:21c

לֹֽא־אֹ֠סִף לְקַלֵּ֨ל ע֤וֹד אֶת־הָֽאֲדָמָה֙

lō'-'ōsif ləqallēl 'ôd 'et-hā'ădāmâ

"I will never again curse the ground

8:21d

בַּעֲב֣וּר הָֽאָדָ֔ם

ba'ăvûr hā'ādām

on account of humans—

8:21e	כִּ֠י יֵ֣צֶר לֵ֧ב הָאָדָ֛ם רַ֖ע מִנְּעֻרָ֑יו
	kî yēṣer lēv hāʾādām raʿ minnəʿūrāyw

even though the intent of the human heart is wicked from their youth.

8:21f	וְלֹֽא־אֹסִ֥ף ע֛וֹד לְהַכּ֥וֹת אֶת־כָּל־חַ֖י
	wəlōʾ-ʾōsīf ʿôd ləhakkôt ʾet-kol-ḥay

I will never again strike down all living things

8:21g	כַּאֲשֶׁ֥ר עָשִֽׂיתִי׃
	kaʾăšer ʿāśîtî.

as I have done.

8:22a	עֹ֖ד כָּל־יְמֵ֣י הָאָ֑רֶץ
	ʿōd kol-yəmê hāʾāreṣ

As long as all the days of the earth—

8:22b	זֶ֣רַע וְ֠קָצִיר
	zeraʿ wəqāṣîr

planting and harvest,

8:22c	וְקֹ֨ר וָחֹ֜ם
	wəqōr wāḥōm

cold and heat,

8:22d	וְקַ֧יִץ וָחֹ֛רֶף
	wəqayiṣ wāḥōref

summer and winter,

8:22e	וְי֥וֹם וָלַ֖יְלָה
	wəyôm wālaylâ

day and night

8:22f	לֹ֥א יִשְׁבֹּֽתוּ׃
	lōʾ yišbōtû.

will not cease.

8:20a	וַיִּ֧בֶן נֹ֛חַ מִזְבֵּ֖חַ לַֽיהוָ֑ה
	Noah built an altar to the Lord

	וַיִּ֧בֶן	and/so/then (he) built	QAL WAYY 3MS	verb
	בנה	way·*yi*·ven		
	נֹ֛חַ	Noah	ABS	noun
	נח	*nō*·aḥ		
	מִזְבֵּ֖חַ	altar	ABS	noun
	מזבח	miz·*bē*·aḥ		
	לַֽיהוָ֑ה	to/for the Lord	ABS W/ PREP לְ	noun
	יהוה	la·YHWH		

This is the first altar anyone builds in the Bible. Like the offerings of Cain and Abel, there is no divine command for Noah's offering—he seems to offer it as an outpouring of thanks as he exits the boat after surviving the flood. Later, in chs. 12–13, Abraham (likewise unprompted) builds several altars, as he journeys from Babylon to the land that will become Israel; and this practice is followed by his descendants (especially Jacob) and also by Moses and Joshua. God's first instructions for offering sacrifices upon an altar come to Israel at Mount Sinai, where he states that an altar can be made of heaped-up dirt or unhewn stones (Exod 20:24–26); subsequent instructions provide for more elaborate forms (e.g., Exod 27:1).

8:20b	וַיִּקַּ֞ח מִכֹּ֣ל ׀ הַבְּהֵמָ֣ה הַטְּהוֹרָ֗ה
	and took from every clean beast

	וַיִּקַּ֞ח	and he took	QAL WAYY 3MS	verb
	לקח	way·yiq·*qaḥ*		
	מִכֹּ֣ל ׀	from all/each/every	CST W/ PREP מִן	noun
	כל	mik·*kōl*		
	הַבְּהֵמָ֣ה	the animals/beasts	ABS W/ DEF. ART.	noun
	בהמה	hab·bə·hē·*mâ*		
	הַטְּהוֹרָ֗ה	clean/pure	FS ATTR W/ DEF. ART.	adj
	טהור	haṭ·ṭə·hô·*râ*		

In 7:2, God commanded Noah to bring seven pairs "from every clean beast" onto the ark. The mention of the concept of ritually "clean" animals there and here shows Noah to be already obeying the law of clean and unclean animals elaborated in the book of Leviticus (ch. 11), a connection that may be reinforced by the phrase אֲשֶׁר יֵאָכֵל in Gen 6:21c (cf. Lev 11:34; 17:13; Deut 12:22).

8:20c	וּמִכֹּל הָעוֹף הַטָּהֹר
	and from every clean bird

	וּמִכֹּל כֹּל *û·mik·kōl*	and from all/each of	CST W/ CONJ וְ + PREP מִן	noun
	הָעוֹף עוֹף *hā·'ôf*	the bird(s)/fowl	ABS W/ DEF. ART.	noun
	הַטָּהֹר טָהוֹר *haṭ·ṭā·hōr*	(the) clean/pure	MS ATTR W/ DEF. ART.	adj

8:20d	וַיַּעַל עֹלֹת בַּמִּזְבֵּחַ:
	and offered up burnt offerings upon the altar.

	וַיַּעַל עלה *way·ya·'al*	and he made to go up/ offered up/sent up	HIPH WAYY 3MS	verb
	עֹלֹת עֹלָה *'ō·lōt*	burnt offerings	ABS	noun
	בַּמִּזְבֵּחַ: מִזְבֵּחַ *bam·miz·bē·aḥ*	on the altar	ABS W/ PREP בְּ + DEF. ART.	noun

Definite articles sometimes function differently in Hebrew from how they do in English. Specifically, it's not uncommon in Hebrew for an element that hasn't yet been mentioned in the story (e.g., this particular altar) to be called "*the* altar" (as if it had already been discussed). In English, of course, we would say "*an* altar."

8:21a	וַיָּ֣רַח יְהוָה֮ אֶת־רֵ֣יחַ הַנִּיחֹ֒חַ֒

The LORD smelled the pleasing smell,			
וַיָּ֣רַח	and/so/then (he) smelled/sniffed	HIPH WAYY 3MS	verb
ריח	way·yā·raḥ		
יְהוָה֮	the LORD	ABS	noun
יהוה	YHWH		
אֶת־	(direct object marker)	---	particle
אֶת	'et-		
רֵ֣יחַ	(the) smell/aroma/odor of	CST	noun
רֵיחַ	rê·aḥ		
הַנִּיחֹ֒חַ֒	the pleasantness/soothing quality	ABS W/ DEF. ART.	noun
נִיחֹחַ	han·nî·ḥō·aḥ		

In a flood story known for millennia in the ancient Near East, narrated as a subplot within the popular Epic of Gilgamesh, the survivor of the flood (Utnapishtim, or Uta-napishtim) exits his boat after the flood and offers a sacrifice, just as Noah does. The epic narrates the reaction of the deities: they "swarmed like flies" around the sacrifice, as they needed to rely on human sacrifices of animals for sustenance. In the biblical conception of animal sacrifice—the exact reasons for which are never systematically explained in the Torah/Pentateuch—Israel's God commands sacrifice and is pleased by its aroma (see the numerous references to this in Exod 29, Lev 1–8, Num 15, 28–29, etc.), but he is never depicted as relying on sacrifices for any purpose.

8:21b	וַיֹּ֤אמֶר יְהוָה֙ אֶל־לִבּ֔וֹ

and the LORD said in his heart,			
וַיֹּ֤אמֶר	and/then/so (he) said	QAL WAYY 3MS	verb
אמר	way·yō'·mer		
יְהוָה֙	the LORD	ABS	noun
יהוה	YHWH		
אֶל־	to/toward	---	prep
אֶל	'el-		

לִבּוֹ לֵב *lib·bô*	his/its heart	CST W/ 3MS SX	noun

The language of saying something "to one's (own) heart" seems to indicate thought or deep consideration (compare 1 Sam 27:1; Isa 44:19).

8:21c	לֹא־אֹסִף לְקַלֵּל עוֹד אֶת־הָאֲדָמָה
	"I will never again curse the ground

לֹא־ לֹא *lō-*	not/never	---	particle
אֹסִף יסף *'ō·sīf*	I will do again/add/increase	HIPH IMPF 1CS	verb
לְקַלֵּל קלל *lə·qal·lēl*	to curse	PIEL INF CST W/ PREP לְ	verb
עוֹד עוֹד *'ôd*	again/still/any more	---	adv
אֶת־ אֵת *'et-*	(direct object marker)	---	particle
הָאֲדָמָה אֲדָמָה *hā·'ă·dā·mâ*	the earth	ABS W/ DEF. ART.	noun

The language for "curse" here (קלל) is different from what it was in ch. 3 (ארר), but the invocation of the "ground" (אֲדָמָה) clearly harks back to the narrative of the judgment there and subsequent expulsion from Eden (3:17, 19, 23; cf. 4:10–12; 5:29).

8:21d	בַּעֲבוּר הָאָדָם
	on account of humans—

בַּעֲבוּר בַּעֲבוּר *ba·'ă·vûr*	on account of/because of	---	prep
הָאָדָם אָדָם *hā·'ā·dām*	humans/the man	ABS W/ DEF. ART.	noun

GOD RESTORES THE EARTH AFTER THE FLOOD

8:21e	כִּי יֵצֶר לֵב הָאָדָם רַע מִנְּעֻרָיו
	even though the intent of the human heart is wicked from their youth.

כִּי כִּי	for/since/because kî	---	conj
יֵצֶר יֵצֶר	(the) intent/plan of yē·ṣer	CST	noun
לֵב לֵב	(the) heart of lēv	CST	noun
הָאָדָם אָדָם	humans/the man hā·'ā·dām	ABS W/ DEF. ART.	noun
רַע רַע	bad/evil/wicked ra'	MS PRED	adj
מִנְּעֻרָיו נְעוּרִים	from his youth/childhood min·nə·'ū·rāyw	CST W/ PREP מִן + 3MS SX	noun

The translation of "even though" for כִּי stretches the normal definition of כִּי in an attempt to understand the sense of the text. The theological and ethical question at stake here concerns why God decided to flood the earth upon seeing the utter wickedness of humanity (Gen 6:5–7) and yet here vows never to do this again—even while he observes that humans are essentially in the same moral mess as before. Some of the language in the present verses harks back to 6:5–7 in a way that strongly suggests the narrator wants to remind us of the situation that prompted the flood in the first place—notice the presence of the terminology for "wickedness" (רַע), "intent of the heart" (יֵצֶר לֵב), and "to his heart" (אֶל־לִבּוֹ) in both passages. The text here implies that Noah's righteousness and his sacrifice affect God so much that they prompt this extraordinary response.

8:21f	וְלֹא־אֹסִף עוֹד לְהַכּוֹת אֶת־כָּל־חַי
	I will never again strike down all living things

וְלֹא־ לֹא	and not/never wə·lō-	--- W/ CONJ וְ	particle
אֹסִף יסף	I will do again/add/increase 'ō·sîf	HIPH IMPF 1CS	verb

עוֹד עוֹד	again/still/any more 'ôd	---	adv
לְהַכּוֹת נכה	to strike down/slay/smite/cut down lə·hak·kôt	HIPH INF CST W/ PREP לְ	verb
אֶת־ אֵת	(direct object marker) 'et-	---	particle
כָּל־ כֹּל	all/each/every kol-	CST	noun
חַי חַי	living (thing) ḥay	MS SUBST	adj

8:21g כַּאֲשֶׁר עָשִׂיתִי׃
as I have done.

כַּאֲשֶׁר אֲשֶׁר	as/just as ka·'ă·šer	--- W/ PREP כְּ	relative pron
עָשִׂיתִי׃ עשה	I did/have done 'ā·śî·tî	QAL PF 1CS	verb

8:22a עֹד כָּל־יְמֵי הָאָרֶץ
As long as all the days of the earth—

עֹד עוֹד	again/still/any more 'ōd	---	adv
כָּל־ כֹּל	all of kol-	CST	noun
יְמֵי יוֹם	(the) days of yə·mê	CST	noun
הָאָרֶץ אֶרֶץ	the earth hā·'ā·reṣ	ABS W/ DEF. ART.	noun

GOD RESTORES THE EARTH AFTER THE FLOOD

8:22b	זֶ֥רַע וְקָצִ֖יר		
	planting and harvest,		
זֶ֥רַע / זֶרַע	seed/seedtime/planting / zeʿ·raʿ	ABS	noun
וְקָצִ֖יר / קָצִיר	and harvest/reaping / wə·qā·ṣîr	ABS W/ CONJ וְ	noun

8:22c	וְקֹ֥ר וָחֹ֖ם		
	cold and heat,		
וְקֹ֥ר / קֹר	and cold / wə·qōr	ABS W/ CONJ וְ	noun
וָחֹ֖ם / חֹם	and hot/warm / wā·ḥōm	ABS W/ CONJ וְ	noun

These are both rare terms: חֹם ("heat") occurs fewer than ten times in the Bible and קֹר ("cold") appears only here. The use of rare terminology is common in Hebrew poetry, and here we find God offering a beautiful poetic statement on the re-created earth, just as he did at various points in the opening chapters of Genesis when he first created the world.

8:22d	וְקַ֥יִץ וָחֹ֖רֶף		
	summer and winter,		
וְקַ֥יִץ / קַיִץ	and summer / wə·qayiṣ	ABS W/ CONJ וְ	noun
וָחֹ֖רֶף / חֹרֶף	and winter / wā·ḥō·ref	ABS W/ CONJ וְ	noun

8:22e	וְי֥וֹם וָלַ֖יְלָה		
	day and night		
וְי֥וֹם / יוֹם	and day / wə·yôm	ABS W/ CONJ וְ	noun

| וָלַיְלָה | and night | ABS W/ CONJ וְ | noun |
| לַיְלָה | wā·**lay**·lâ | | |

8:22f		לֹא יִשְׁבֹּֽתוּ׃	
		will not cease.	
	לֹא not	---	particle
	לא lō'		
	יִשְׁבֹּֽתוּ׃ (they) will cease/stop	QAL IMPF 3MP	verb
	שבת yiš·**bō**·tû		

The use of the verb שבת here recalls the Sabbath in Gen 2:2–3 and calls our attention back to the goodness of God's original creation and its cycles of nature, work, and rest.

9:1–4

9:1a
וַיְבָ֣רֶךְ אֱלֹהִ֔ים אֶת־נֹ֖חַ וְאֶת־בָּנָ֑יו
wayəvārek ʾĕlōhîm ʾet-nōaḥ wəʾet-bānāyw

God blessed Noah and his sons,

9:1b
וַיֹּ֥אמֶר לָהֶ֖ם
wayyōʾmer lāhem

and said to them,

9:1c
פְּר֥וּ וּרְב֖וּ וּמִלְא֥וּ אֶת־הָאָֽרֶץ׃
pərû ûrəvû ûmilʾû ʾet-hāʾāreṣ.

"Be fruitful and multiply and fill the earth!

9:2a
וּמוֹרַאֲכֶ֤ם וְחִתְּכֶם֙ יִֽהְיֶ֔ה
ûmôrāʾăkem wəḥittəkem yihye

Fear and terror of you will be

9:2b
עַ֚ל כָּל־חַיַּ֣ת הָאָ֔רֶץ
ʿal kol-ḥayyat hāʾāreṣ

upon all the living things of the earth

9:2c
וְעַ֖ל כָּל־ע֣וֹף הַשָּׁמָ֑יִם
wəʿal kol-ʿôf haššāmāyim

and upon all the birds of the air

9:2d
בְּכֹל֙ אֲשֶׁ֣ר תִּרְמֹ֣שׂ הָֽאֲדָמָ֔ה
bəkōl ʾăšer tirmōś hāʾădāmâ

and on all things that creep upon the ground

9:2e
וּֽבְכָל־דְּגֵ֥י הַיָּ֖ם בְּיֶדְכֶ֥ם נִתָּֽנוּ׃
ûvəkol-dəgê hayyām bəyedkem nittānû.

**and on all the fish of the sea—
they are given into your hand.**

9:3a	כָּל־רֶ֙מֶשׂ֙ אֲשֶׁ֣ר הוּא־חַ֔י
	kol-remeś 'ăšer hû-ḥay
	Every creeping thing that lives—
9:3b	לָכֶ֥ם יִהְיֶ֖ה לְאָכְלָ֑ה
	lākem yihye lə'oklâ
	it is for you, for food.
9:3c	כְּיֶ֣רֶק עֵ֔שֶׂב נָתַ֥תִּי לָכֶ֖ם אֶת־כֹּֽל׃
	kəyereq 'ēśev nātattî lākem 'et-kōl.
	Just as with pieces of green vegetation,
	I have given you everything—
9:4a	אַךְ־בָּשָׂ֕ר בְּנַפְשׁ֥וֹ דָמ֖וֹ
	'ak-bāśār bənafšô dāmô
	however, meat with its life, its blood,
9:4b	לֹ֥א תֹאכֵֽלוּ׃
	lō' tōkēlû.
	you shall not eat.

9:1a	וַיְבָ֣רֶךְ אֱלֹהִ֔ים אֶת־נֹ֖חַ וְאֶת־בָּנָ֑יו
	God blessed Noah and his sons,

וַיְבָ֣רֶךְ	and/so/then (he) blessed	PIEL WAYY 3MS	verb
ברך	*wa·yə·vā·rek*		
אֱלֹהִ֔ים	God	ABS	noun
אֱלֹהִים	*ĕ·lō·hîm*		
אֶת־	(direct object marker)	---	particle
אֵת	*'et-*		
נֹ֖חַ	Noah	ABS	noun
נֹחַ	*nō·aḥ*		

GOD RESTORES THE EARTH AFTER THE FLOOD

וְאֶת־	and (+ direct object marker)	---	particle
אֵת	wə·'et-	W/ CONJ וְ	
בָּנָיו	his sons	CST	noun
בֵּן	bā·nāyw	W/ 3MS SX	

The verb בר״ך appears here for the first time since God's initial blessing of the various parts of his creation, including creatures of sky and sea (1:22), the seventh day (2:3), and humanity (1:28; cf. 5:2). With the invocation of this term here, God reaffirms his blessing on and approval of humanity. This theme of blessing continues through Genesis—extending to Abraham (12:2–3; 14:19–20), Sarah (17:16), Hagar and Ishmael (17:20), and the rest of the ancestors, all the way through to Jacob's deathbed blessing of his sons (49:28), most notably Joseph and his sons Ephraim and Manasseh (48:15–16, 20; 49:25).

9:1b וַיֹּאמֶר לָהֶם

and said to them,

וַיֹּאמֶר	and/so/then he said	QAL WAYY 3MS	verb
אמר	way·yō·mer		
לָהֶם	to them	---	prep
לְ	lā·hem	W/ 3MP SX	

9:1c פְּרוּ וּרְבוּ וּמִלְאוּ אֶת־הָאָרֶץ׃

"Be fruitful and multiply and fill the earth!

פְּרוּ	bear fruit/be fruitful	QAL IMPV MP	verb
פרה	pə·rû		
וּרְבוּ	and be many/multiply	QAL IMPV MP	verb
רבה	û·rə·vû	W/ CONJ וְ	
וּמִלְאוּ	and fill	QAL IMPV MP	verb
מלא	û·mil·'û	W/ CONJ וְ	
אֶת־	(direct object marker)	---	particle
אֵת	'et-		
הָאָרֶץ׃	the earth/land	ABS	noun
אֶרֶץ	hā·'ā·res	W/ DEF. ART.	

Genesis 9:1 in its entirety echoes almost verbatim Gen 1:28 (cf. 1:22), where God blessed (וַיְבָרֶךְ) humankind after creating them, "said to them" (וַיֹּאמֶר לָהֶם), and then issued the command to "be fruitful and multiply and fill the earth" (פְּרוּ וּרְבוּ וּמִלְאוּ אֶת־הָאָרֶץ). The effect could not be clearer: creation is happening all over again after the divine "reset" of the flood. (See also the commentary on 1:28 above for more on this theme of procreating as an act of creation.)

9:2a	וּמוֹרַאֲכֶם וְחִתְּכֶם יִהְיֶה		
	Fear and terror of you will be		
	וּמוֹרַאֲכֶם and fear/dread/terror of you	CST	noun
	מוֹרָא û·mô·ra·ʾă·ḵem	W/ CONJ ו + 2MP SX	
	וְחִתְּכֶם and fear/dread/terror of you	CST	noun
	חַת wə·ḥit·tə·ḵem	W/ CONJ ו + 2MP SX	
	יִהְיֶה (it) will be	QAL IMPF 3MS	verb
	היה yih·ye		

In contrast to the repetition of phraseology from Gen 1 here in 9:1–3, which emphasizes that what now occurs after the flood is a new creation, the concept of "fear" and "terror" in this phrase is striking and unparalleled in the Bible's initial creation account. Adam had been "afraid" (ירא) of God in the garden (3:10), and humans were to "subdue" the earth and "rule over" it (1:28); but the notion that the living things of the earth will now live in "fear" and "terror" of humans is new and reflects the stark reality of the violence and brokenness that are present on earth after Gen 3 and that persist even after the flood. Thus, the idea of starting creation anew is already complicated and portends further struggle.

9:2b	עַל כָּל־חַיַּת הָאָרֶץ		
	upon all the living things of the earth		
	עַל over/upon/against	---	prep
	עַל ʿal		
	כָּל־ all/each/every	CST	noun
	כֹּל kol-		

חַיַּת חַיָּה	living thing/being/animal of ḥay·*yat*	CST	noun
הָאָ֫רֶץ אֶ֫רֶץ	the earth/land hā·'ā·reṣ	ABS W/ DEF. ART.	noun

9:2c וְעַל כָּל־עוֹף הַשָּׁמַ֫יִם

and upon all the birds of the air

וְעַל עַל	and over/upon/against wə·'al	--- W/ CONJ וְ	prep
כָּל־ כֹּל	all/each/every kol-	CST	noun
עוֹף עוֹף	bird(s)/fowl of 'ôf	CST	noun
הַשָּׁמַ֫יִם שָׁמַ֫יִם	the heavens/skies/air above haš·šā·*māyim*	ABS W/ DEF. ART.	noun

9:2d בְּכֹל אֲשֶׁר תִּרְמֹשׂ הָאֲדָמָה

and on all things that creep upon the ground.

בְּכֹל כֹּל	on every(thing) bə·ḵōl	ABS W/ PREP בְּ	noun
אֲשֶׁר אֲשֶׁר	that/which 'ă·šer	---	relative pron
תִּרְמֹשׂ רמשׂ	(it) creeps tir·*mōś*	QAL IMPF 3FS	verb
הָאֲדָמָה אֲדָמָה	the ground hā·'ă·dā·*mâ*	ABS W/ DEF. ART.	noun

9:2e

וּבְכָל־דְּגֵי הַיָּם בְּיֶדְכֶם נִתָּנוּ

and on all the fish of the sea—
they are given into your hand.

וּבְכָל־ כֹּל	and on all/each/every *û·və·ḵol-*	CST W/ CONJ וְ + PREP בְּ	noun
דְּגֵי דָּג	(the) fish of *də·ḡê*	CST	noun
הַיָּם יָם	the sea *hay·yām*	ABS W/ DEF. ART.	noun
בְּיֶדְכֶם יָד	in your hand/power *bə·yeḏ·ḵem*	CST W/ PREP בְּ + 2MP SX	noun
נִתָּנוּ׃ נתן	they are given *nit·tā·nû*	NIPH PF 3CP	verb

The phrase "given into your hand" (taking יָד in the sense of "agency" or "power") echoes the notion of subduing and ruling over the animal kingdom from Gen 1:28. We might also see an ominous undertone to this phrase (recalling the comment at 9:2a above), since it often appears in passages where people are "given into the hand of" their enemies (e.g., Gen 14:20; Lev 26:25; Judg 2:15; 2 Kgs 21:14).

9:3a

כָּל־רֶמֶשׂ אֲשֶׁר הוּא־חַי

Every creeping thing that lives—

כָּל־ כֹּל	all/each/every *kol-*	CST	noun
רֶמֶשׂ רֶמֶשׂ	creeping thing *re·meś*	ABS	noun
אֲשֶׁר אֲשֶׁר	that/which *ʾă·šer*	---	relative pron
הוּא־ הוּא	(it) *hû-*	---	personal pron
חַי חַי	lives/living/alive *ḥay*	MS PRED	adj

GOD RESTORES THE EARTH AFTER THE FLOOD

9:3b

לָכֶם יִהְיֶה לְאָכְלָה

it is for you, for food.

לָכֶם / לְ	to you / *lā·kem*	--- / W/ 2MP SX	prep
יִהְיֶה / היה	it will be/become / *yih·ye*	QAL IMPF 3MS	verb
לְאָכְלָה / אׇכְלָה	as/for food / *lə·'ok̲·lâ*	ABS / W/ PREP לְ	noun

9:3c

כְּיֶרֶק עֵשֶׂב נָתַתִּי לָכֶם אֶת־כֹּל׃

Just as with green things, I have given you everything—

כְּיֶרֶק / יֶרֶק	herb/green/greenery / *kə·ye·req*	CST / W/ PREP כְּ	noun
עֵשֶׂב / עֵשֶׂב	green thing/shrub/grass/ vegetation / *'ē·śev*	ABS	noun
נָתַתִּי / נתן	I give/am giving/have given / *nā·tat·tî*	QAL PF 1CS	verb
לָכֶם / לְ	to you / *lā·kem*	--- / W/ 2MP SX	prep
אֶת־ / אֵת	(direct object marker) / *'et-*	---	particle
כֹּל׃ / כֹּל	all/each/every/everything / *kōl*	ABS	noun

The notion that here God has given Noah and his descendants "everything" significantly expands upon Gen 1:29–30, where God permitted all plants but (by implication) no animals as food for the first humans. Since Gen 1–8 contains no laws or narratives about eating meat, the simplest reading of the present text is that here for the first time God allows humans to eat meat—though with the caveat that (uncooked?) blood is never to serve as food (on which see below).

9:4a	אַךְ־בָּשָׂר בְּנַפְשׁוֹ דָמוֹ
	however, meat with its life, its blood,

אַךְ־	only/certainly/nevertheless/ indeed	---	adv
אַךְ	'aḵ-		
בָּשָׂר	meat/flesh	ABS	noun
בָּשָׂר	bā·śār		
בְּנַפְשׁוֹ	in/with its breath/ spirit/soul	CST W/ PREP בְּ + 3MS SX	noun
נֶפֶשׁ	bə·naf·šô		
דָמוֹ	its/his blood	CST W/ 3MS SX	noun
דָּם	dā·mô		

"Its blood" is used here in apposition to (i.e., immediately afterward, for clarification) the phrase "its life," apparently indicating that an animal's blood is its "life." The association of life and blood (דָּם) here and in the next two verses echoes back to ch. 4 (vv. 10–11), where the only other references to blood (דָּם) in Gen 1–11 occur, in reference to Abel's blood, which cries out from the ground to God for justice. To spill another's blood is to take a life.

9:4b	לֹא תֹאכֵלוּ׃
	you shall not eat.

לֹא	not/no	---	particle
לֹא	lō'		
תֹאכֵלוּ׃	you shall/will/could/should eat/consume	QAL IMPF 2MP	verb
אכל	tō'·ḵē·lû		

In terms of the overarching biblical narrative, Gen 9:4 serves as the root of the laws related to blood later given to Israel. For example, Lev 17:10–13 echoes this Noahide blood commandment and extends it, clarifying the reason for it and elaborating a punishment for transgressing it:

> If anyone of the house of Israel or of the aliens who reside among them eats any blood, I will set my face against that person who eats blood and will cut that person off from the people. For the life

of the flesh is in the blood, and I have given it to you for making atonement for your lives on the altar, for, as life, it is the blood that makes atonement. (Lev 17:10–11 NRSVue)

Deuteronomy 12:15–16 and 15:23 also reiterate the prohibition on eating blood and clarify that blood must be "poured out . . . on the ground like water" before cooking or eating. (Presumably, even though some blood would technically remain in the meat even after all the free-flowing blood had been poured out, the rest of the blood would be cooked, assuring correct adherence to this law.)

In a number of other places, the Old Testament enshrines the idea that blood is sacred and needs to be used for sacred purposes (e.g., Exod 23:18; 24:8; Lev 1:5) or that blood is a type of "pollution" or "impurity" (e.g., Lev 15:19; Num 35:33). The idea shows up in narrative as well: for example, Judg 14 tells a story in which Samson eats from a carcass, possibly eating food tainted with blood, and 1 Sam 14 recounts a time when King Saul's famished troops more explicitly violate one or another of these various commands by eating food with its blood.

9:5–7

9:5a

וְאַ֨ךְ אֶת־דִּמְכֶ֤ם לְנַפְשֹֽׁתֵיכֶם֙ אֶדְרֹ֔שׁ

wə'ak 'et-dimkem lənafšōtêkem 'edrōš

Indeed, your blood, for your lives, I will require—

9:5b

מִיַּ֥ד כָּל־חַיָּ֖ה אֶדְרְשֶׁ֑נּוּ

miyyad kol-ḥayyâ 'edrəšennû

from the hand of every living thing, I will require it.

9:5c

וּמִיַּ֣ד הָֽאָדָ֗ם מִיַּד֙ אִ֣ישׁ אָחִ֔יו

ûmiyyad hā'ādām miyyad 'îš 'āḥîw

**And from the hand of human beings,
from the hand of each one for his fellow,**

9:5d

אֶדְרֹ֖שׁ אֶת־נֶ֥פֶשׁ הָֽאָדָֽם׃

'edrōš 'et-nefeš hā'ādām.

I will require the life of human beings.

9:6a

שֹׁפֵךְ֙ דַּ֣ם הָֽאָדָ֔ם

šōfēk dam hā'ādām

The one who pours out the blood of a human—

9:6b

בָּֽאָדָ֖ם דָּמ֣וֹ יִשָּׁפֵ֑ךְ

bā'ādām dāmô yiššāfēk

by a human will his blood be poured out.

9:6c

כִּ֚י בְּצֶ֣לֶם אֱלֹהִ֔ים עָשָׂ֖ה אֶת־הָאָדָֽם׃

kî bəṣelem 'ĕlōhîm 'āśâ 'et-hā'ādām.

For in the image of God he made humans.

9:7a

וְאַתֶּ֖ם פְּר֣וּ וּרְב֑וּ

wə'attem pərû ûrəvû

And as for you: be fruitful and multiply,

GOD RESTORES THE EARTH AFTER THE FLOOD

9:7b	שִׁרְצ֣וּ בָאָ֔רֶץ
	širṣû vāʾāreṣ
	swarm upon the earth
9:7c	וּרְבוּ־בָֽהּ׃
	ûrəvû-vāh.
	and multiply in it.

9:5a	וְאַ֨ךְ אֶת־דִּמְכֶ֤ם לְנַפְשֹֽׁתֵיכֶם֙ אֶדְרֹ֔שׁ
	Indeed, your blood, for your lives, I will require—

וְאַ֨ךְ	and only/certainly/ indeed	---	adv
אַךְ	*wə·ʾak*	W/ CONJ וְ	
אֶת־	(direct object marker)	---	particle
אֵת	*ʾet-*		
דִּמְכֶ֤ם	your blood	CST	noun
דָּם	*dim·kem*	W/ 2MP SX	
לְנַפְשֹֽׁתֵיכֶם֙	to/for your breaths/lives/ spirits/souls	CST W/ PREP לְ + 2MP SX	noun
נֶפֶשׁ	*lə·naf·šō·tê·kem*		
אֶדְרֹ֔שׁ	I will require/seek	QAL IMPF 1CS	verb
דרשׁ	*ʾed·rōš*		

The word "require" (דרשׁ) here and in the following phrases implies a reckoning, a sense of justice, a need to answer (compare Ezek 33:6 for similar language). The verb דרשׁ often carries with it a ritual sense, as with reference to a person "seeking" answers from God at a shrine or temple, and it can denote a sacred type of seeking that goes beyond the mundane. Human life is sacred to God, and humans cannot take life or shed blood without answering to God for what occurs.

9:5b

מִיַּד כָּל־חַיָּה אֶדְרְשֶׁנּוּ

from the hand of every living thing, I will require it.

מִיַּד	from (the) hand/possession of	CST	noun
יָד	miy·yad	W/ PREP מִן	
כָּל־	all/each/every	CST	noun
כֹּל	kol-		
חַיָּה	living thing/being/animal/beast	ABS	noun
חַיָּה	ḥay·yâ		
אֶדְרְשֶׁנּוּ	I will require/seek it	QAL IMPF 1CS W/ 3MS SX	verb
דרשׁ	'ed·rə·šen·nû		

9:5c

וּמִיַּד הָאָדָם מִיַּד אִישׁ אָחִיו

And from the hand of human beings,
from the hand of each one for his fellow,

וּמִיַּד	and from (the) hand/possession of	CST W/ CONJ וְ + PREP מִן	noun
יָד	û·miy·yad		
הָאָדָם	the man/human/humanity	ABS W/ DEF. ART.	noun
אָדָם	hā·'ā·dām		
מִיַּד	from (the) hand/possession of	CST W/ PREP מִן	noun
יָד	miy·yad		
אִישׁ	man	ABS	noun
אִישׁ	'îš		
אָחִיו	his brother	CST W/ 3MS SX	noun
אָח	'ā·ḥîw		

The phrase אִישׁ אָחִיו (lit., "man his brother") appears elsewhere in the Bible (Joel 2:8; Zech 7:10) and here means "each one for his fellow (man)." The reference to "brother" here, more specifically, calls our attention back to the Cain and Abel story ("Where is your brother?", "Am I my brother's keeper?", "Your brother's blood screams out"). The present verse can thus be read to suggest that all human beings are "brothers," part of one human family. Interestingly, whereas in Gen 4 God says he will protect Cain from retribution for his killing of Abel, here in Gen 9 God himself promises to bring retribution against the individual who murders his brother.

9:5d	אֶדְרֹשׁ אֶת־נֶפֶשׁ הָאָדָם:		
	I will require the life of human beings.		
	אֶדְרֹשׁ — I will require/seek דרשׁ — 'ed·rōš	QAL IMPF 1CS	verb
	אֶת־ — (direct object marker) אֵת — 'et-	---	particle
	נֶפֶשׁ — (the) breath/life/soul of נֶפֶשׁ — ne·feš	CST	noun
	הָאָדָם: — the man/human/humanity אָדָם — hā·'ā·dām	ABS W/ DEF. ART.	noun

9:6a	שֹׁפֵךְ דַּם הָאָדָם		
	The one who pours out the blood of a human—		
	שֹׁפֵךְ — pouring/spilling/one who pours/spills שׁפך — šō·fēḵ	QAL (CST) PTCP MS	verb
	דַּם — (the) blood of דָּם — dam	CST	noun
	הָאָדָם — the man/human/humanity אָדָם — hā·'ā·dām	ABS W/ DEF. ART.	noun

9:6b	בָּאָדָם דָּמוֹ יִשָּׁפֵךְ		
	by a human will his blood be poured out.		
	בָּאָדָם — by the man/human/humanity אָדָם — bā·'ā·dām	ABS W/ PREP בְּ + DEF. ART.	noun

דָּמוֹ דָּם	his blood dā·mô	CST W/ 3MS SX	noun
יִשָּׁפֵךְ שפך	(it) will be poured/spilled yiš·šā·fēḵ	NIPH IMPF 3MS	verb

This formulation anticipates the famous *lex talionis* ("law of retaliation") of later biblical law, which stipulates kind-for-kind punishment: e.g., an eye for an eye, a tooth for a tooth (Exod 21:24; Lev 24:20; Deut 19:21; and note Jesus' take on this in the Sermon on the Mount in Matt 5:38). The kind-for-kind punishment here is reinforced on a literary level through the fact that this statement in 9:6a–b has been constructed in the form of a chiasm (whereby the crime and the punishment literally mirror each other):

[A] the one who pours out (שפך)
   [B] the blood of (דָּם)
      [C] a human (אָדָם)—
      [C'] by a human (אָדָם)
   [B'] his blood (דָּם)
[A'] will be poured out (שפך).

In the context of the end of the flood, after which God has personally taken retribution on humans for their wickedness, God's statement here in vv. 5–6 could be seen as a decision to share the responsibility of enacting justice on earth with humans in a new and expanded way, clarifying that humans will (or can? or should?) enact retribution for murder on each other.

9:6c — כִּי בְּצֶלֶם אֱלֹהִים עָשָׂה אֶת־הָאָדָם׃

For in the image of God he made humans.

כִּי כִּי	for/since/because kî	---	conj
בְּצֶלֶם צֶלֶם	in the image of bə·ṣe·lem	CST W/ PREP בְּ	noun
אֱלֹהִים אֱלֹהִים	God ʾĕ·lō·hîm	ABS	noun

עָשָׂה עשה	he made 'ā·śâ	QAL PF 3MS	verb
אֶת־ אֵת	(direct object marker) 'et-	---	particle
הָאָדָם: אָדָם	the man/human/humanity hā·'ā·dām	ABS W/ DEF. ART.	noun

God repeats the creation pronouncement of Gen 1:26–27 (see comments above). The reaffirmation is stunning and indeed beautiful: even after the flood and in light of the corruption that has characterized the world after the events in the Garden of Eden, God still declares that humans are made in the divine image.

9:7a — וְאַתֶּם פְּרוּ וּרְבוּ

And as for you: be fruitful and multiply,

וְאַתֶּם אַתֶּם	and you all wə·'at·tem	W/ CONJ וְ	personal pron
פְּרוּ פרה	bear fruit/be fruitful pə·rû	QAL IMPV MP	verb
וּרְבוּ רבה	and be many/multiply û·rə·vû	QAL IMPV MP W/ CONJ וְ	verb

See comment above at 9:1.

9:7b — שִׁרְצוּ בָאָרֶץ

swarm upon the earth

שִׁרְצוּ שׁרץ	swarm/teem/proliferate šir·ṣû	QAL IMPV MP	verb
בָאָרֶץ אֶרֶץ	in/upon the earth vā·'ā·reṣ	ABS W/ PREP בְּ + DEF. ART.	noun

9:7c	וּרְבוּ־בָֽהּ׃		
	and multiply in it.		
וּרְבוּ־	and be many/multiply	QAL IMPV MP	verb
רבה	*û·rə·vû-*	W/ CONJ וְ	
בָֽהּ׃	in it/her	---	prep
בְּ	*vāh*	W/ 3FS SX	

Not only has the image of God been retained in humans after the flood, but God reaffirms the command for humans to multiply on the earth (Gen 1:28). This observation takes on additional richness when we consider the use of the verb שׁרץ from the previous clause. In Gen 1:20–21, שׁרץ describes the things that swim in the sea that God originally creates. Genesis 7:21 says that all swarming things died in the flood (though the fate of sea creatures is not exactly specified), but in 8:17 God commands Noah to bring all the animals (birds, beasts, and creeping things) out so that they may "swarm" (שׁרץ) on the earth. Then, here in 9:7, God reiterates this command, but now to Noah and the human family as a whole. Note also that Exod 1:7 draws on this same "be fruitful and multiply" language from Genesis to describe Israel growing into a great nation, and uses this same term for "swarm."

From Text to Sermon

As you meditate on this passage and contemplate
how you might teach or preach it to others,
consider the following areas of emphasis.

 Historical and Literary Context. Compare the language of re-creation in ch. 9 of Genesis with the language of the original creation in chs. 1–2. The allusions to those earlier chapters, including the echoing of exact words and phrases, suggests that in Gen 1–11 creation is understood as an ongoing activity—and by implication, it is ongoing for us today, with all its holiness and obligations.

The staggering scope of the divine violence portrayed in the flood story may be compared, on ethical terms, with other similar moments of totalizing death, such as the (attempted) eradication of the Canaanites from the land narrated in the book of Joshua. We are in good company (with many readers past and present) when we find ourselves wrestling with such challenging biblical stories and thinking about how to interpret and preach them with wisdom and sensitivity. In 9:11, God provides Noah with a new type of covenant (בְּרִית), promising to never again flood the earth and placing a rainbow in the sky to serve as a physical marker of the agreement. Curiously, despite the fact that the flood has been such a popular story in readers' imaginations throughout the centuries, the Old Testament itself rarely refers back to it: outside of Gen 1–11, the specific word for "flood" used in this story (מַבּוּל) only appears again in Ps 29:10, and specific reference to Noah is found in only a couple of contexts in the Old Testament (Isa 54:9 and Ezek 14:14, 20; see the "From Text to Sermon" section for Gen 6:1–22 above for further comment on this).

 Bridge to the Gospel. You may wish to point out to your listeners major themes in the New Testament that resonate with God's words to Noah after the flood. The focus in Gen 9 on blood and the power of blood in terms of justice sets the stage for the long biblical conversation on the power of blood, which runs from this text through the book of Exodus and the Passover narrative; through biblical law and the violent, tragic story of Israel; to Jesus and the cup of wine at the Last Supper; to texts that interpret Jesus' blood as bringing salvation to all humankind (e.g., Rom 5:9; Eph 1:7; Heb 9:12–14); and finally to the book of Revelation, which speaks of martyrs' blood, natural elements (moon and waters) turned to blood, robes dipped in blood, and the salvific "blood of the Lamb," i.e., Jesus (e.g., Rev 6:10; 7:14; 8:9; 17:6; 19:13).

It may surprise your audience to learn that the command to abstain from eating blood is not limited to the Old Testament but reappears in Acts 15 (vv. 20, 29; cf. 21:25), where an agreement reached by James, Paul, and Barnabas requires Christian believers to (among other things) not eat meat with blood in it. Regardless of how Christians today interpret the Acts compromise about abstaining from blood, it is instructive to see the early church referring to a ritual-ethical practice that has its narrative origin in Gen 9.

 Illustrations. As we think about how to illustrate the themes of Gen 9 with more contemporary storytelling and art, the rich world of film again comes to mind, especially the many cinematic plotlines that deal with the reciprocity of justice (either fulfilled or denied). Classic films in the "noir" genre, such as *Out of the Past* (1947) and *The Long Goodbye* (1973), treat themes of crime, punishment, and death in a stark and sometimes ambiguous manner, evoking the central covenantal statement God makes to Noah, whereby God declares blood to be sacred and mysteriously promises (without specifying how or when) that murder will be met with the reciprocal spilling of blood. Contemporary films in the "Western" genre, such as *The Revenant* (2015) and *True Grit* (the original 1969 version or the 2010 remake), depict wounded characters in search of blood-for-blood justice. Viewers of films like these can consider how the search for justice either can turn into (unholy) vengeance or can rightly fulfill the demands of ethical reciprocity.

GENESIS 11:1–9

THE TOWER OF CONFUSION

In this final story within the "primeval history" narrated in Gen 1–11, recurrent themes from these chapters come to a head once again, as human growth and movement lead to the crossing of boundaries and to divinely executed consequences. As is typical of these chapters, all of this is told in an enigmatic, sparse narrative.

LARGER LITERARY CONTEXT ▸ 11:1–9

11:1–2

1a וַיְהִי כָל־הָאָרֶץ שָׂפָה אֶחָת
wayəhî kol-hā'āreṣ śāfâ 'eḥāt

Now all the earth had one language,

1b וּדְבָרִים אֲחָדִים׃
ûdəvārîm 'ăḥādîm.

the same words.

2a וַיְהִי בְּנָסְעָם מִקֶּדֶם
wayəhî bənos'ām miqqedem

It so happened that they journeyed from the east

2b וַיִּמְצְאוּ בִקְעָה בְּאֶרֶץ שִׁנְעָר
wayyimṣə'û viq'â bə'ereṣ šin'ār

and found a plain in the land of Shinar,

2c וַיֵּשְׁבוּ שָׁם׃
wayyēšəvû šām.

and they settled there.

1a	וַיְהִי כָל־הָאָרֶץ שָׂפָה אֶחָת		
	Now all the earth had one language,		
	וַיְהִי *wa·yə·hî* / היה	and it was	QAL WAYY 3MS	verb
	כָל־ *kol-* / כֹּל	all	CST	noun
	הָאָרֶץ *hā·'ā·reṣ* / אֶרֶץ	the earth	ABS W/ DEF. ART.	noun

שָׂפָ֖ה שָׂפָה	lip/language/speech śā·fâ	ABS	noun
אֶחָ֑ת אֶחָד	one 'e·ḥāt	ABS	cardinal number

1b	וּדְבָרִ֖ים אֲחָדִֽים׃		
	the same words.		
	וּדְבָרִ֖ים דָּבָר	and words û·də·vā·rîm	ABS W/ CONJ וְ	noun
	אֲחָדִֽים׃ אֶחָד	one/same 'ă·ḥā·dîm	ABS	cardinal number

Up to this point, human language has been a given, with scant reference to any particular language (see Gen 10:20). Presumably, on a straightforward reading, the narrators of Genesis assume the world's original language is Hebrew—though this is nowhere stated. Often in biblical narrative, dialogue among people who could or should (historically) be speaking different languages is flattened into a single language, Hebrew. For example, the Egyptian Pharaoh, Moses, Moses' (non-Egyptian) father-in-law and wife, and the Hebrew people all seem to speak the same language, which is straightforwardly presented as Hebrew in the narrative of Exodus. And the Philistines, who may (at least originally) have spoken a language closer to the Indo-European languages (like Greek) than to the Semitic languages (like Hebrew) only speak in the Bible with words that are straightforwardly comprehensible to Israelites. When characters speak more than one language, this typically serves the narrative development: for example, in 2 Kgs 18:27–37 (// Isa 36:2–20), when an Assyrian official strategically toggles between two distinct (though still both Semitic) languages, and in Gen 42:23, when Joseph speaks to his brothers using an interpreter (so they will not know that he understands them). One could simply accept the general use of Hebrew as a universal language in biblical stories as a narrative device, similar to how movies will often flatten language differences for dramatic simplicity; or one could assume either that the characters in these stories were multilingual, or perhaps that they communicated by means of some kind of translation process (as in the case of Gen 42:23) that the biblical narrator rarely mentions.

2a	וַיְהִי בְּנָסְעָם מִקֶּדֶם
	It so happened that they journeyed from the east

	וַיְהִי	and it was	QAL WAYY 3MS	verb
	היה	wa·yə·hî		
	בְּנָסְעָם	in their journeying/ traveling/setting out	QAL INF CST W/ PREP בְּ + 3MP SX	verb
	נסע	bə·nos·ʿām		
	מִקֶּדֶם	from (the) east	ABS W/ PREP מִן	noun
	קֶדֶם	miq·qe·dem		

The invocation of the cardinal direction "east," the direction toward which Adam and Eve are expelled from Eden (Gen 3:24), recalls that pivotal event as well as Cain's wandering further away from God, in which he too travels "east of Eden" (4:16; see the "From Text to Sermon" section for Gen 4:1–16 above). The directions east and west take on a meaningful symbolism as the biblical narrative continues—for example, as Abraham and Sarah journey west to reach the land God had promised to them, thereby reversing the movement of expulsion out of the garden. Much later in the narrative, as a "second expulsion," God's people are driven out of their temple and land by the Babylonians in the early sixth century BCE to go east, into exile in Babylon. And the subsequent return home, narrated in or alluded to in the books of Isaiah (chs. 40–55) and Ezra, reenacts the Abrahamic journey west, back to the land.

2b	וַיִּמְצְאוּ בִקְעָה בְּאֶרֶץ שִׁנְעָר
	and found a plain in the land of Shinar,

	וַיִּמְצְאוּ	and they found/discovered	QAL WAYY 3MP	verb
	מצא	way·yim·ṣə·ʾû		
	בִקְעָה	valley/plain	ABS	noun
	בִּקְעָה	viq·ʿâ		
	בְּאֶרֶץ	in (the) land of	CST W/ PREP בְּ	noun
	אֶרֶץ	bə·ʾe·reṣ		
	שִׁנְעָר	Shinar	ABS	noun
	שִׁנְעָר	šin·ʿār		

Genesis 10:10 has identified "Shinar" as the location of Babel (Babylon), Erech (presumably Uruk, in the heart of Mesopotamia), and Akkad (also in Mesopotamia). Thus, the narrative movement from the Garden of Eden has people moving farther and farther east, away from God, until they plan to settle in the heart of the land out of which God will soon call Abram and Sarai.

2c	וַיֵּשְׁבוּ שָׁם:		
	and they settled there.		
	וַיֵּשְׁבוּ	and they settled/lived/remained	QAL WAYY 3MP	verb
	ישׁב	*way·yē·šə·vû*		
	שָׁם:	there	---	adv
	שָׁם	*šām*		

No comment is made about why this group (envisioned by the narrator as either a subset of the human population living at this time or the entire population) undertakes this migration, or why they settle where they do. The fact that they end up in the heart of Babylon (later explicitly identified with the city they end up building) serves as literary foreshadowing that—perhaps mystically or spiritually—connects their place of confusion and overreach with the Babylonians (who, in 2 Kgs 25 are described as invading Jerusalem, burning down the temple, and taking Israel captive into exile).

11:3–4

3a
וַיֹּאמְר֞וּ אִ֣ישׁ אֶל־רֵעֵ֗הוּ
wayyōʼmərû ʼîš ʼel-rēʻēhû
Each man said to his fellow,

3b
הָ֚בָה נִלְבְּנָ֣ה לְבֵנִ֔ים
hāvâ nilbənâ ləvēnîm
"Come, let us build bricks,

3c
וְנִשְׂרְפָ֖ה לִשְׂרֵפָ֑ה
wəniśrəfâ liśrēfâ
and let us bake them hard."

3d
וַתְּהִ֨י לָהֶ֤ם הַלְּבֵנָה֙ לְאָ֔בֶן
wattəhî lāhem halləvēnâ ləʼāven
So they had for themselves bricks for stone

3e
וְהַ֣חֵמָ֔ר הָיָ֥ה לָהֶ֖ם לַחֹֽמֶר׃
wəhaḥēmār hāyâ lāhem laḥōmer.
and bitumen for mortar.

4a
וַיֹּאמְר֞וּ
wayyōʼmərû
They said,

4b
הָ֣בָה ׀ נִבְנֶה־לָּ֣נוּ עִ֗יר
hāvâ nivne-lānû ʻîr
"Come, let us build for ourselves a city,

4c
וּמִגְדָּל֙ וְרֹאשׁ֣וֹ בַשָּׁמַ֔יִם
ûmigdāl wərōʼšô vaššāmayim
and a tower whose top is in the heavens!

4d

וְנַעֲשֶׂה־לָּנוּ שֵׁם
wənaʿăśe-lānû šēm

And let us make a name for ourselves,

4e

פֶּן־נָפוּץ עַל־פְּנֵי כָל־הָאָרֶץ׃
pen-nāfûṣ ʿal-pənê kol-hāʾāreṣ.

lest we be scattered across the face of the entire earth!"

3a

וַיֹּאמְרוּ אִישׁ אֶל־רֵעֵהוּ

Each man said to his fellow,

וַיֹּאמְרוּ אמר	and they said/spoke way·yō'·mə·rû	QAL WAYY 3MP	verb
אִישׁ אִישׁ	man/each ʾîš	ABS	noun
אֶל־ אֶל	to/toward ʾel-	---	prep
רֵעֵהוּ רֵעַ	his fellow/companion rē·ʿē·hû	CST W/ 3MS SX	noun

3b

הָבָה נִלְבְּנָה לְבֵנִים

"Come, let us build bricks,

הָבָה יהב	come/give hā·vâ	QAL IMPV MS	verb
נִלְבְּנָה לבן	let us make bricks nil·bə·nâ	QAL COHORT 1CP	verb
לְבֵנִים לְבֵנָה	bricks lə·vē·nîm	ABS	noun

No building construction tactics of any kind for a building of this type have been mentioned in the biblical text up to this point (but note the reference to acts of making clothes and the development of culture in Gen 3:7 and 4:20–22, and of course Noah's construction of the boat in Gen 6). Perhaps the narrator intends to suggest that the group is inventing brickmaking at this very moment, along with using bitumen and mortar (see later in v. 3), but this is not completely clear.

3c	וְנִשְׂרְפָה לִשְׂרֵפָה			
	and let us bake them hard."			
	וְנִשְׂרְפָה שׂרף	and let us burn/bake wə·niś·rə·fâ	QAL COHORT 1CP W/ CONJ וְ	verb
	לִשְׂרֵפָה שְׂרֵפָה	to burning/baking liś·rē·fâ	ABS W/ PREP לְ	noun

Baking clay bricks would increase their durability, and this statement thus reinforces the permanent, strong status the group wishes to achieve.

3d	וַתְּהִי לָהֶם הַלְּבֵנָה לְאָבֶן			
	So they had for themselves bricks for stone			
	וַתְּהִי היה	and (it) was wat·tə·hî	QAL WAYY 3FS	verb
	לָהֶם לְ	to/for them lā·hem	--- W/ 3MP SX	prep
	הַלְּבֵנָה לְבֵנָה	the brick/bricks hal·lə·vē·nâ	ABS W/ DEF. ART.	noun
	לְאָבֶן אֶבֶן	to/for/as stone lə·'ā·ven	ABS W/ PREP לְ	noun

"Bricks for stone" seems to indicate that the people were using bricks as their primary building material, used in the way one might more primitively pile stone upon stone. The group is apparently doing their best to make this structure as durable as possible.

3e

וְהַחֵמָר הָיָה לָהֶם לַחֹמֶר:
and bitumen for mortar.

וְהַחֵמָר חֵמָר	and the bitumen wə·ha·ḥē·**mār**	ABS W/ CONJ וְ + DEF. ART.	noun
הָיָה היה	(it) was hā·yâ	QAL PF 3MS	verb
לָהֶם לְ	to/for them lā·hem	--- W/ 3MP SX	prep
לַחֹמֶר: חֹמֶר	for/as the mortar la·ḥō·mer	ABS W/ PREP לְ + DEF. ART.	noun

The terms used in this passage for "brick" (לְבֵנָה) and "mortar" (חֹמֶר) do not appear frequently in the Old Testament—but notably, this same combination comes up in Exod 1:14 to describe the harsh slave labor the Hebrews experience in Egypt (i.e., using brick and mortar in Egyptian building projects). Note also the further description of the drama around the Hebrew slaves and brickmaking in Exod 5. Both of these empires, Babylon and Egypt, defy God's will in their attempt to enrich and enlarge themselves.

4a

וַיֹּאמְרוּ
They said,

וַיֹּאמְרוּ אמר	and/then they said/spoke way·yō'·mə·rû	QAL WAYY 3MP	verb

4b

הָבָה ׀ נִבְנֶה־לָּנוּ עִיר
"Come, let us build for ourselves a city,

הָבָה ׀ יהב	come/give hā·vâ	QAL IMPV MS	verb
נִבְנֶה־ בנה	let us build/construct niv·ne-	QAL COHORT 1CP	verb
לָּנוּ לְ	to/for us/ourselves lā·nû	--- W/ 1CP SX	prep

עִיר	city	ABS	noun
עִיר	'îr		

The ambition to build a tower is thus far unprecedented in Gen 1–11, though cities have appeared—notably one built by Cain, the first murderer (in 4:17), and one built by the Assyrians (10:11–12, where the nation is represented by one man, Nimrod), a group that would become one of Israel's primary enemies (e.g., 2 Kgs 15–17). We thus begin to experience an even deeper sense of foreboding, as the story ever more clearly foreshadows the themes of hubris, conflict, and destruction that will loom large in the biblical story as a whole.

4c — וּמִגְדָּל וְרֹאשׁוֹ בַשָּׁמַיִם

and a tower whose top is in the heavens!

וּמִגְדָּל	and tower	ABS	noun
מִגְדָּל	û·mig·dāl	W/ CONJ וְ	
וְרֹאשׁוֹ	and its head/top	CST	noun
רֹאשׁ	wə·rō'·šô	W/ CONJ וְ + 3MS SX	
בַשָּׁמַיִם	in the heavens/skies	ABS	noun
שָׁמַיִם	vaš·šā·mayim	W/ PREP בְּ + DEF. ART.	

Did the builders imagine that the top of their tower would literally reach the divine realm? Perhaps; ancient Near Eastern people generally believed that deities lived in (or could inhabit) the skies (for example, שָׁמַיִם does not necessarily—at least in most contexts—indicate the Christian conception of "heaven," but rather the sky above the earth in all its height). In light of the following phrases, however, it is just as likely that the group's exclamation here simply signals an attempt to make a widely visible marker of their presence—something that would put them "on the map" and spread their fame. Throughout the history of this text's interpretation, especially in the modern age of archaeological and linguistic discoveries related to ancient Mesopotamia, some have interpreted the tower they build as a Babylonian "ziggurat," i.e., a pyramidal or tiered religious structure made of durable baked bricks whose peak (i.e., רֹאשׁ, "head" or "top") was a site where sacred transactions between the human and divine realms were brokered. Some of these structures are still visible today in Iraq, such as the partly reconstructed Ziggurat of Ur.

Later in Genesis, the staircase in Jacob's dream also has a top (רֹאשׁ) that leads to heaven (הַשָּׁמַיְמָה) (Gen 28:12). In a text like Genesis, which has so many echoes and cross-references, we are not stretching too far here to see a connection: Jacob's story, like the story of Pentecost in Acts (see the "From Text to Sermon" section below), seems to reverse the Babel story. Whereas the Babel builders tried to "get up to heaven" and make a name for themselves on their own, God appears to Jacob, with "heaven coming down to earth," and then renames Jacob with a special new name, Israel.

4d	וְנַעֲשֶׂה־לָּנוּ שֵׁם		
	And let us make a name for ourselves,		
וְנַעֲשֶׂה־ עשׂה	and let us make *wə·na·ʿă·śe-*	QAL COHORT 1CP W/ CONJ וְ	verb
לָּנוּ לְ	to/for us/ourselves *lā·nû*	--- W/ 1CP SX	prep
שֵׁם שֵׁם	name/fame/renown *šēm*	ABS	noun

The term "name" (שֵׁם) can also be translated as "fame" or "renown" (see the use of the same term in this way in Gen 6:4). Their desire to make their own "name" can be contrasted with God's promise to Abraham later in Genesis to make a "name" for him (12:2) and with God's promise even later in the biblical narrative that he will establish an everlasting "name" for David and his kingdom (2 Sam 7:9).

4e	פֶּן־נָפוּץ עַל־פְּנֵי כָל־הָאָרֶץ:		
	lest we be scattered across the face of the entire earth!"		
פֶּן־ פֶּן	lest/otherwise *pen-*	---	conj
נָפוּץ פוץ	we will be scattered/ spread out *nā·fûṣ*	QAL IMPF 1CP	verb
עַל־ עַל	on/upon *ʿal-*	---	prep

פְּנֵי פָּנֶה	(the) face/surface of pə·nê	CST	noun
כָּל־ כֹּל	all/(the) entirety of kol-	CST	noun
הָאָֽרֶץ׃ אֶרֶץ	the earth hā·'ā·reṣ	ABS W/ DEF. ART.	noun

Why are the people afraid of being scattered? In Gen 1:28, God had charged humanity with "filling" (מלא) the earth, and we might see their desire here as something of an opposite movement—the people seek to huddle together, refusing the divine command.

11:5–7

5a וַיֵּ֣רֶד יְהוָ֔ה לִרְאֹ֥ת אֶת־הָעִ֖יר וְאֶת־הַמִּגְדָּ֑ל
wayyēred YHWH lirʾōt ʾet-hāʿîr wǝʾet-hammigdāl

Then the Lord came down to see the city and the tower

5b אֲשֶׁ֥ר בָּנ֖וּ בְּנֵ֥י הָאָדָֽם׃
ʾăšer bānû bǝnê hāʾādām.

that the sons of man had built.

6a וַיֹּ֣אמֶר יְהוָ֗ה
wayyōʾmer YHWH

Then the Lord said,

6b הֵ֣ן עַ֤ם אֶחָד֙ וְשָׂפָ֤ה אַחַת֙ לְכֻלָּ֔ם
hēn ʿam ʾeḥād wǝśāfâ ʾaḥat lǝkullām

"This is one people, with one language for all of them—

6c וְזֶ֖ה הַחִלָּ֣ם לַעֲשׂ֑וֹת
wǝze haḥillām laʿăśôt

and this is only the beginning of what they can do!

6d וְעַתָּה֙ לֹֽא־יִבָּצֵ֣ר מֵהֶ֔ם
wǝʿattâ lōʾ-yibbāṣēr mēhem

Now nothing will be impossible for them

6e כֹּ֛ל אֲשֶׁ֥ר יָזְמ֖וּ לַעֲשֽׂוֹת׃
kōl ʾăšer yāzǝmû laʿăśôt.

out of anything that they devise to do!

7a הָ֚בָה נֵֽרְדָ֔ה
hāvâ nērǝdâ

Come, let us go down

7b	וְנָבְלָ֣ה שָׁ֔ם שְׂפָתָ֑ם
	vənāvəlâ šām śəfātām

and let us confuse their language there,

7c	אֲשֶׁר֙ לֹ֣א יִשְׁמְע֔וּ אִ֖ישׁ שְׂפַ֥ת רֵעֵֽהוּ׃
	'ăšer lō' yišmə'û 'îš śəfat rē'ēhû.

so that each cannot understand the language of his fellow."

5a	וַיֵּ֣רֶד יְהוָ֔ה לִרְאֹ֥ת אֶת־הָעִ֖יר וְאֶת־הַמִּגְדָּ֑ל

Then the LORD came down to see the city and the tower

וַיֵּ֣רֶד	and/then (he) came down/descended	QAL WAYY 3MS	verb
ירד	way·yē·red		
יְהוָ֔ה	the LORD	ABS	noun
יהוה	YHWH		
לִרְאֹ֥ת	to see/look at	QAL INF CST W/ PREP לְ	verb
ראה	lir·'ōt		
אֶת־	(direct object marker)	---	particle
אֵת	'et-		
הָעִ֖יר	the city	ABS W/ DEF. ART.	noun
עיר	hā·'îr		
וְאֶת־	and (+ direct object marker)	--- W/ CONJ וְ	particle
אֵת	wə·'et-		
הַמִּגְדָּ֑ל	the tower	ABS W/ DEF. ART.	noun
מִגְדָּל	ham·mig·dāl		

This clause is located at the center of a literary structure that is common in Hebrew prose and poetry: chiasm. Chiastic (or concentric) structures present a progression of statements that lead to a "center" (often the focus), which is then followed by statements that mirror—in reverse order (and sometimes through only small connections)—the original statements:

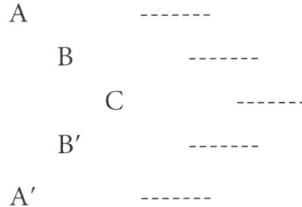

In this story of the tower and city, the chiastic elements can be understood as follows (there are different ways to plot out the structure; for a representative example, which is followed here, see Waltke and Fredricks 2016:176):

    all the earth (v. 1)
        people settle "there" (v. 2)
            his fellow (v. 3)
                "come now . . . let us . . ." (vv. 3–4)
                    city and tower (v. 4)
                        the Lord came down to see (v. 5)
                    city and tower (v. 5)
                "come now . . . let us . . ." (v. 7)
            his fellow (v. 7)
        people scatter from "there" (v. 8)
    all the earth (v. 9)

That the Lord must *descend* to the city and the tower implies that he is not with the people in their quest, and the presence of this statement at the center of the chiasm puts a fine (and somewhat humorous) point on the fact that, despite their concerted efforts, the people completely fail in their goal of reaching the divine realm.

Many interpreters see a (large-scale) chiastic structure as well in the story of the flood, one that spans chs. 6–9 and turns upon the central clause in 9:1: "But God remembered Noah . . ." The point of that pivotal clause seems to be that it is not human striving on which history turns, but God's own acts of seeing and memory. In other words, the chiastic structure of these chapters, like that of Gen 11:1–9, presents human history and divine involvement as structured and controlled. When the Lord sees or remembers, he will act.

5b

	אֲשֶׁ֥ר בָּנ֖וּ בְּנֵ֥י הָאָדָֽם׃		
	that the sons of man had built.		
אֲשֶׁ֥ר אֲשֶׁר	that/which 'ă·šer	---	relative pron
בָּנ֖וּ בנה	(they) built/constructed bā·nû	QAL PF 3CP	verb
בְּנֵ֥י בֵּן	(the) sons of bə·nê	CST	noun
הָאָדָֽם׃ אָדָם	the man/humans/humanity hā·'ā·dām	ABS W/ DEF. ART.	noun

The use here of the phrase בְּנֵי הָאָדָם ("the sons of man" or "mortals")—the only appearance of this expression in the book of Genesis—underscores the fallible identity of the builders vis-à-vis God's divine identity. The point that these humans' identity is tied up with their failed building project is further highlighted by the soundplay between the adjacent words "sons" (בְּנֵי) and "they built" (בָּנוּ).

6a

	וַיֹּ֣אמֶר יְהוָ֗ה		
	Then the LORD said,		
וַיֹּ֣אמֶר אמר	and/then (he) said way·yō'·mer	QAL WAYY 3MS	verb
יְהוָ֗ה יהוה	the LORD YHWH	ABS	noun

6b

	הֵ֣ן עַ֤ם אֶחָד֙ וְשָׂפָ֤ה אַחַת֙ לְכֻלָּ֔ם		
	"This is one people, with one language for all of them—		
הֵ֣ן הֵן	look/behold hēn	---	particle
עַ֤ם עַם	people 'am	ABS	noun
אֶחָד֙ אֶחָד	one 'e·ḥād	ABS	cardinal number

וְשָׂפָ֥ה	and lip/language/speech	ABS	noun
שָׂפָה	wə·śā·fâ	W/ CONJ וְ	
אַחַ֖ת	one	ABS	cardinal number
אֶחָד	'a·ḥat		
לְכֻלָּ֑ם	to/for all of them	CST	noun
כֹּל	lə·ḵul·lām	W/ PREP לְ + 3MP SX	

6c — וְזֶ֖ה הַחִלָּ֣ם לַעֲשׂ֑וֹת

and this is only the beginning of what they can do!

וְזֶ֖ה	and this	---	demonstr pron
זֶה	wə·ze	W/ CONJ וְ	
הַחִלָּ֣ם	their beginning/to begin	HIPH INF CST	verb
חלל	ha·ḥil·lām	W/ 3MP SX	
לַעֲשׂ֑וֹת	to do/make	QAL INF CST	verb
עשׂה	la·'ă·śôt	W/ PREP לְ	

6d — וְעַתָּה֙ לֹא־יִבָּצֵ֣ר מֵהֶ֔ם

Now nothing will be impossible for them

וְעַתָּה֙	and now	---	adv
עַתָּה	wə·'at·tâ	W/ CONJ וְ	
לֹא־	not	---	particle
לֹא	lō-		
יִבָּצֵ֣ר	it will be impossible/inaccessible	NIPH IMPF 3MS	verb
בצר	yib·bā·ṣēr		
מֵהֶ֔ם	from them	---	prep
מִן	mē·hem	W/ 3MP SX	

THE TOWER OF CONFUSION

6e	כֹּל אֲשֶׁר יָזְמוּ לַעֲשׂוֹת:
	out of anything that they devise to do!

	כֹּל כֹּל	all/each/every/everything kōl	ABS	noun
	אֲשֶׁר אֲשֶׁר	that/which 'ă·šer	---	relative pron
	יָזְמוּ זמם	they devise/scheme/purpose yā·zə·mû	QAL IMPF 3MP	verb
	לַעֲשׂוֹת: עשׂה	to do/make la·'ă·śôt	QAL INF CST W/ PREP לְ	verb

The Lord recognizes the startling possibility of what humans might achieve through their scheming. And indeed, the verb זמם does not indicate normal, routine planning but rather devising, concocting, scheming, and so on. Based on two other parallel situations we have already encountered wherein humans have crossed a boundary and made an illicit achievement (3:22–24; 6:1–4), we are prepared for the divine reaction: God will reestablish the boundary and limit human overreach.

7a	הָבָה נֵרְדָה
	Come, let us go down

	הָבָה יהב	come/give hā·vâ	QAL IMPV MS	verb
	נֵרְדָה ירד	let us go down/descend nê·rə·dâ	QAL COHORT 1CP	verb

The first-person plural language mirrors the language of the people in vv. 3–4 and also recalls God's plural exhortation in Gen 1:26, "Let us make humans . . ." (see the commentary there for discussion of God's use of such first-person plural verb forms). Whereas the builders said, "Come, let us build and reach heaven," God is saying the opposite: "Come, let us go down and frustrate their plans."

7b	וְנָבְלָה שָׁם שְׂפָתָם
	and let us confuse their language there,

וְנָבְלָה בלל	and let us confuse/mix və·nā·və·lâ	QAL COHORT 1CP W/ CONJ וְ	verb
שָׁם שָׁם	there šām	---	adv
שְׂפָתָם שָׂפָה	their lip/language/speech śə·fā·tām	CST W/ 3MP SX	noun

The word וְנָבְלָה ("and let us confuse") scrambles the letters of לְבֵנָה ("brick"), used earlier in the narrative. This seems intentional, as it reinforces the point that by "confusing" their language God is going to undo the "brickwork" they have put together.

7c	אֲשֶׁר לֹא יִשְׁמְעוּ אִישׁ שְׂפַת רֵעֵהוּ׃
	so that each cannot understand the language of his fellow."

אֲשֶׁר אֲשֶׁר	that/which 'ă·šer	---	relative pron
לֹא לֹא	not lō'	---	particle
יִשְׁמְעוּ שמע	they will/can/should hear/listen yiš·mə·'û	QAL IMPF 3MP	verb
אִישׁ אִישׁ	man/each 'îš	ABS	noun
שְׂפַת שָׂפָה	(the) lip/language/speech of śə·fat	CST	noun
רֵעֵהוּ׃ רֵעַ	his fellow/companion rē·'ē·hû	CST W/ 3MS SX	noun

The word "hear" (שמע) in this context clearly means "understand."

11:8–9

8a וַיָּ֧פֶץ יְהוָ֛ה אֹתָ֖ם מִשָּׁ֑ם
wayyāfeṣ YHWH 'ōtām miššām

So the Lord scattered them from there

8b עַל־פְּנֵ֣י כָל־הָאָ֑רֶץ
'al-pǝnê kol-hā'āreṣ

upon the face of all the earth,

8c וַֽיַּחְדְּל֖וּ לִבְנֹ֥ת הָעִֽיר׃
wayyaḥdǝlû livnōt hā'îr.

and they ceased building the city.

9a עַל־כֵּ֞ן קָרָ֤א שְׁמָהּ֙ בָּבֶ֔ל
'al-kēn qārā' šǝmāh bāvel

This is why its name is called "Babylon"—

9b כִּי־שָׁ֛ם בָּלַ֥ל יְהוָ֖ה שְׂפַ֣ת כָּל־הָאָ֑רֶץ
kî-šām bālal YHWH śǝfat kol-hā'āreṣ

because there God mixed up the language of all the earth,

9c וּמִשָּׁם֙ הֱפִיצָ֣ם יְהוָ֔ה
ûmiššām hěfiṣām YHWH

and from there the Lord scattered them

9d עַל־פְּנֵ֖י כָּל־הָאָֽרֶץ׃
'al-pǝnê kol-hā'āreṣ.

upon the face of all the earth.

8a	וַיָּ֨פֶץ יְהוָ֧ה אֹתָ֛ם מִשָּׁ֖ם		
	So the Lord scattered them from there		
וַיָּ֨פֶץ / פוץ	and/so/then (he) scattered / way·yā·feṣ	HIPH WAYY 3MS	verb
יְהוָ֧ה / יהוה	the Lord / YHWH	ABS	noun
אֹתָ֛ם / אֵת	(direct object marker +) them / ʾō·tām	--- W/ 3MP SX	particle
מִשָּׁ֖ם / שָׁם	from there / miš·šām	--- W/ PREP מִן	adv

Elsewhere in the Bible the Hiphil of פוץ signals judgment and defeat; it refers to routing defeated armies and God sending a nation into exile (e.g., Gen 49:7; Num 10:35; Deut 4:27).

8b	עַל־פְּנֵ֣י כָל־הָאָ֑רֶץ		
	upon the face of all the earth,		
עַל־ / עַל	on/upon / ʿal-	---	prep
פְּנֵ֣י / פָּנֶה	(the) face/surface of / pə·nê	CST	noun
כָל־ / כֹּל	all/(the) entirety of / kol-	CST	noun
הָאָ֑רֶץ / אֶרֶץ	the earth / hā·ʾā·reṣ	ABS W/ DEF. ART.	noun

See the comment above at Gen 4:14b regarding the negative associations that accompany the phrase "upon the face of the earth/ground."

8c	וַֽיַּחְדְּל֖וּ לִבְנֹ֥ת הָעִֽיר׃		
	and they ceased building the city.		
וַֽיַּחְדְּל֖וּ / חדל	and/then they ceased/ stopped / way·yaḥ·də·lû	QAL WAYY 3MP	verb

THE TOWER OF CONFUSION

לִבְנֹ֖ת	to build/construct/ building/constructing	QAL INF CST W/ PREP לְ	verb
בנה	liv·nōt		
הָעִֽיר׃	the city	ABS W/ DEF. ART.	noun
עיר	hā·'îr		

9a   עַל־כֵּ֛ן קָרָ֥א שְׁמָ֖הּ בָּבֶ֑ל

This is why its name is called "Babylon"—

עַל־כֵּ֛ן	therefore [lit., on/upon thus]	---	adv
עַל־כֵּן	'al-kēn		
קָרָ֥א	he called	QAL PF 3MS	verb
קרא	qā·rā'		
שְׁמָ֖הּ	its name/fame/renown	CST W/ 3FS SX	noun
שֵׁם	šə·māh		
בָּבֶ֑ל	Babel	ABS	noun
בָּבֶל	bā·vel		

Old Testament narratives often use the phrase עַל־כֵּן to signal an etiology (i.e., a story of origins or a historical explanation; see, e.g., Gen 2:24; 10:9).

In Hebrew, the word בָּבֶל is the term for "Babylon." Literally, this clause would be rendered "Therefore he called its name 'Babylon,'" using an impersonal construction (i.e., "one called"; note that "God" is not the subject of "he called"). The clause is best rendered in English with a passive construction: "its name is called."

Although the name of this city/empire occurs frequently in the Old Testament, it will not appear again until 2 Kgs 17, which describes the Assyrians moving people from Babylon into the destroyed Northern Kingdom of Israel, and then in 2 Kgs 20–25, which narrates the Babylonians' destruction of the Southern Kingdom of Judah and its capital, Jerusalem. On the connection between this later city/empire of Babylon and the city in Gen 11, see the comment on v. 2c above.

9b	כִּי־שָׁם בָּלַל יְהוָה שְׂפַת כָּל־הָאָרֶץ
	because there God mixed up the language of all the earth,

כִּי־	for/since/because	---	conj
kî-			
שָׁם	there	---	adv
šām			
בָּלַל	(he) mixed/confused	QAL PF 3MS	verb
bā·lal			
יְהוָה	the Lord	ABS	noun
YHWH			
שְׂפַת	(the) lip/language/speech of	CST	noun
śə·fat			
כָּל־	all/(the) entirety of	CST	noun
kol-			
הָאָרֶץ	the earth	ABS W/ DEF. ART.	noun
hā·'ā·reṣ			

The narrator here plays on the similarity of the verb בלל, "to mix up, confuse" (which is also the root of וְנָבְלָה in v. 7b above), and the name בָּבֶל, "Babylon." The Babylonians sought religious connection to their deities, fame, and a mighty heroic name for themselves—but in the end they receive only confusion.

9c	וּמִשָּׁם הֱפִיצָם יְהוָה
	and from there the Lord scattered them

וּמִשָּׁם	and from there	W/ CONJ וְ + PREP מִן	adv
û·miš·šām			
הֱפִיצָם	(he) scattered them	HIPH PF 3MS W/ 3MP SX	verb
hĕ·fî·ṣām			
יְהוָה	the Lord	ABS	noun
YHWH			

9d	עַל־פְּנֵי כָל־הָאָֽרֶץ׃		
	upon the face of all the earth.		
עַל־ / עַל	on/upon / 'al-	---	prep
פְּנֵי / פָּנֶה	(the) face/surface of / pə·nê	CST	noun
כָל־ / כֹּל	all/(the) entirety of / kol-	CST	noun
הָאָֽרֶץ׃ / אֶרֶץ	the earth / hā·'ā·reṣ	ABS W/ DEF. ART.	noun

Although Gen 11 continues for several more verses—giving us the genealogy of Noah's son Shem, leading to Abraham—the phrase "all the earth" is an appropriate end-marker to the epic story of Gen 1–11. This story begins with the creation of the heavens and the earth and ends with humans being scattered over the face of that same earth, lost and fractured but still connected to and cared for by the God who created them. The reference to the name of שֵׁם ("Shem") in Gen 11:10, progenitor of the "Shemites" (Semitic people, in biblical terms), offers a telling contrast to the שֵׁם ("name") that the tower builders had sought to find for themselves (i.e., in Hebrew, the proper noun "Shem" and the word "name" are the same word). God's first promise to Abram in Gen 12:2 also involves the invocation of a שֵׁם ("name"): "I will make of you a great nation, and I will bless you and make your name [שֵׁם] great, so that you will be a blessing" (NRSVue). Genesis 1–11 teaches us that only God can give us that true name and a lasting, faithful identity.

From Text to Sermon

*As you meditate on this passage and contemplate
how you might teach or preach it to others,
consider the following areas of emphasis.*

 Historical and Literary Context. When thinking about the broader historical and literary context, it is helpful to consider the role of Babylon in the Bible and what we know of the ancient Babylonians and their religious world. Immediately preceding the Tower of Babel story, in Gen 10, the "table of nations" tells of the ancient history of Babylon, a people descended from a "mighty warrior" and hunter named Nimrod. Indeed, the other descendants in this group include Egypt, Assyria, Canaan, and the Philistines—all of whom will become significant oppressors of Israel in the biblical narrative (Egypt in the Exodus story and beyond; the Assyrians in the eighth century BCE, as narrated in the books of Isaiah and 2 Kings; the Canaanites in the books of Joshua and Judges; and the Philistines in 1 Samuel). These peoples are all said to have descended from Noah's son Ham, who in an enigmatic scene after the flood (9:18–27) sees his father naked and tells his brothers about this, thereby committing, according to the narrative, a grave infraction. Moreover, in the construction of a tower and, notably, a "city," the builders in Gen 11 follow in the tradition of Cain, the first city builder. In the Old Testament, we find a long tradition of the city being a symbol of sin and arrogance (a tradition that runs from the Tower of Babel story to Sodom and Gomorrah in Gen 19 and on to the frequent prophetic condemnation of major cities, of which Nahum is a prominent example). However, cities can be presented as sites of great possibility not only for ruin but also for righteousness (see, e.g., Isa 1, esp. vv. 21 and 26), and the city of Jerusalem in particular is held up as the site God has chosen for his king and temple to be located. In the book of Jonah, the city that Jonah finds so abominable, Nineveh, ends up repenting and turning to God in a stunning fashion.

Archaeological work on the ancient city of Babylon and its surrounding territory has revealed the remains of a monumental empire, famous for its architecture, art, and technological achievements. The Babylonians' polytheistic religions and rich literary traditions were among the most advanced and intricate of the ancient world, bolstered by the power of empire. Regardless of this splendor, the Tower of Babel story tells of this empire's past and also its future—indeed, as the biblical story unfolds,

Babel/Babylon is revealed to not be limited to only one place in the past; rather, in the biblical idiom, it is symbolic of all oppressors and of all who are morally confused.

Bridge to the Gospel. As a bridge to the preaching of the gospel in the New Testament, we should meditate on the rich symbolic reversal of the misunderstanding of languages that occurs on the day of Pentecost, as narrated in Acts 2. After Jesus ascends to heaven, his followers wait for the coming of the Holy Spirit. When the Spirit arrives, Jesus' followers—empowered by that Spirit—speak "in tongues," i.e., in languages not their own:

> And at this sound the crowd gathered and was bewildered, because each one heard them speaking in the native language of each. Amazed and astonished, they asked, "Are not all these who are speaking Galileans? And how is it that we hear, each of us, in our own native language? Parthians, Medes, Elamites, and residents of Mesopotamia, Judea and Cappadocia, Pontus and Asia, Phrygia and Pamphylia, Egypt and the parts of Libya belonging to Cyrene, and visitors from Rome, both Jews and proselytes, Cretans and Arabs—in our own languages we hear them speaking about God's deeds of power."
>
> (Acts 2:6–11 NRSVue)

The long list of different peoples and languages in this passage offers a panoramic view of the ancient Near Eastern and Mediterranean world, and suggests that through the power of the gospel the curse of confusion and misunderstanding perpetrated at Babel has now been addressed. Instead of humans engaging in upward striving to make a "name" for themselves, God now makes his name known in the person of Jesus to all people, in their own languages.

As a symbolic city, Babylon makes a climactic reappearance in the Bible's final book, Revelation. As a cipher for the Roman Empire, which ruled over the world of early Christianity, Babylon stands for all that is corrupt—the impulse to persecute God's people, commit idolatry, and revolt against God, all of which leads to an epic, final showdown of cosmic proportions. Evoking the prophetic condemnation of Babylon found in Isa 21, Rev 18 narrates the final downfall of Babylon, which precedes the establishment of God's righteous city on earth, the New Jerusalem.

Illustrations. As you think about how to illustrate the themes of Gen 11 with more contemporary examples, consider how the Tower of Babel has remained a potent cultural symbol of group confusion, of the arrogant desire of totalitarian (forced, false) unity, and of the ultimate futility of all human effort to reach God through humanity's own devices. These themes find expression in what is probably the most famous artistic depiction of the Tower of Babel scene, by the Flemish master Pieter Bruegel the Elder, which he completed in 1563 and which survives in two versions. In both, the tower stands upon the seashore, surrounded by urban development and frantic workers; the bottom of the tower is stately and refined, the product of a wonderful achievement, but the top is decrepit and unfinished, demonstrating the failure of hubris. Or to take an example from cinema, the 2006 drama *Babel*, directed by Alejandro González Iñárritu, earned seven Academy Award nods and won the Golden Globe for best picture. This dark, complex, and nonlinear film explores themes of alienation and miscommunication in troubled, multinational contexts. Finally, in our contemporary world, we have seen developments resonant with the themes of the Tower of Babel story in the dominance of social media and Internet culture—technologies that offer the promise of connection and success but also lead many to deception and division. The biblical story offers a powerful reminder that it is ultimately God, not human scheming or striving, who is the key to the flourishing of the human family.

WORKS CITED

Alter, Robert. 1997. *Genesis: Translation and Commentary*. New York: Norton.

Barr, James. 1961. *The Semantics of Biblical Language*. Oxford: Oxford University Press.

Bonhoeffer, Dietrich. 2015 [orig. 1954]. *Life Together*. London: SCM.

Schloen, David. 2001. *The House of the Father as Fact and Symbol: Patrimonialism in Ugarit and the Ancient Near East*. SAHL 2. Winona Lake, IN: Eisenbrauns.

Speiser, E. A. 1964. *Genesis: A New Translation with Introduction and Commentary*. AB 1. Garden City, NY: Doubleday.

Steinbeck, John. 2002 [orig. 1952]. *East of Eden*. New York: Penguin.

Waltke, Bruce K., with Cathi J. Fredricks. 2016. *Genesis: A Commentary*. Grand Rapids: Zondervan.

INDEX OF BIBLICAL REFERENCES

NOTE: The primary purpose of a Scripture index in a book like this, where biblical passages are being treated directly, is not to present the reader with every biblical reference found in the book, but to offer ones that lie outside the range of each of the passages treated. Hence, this index presents references to such outside passages, plus verses from the passages treated in this book *but only when these are cross-referenced in a discussion of another verse found in these passages.*

OLD TESTAMENT

Genesis
1   57, 59–61, 64, 80, 110, 178, 186, 199, 209, 231
1–2   24, 51, 127, 244
1–3   103, 121
1–8   234
1–9   179
1:2   5, 16
1:3–5   5
1:9   201
1:9–13   34
1:14–19   5
1:20–21   243
1:22   27–28, 51, 230–31
1:26   5, 26, 29, 41, 61, 128, 264
1:26–27   42, 130, 242
1:27   23, 208
1:28   26, 41, 51, 230–31, 233, 243, 258
1:28–31   89
1:29   36, 211
1:29–30   42, 234
1:30   61
1:31   161
2   91, 110
2:2–3   227
2:3   230
2:4   59
2:7   61–63, 80
2:8–9   89
2:9   13
2:15–17   89
2:16   211, 213
2:17   91, 96
2:18   13
2:19   71
2:19–20   87
2:20   80, 121
2:21–22   80
2:23   27, 76
2:24   81, 268
3   41, 104, 133, 135, 157, 186, 223, 231
3–4   95
3:1   78, 112
3:1–7   110
3:6   96, 177
3:7   95, 254
3:8   110
3:10   231
3:11   213
3:13   156
3:14   157
3:14–19   27, 110
3:14–21   102
3:16   123–24
3:17   69, 111–12, 128, 157, 175, 213
3:19   223
3:20   121
3:22   95, 102
3:22–24   264
3:23   223
3:24   161, 250
4   41, 186, 191, 240
4–11   130
4:1   59, 95, 97
4:1–16   250
4:2   175
4:3   174
4:7   118, 130
4:7–8   169
4:9   95
4:10–11   235
4:10–12   223
4:12   175
4:14   201, 267
4:16   250
4:17   95, 97, 163, 256
4:20–22   254
4:23–24   27, 164
4:25   23, 95, 97, 121
5   174
5:1   41
5:2   208, 230
5:28–29   190
5:29   190, 223
6   215, 254
6–9   187, 192, 214, 261
6:1–2   180, 182
6:1–4   185, 214, 264
6:1–22   244
6:2   98
6:4   175, 257
6:5–7   224
6:5–8   190
6:5–9   185
6:5–10   183
6:5–9:29   181
6:7   161
6:8–9   190, 203
6:11–12   192
6:11–13   190
6:13   200
6:18   207
6:21   213, 221
6:22   213
7:2   221
7:4   161
7:5   213
7:11   8

7:21   243
7:23   161
8:17   28, 243
9   36, 202, 244
9:1   28, 41, 242, 261
9:1–3   231
9:4   235
9:5–6   241
9:6   41
9:6–7   27
9:7   28, 41
9:11   187, 214, 244
9:15   214
9:15–17   187
9:18–27   271
9:20   190
9:26   59
9:28–29   179
10   271
10:9   75, 268
10:10   251
10:11–12   256
10:20   249
11   160, 179
11:1–9   261
11:2   268
11:3–4   264
11:7   5, 269
11:9   75
11:10   270
12   213
12–13   220
12–50   41
12:1–3   27, 41
12:2   257, 270
12:2–3   230
14:19–20   230
14:20   233
15   202
15:1   59
15:12   70
16:14   75
17   202
17:6   28, 41
17:16   230
17:20   28, 230
18   80
18:22–33   203
19   271
19:22   75
19:32   135
21:19   96
21:31   75
22   154, 213
23:1   179
25:7–8   180
25:29–34   101

25:30   75
26:22   28
26:33   75
28:3   28, 41
28:12   257
29:34–35   75
30:6   75
31:48   75
31:51–54   202
32:21 [32:20]   144
32:33 [32:32]   75
33:17   75
35:11   28, 41
35:28   180
41:27   28
41:38   9
42:23   249
45:7   207
47:28   180
48:4   28
48:15–16   230
48:20   230
49:7   267
49:9   146
49:25   230
49:28   230
49:33   180
50:11   75
50:20   207
50:22   180

Exodus
1:7   243
1:14   255
2:3   192
2:5   192
3:13–15   59
5   255
10:15   8
12   17, 54
13:15   60
14:8   60
16   48
18:4   62
20   53–54
20:1–6   23
20:5–6   204
20:9–10   48
20:24–26   220
21:24   192, 241
23:16–19   142
23:18   236
24:8   236
25–26   80
27:1   220
29   222
31:3   9

31:14–15   53
32:12   161
35–36   49
35:2   53

Leviticus
1–8   222
1:5   236
2:1–16   142
6:7–11 [6:14–18]   142
10:10   13
11   221
11:34   221
15:19   236
17:10–11   236
17:10–13   235
17:13   221
19:2   129
23   48
24:20   241
25:43   24
26:20   159
26:25   233

Numbers
7:86   179
8:14   13
10:35   267
13:33   181
15   222
15:32–36   53
16:30   158
22   87
28–29   48, 222
32:22   29
33:52   23
35:33   236

Deuteronomy
1:39   97–98
4–5   23
4:27   267
5   54
5:13–14   48
5:15   54
6:15   161
7:2   214
7:26   214
8:7   8
12:15–16   236
12:22   221
13:13–19 [13:12–18]   214
15:23   236
19:21   241
20:17   214
28:5   51
28:16   157

28:19   157
32:8   175
32:10   7
32:11   9
33:7   62
33:13   51
33:29   62
34:7   179

Joshua
6–12   214
7:16–26   204
18:1   29

Judges
2:15   233
11:39   135
14   236
19   168
20:1   97

1 Samuel
1:19   135
2:22   135
6:5   23
9:13   51
12:21   7
14   236
26:12   70
27:1   223

2 Samuel
5:20   199
7:9   257
8:11   29
11:2–5   98
13–14   168
14:7   161
22:12   8
24:15   97

1 Kings
5:4 [4:24]   24
5:30 [5:16]   24
7   49
9:14   179
10:10   179
21   168

2 Kings
6:17–20   96
8:5   207
11:18   23
15–17   256
17   268
18:27–37   249
20–25   268

21:14   233
25   251

1 Chronicles
28–29   49

2 Chronicles
3:4   179
5:12   179
23:10   29

Nehemiah
5:5   29
6   49
9:2   13
10:36 [10:35]   142

Job
1:6   175
1:10   51
2:1   175
4:13   70
12:11   101
20:14   101
22:11   199
26   16
33:15   70
34:3   101
38:7   175
42:7–9   203

Psalms
8:4–10 [3–9]   81
22:25 [22:24]   162
27:9   162
29:1   175
29:10   199, 244
74   16
78:18   101
82:6   175
89:7 [89:6]   175
102:3 [102:2]   162
110:2   24
121:1–2   62
128:3   28
139   17
146:8   96

Proverbs
15:11   88
20:21   51
23:3   101
23:19–21   101
30:22   101

Ecclesiastes
1:2   130, 137

2:13   8
12:12   130

Song of Songs
7:11 [7:10]   118

Isaiah
1   271
1:21   271
1:26   74, 271
9:5 [9:6]   183
11:1   28
13:20–21   146
14   86
14:12   86
21   272
24:19–20   160
29:10   70
29:21   7
32:5   74
35:5   96
35:8   74
36:2–20   249
40–55   5, 17, 62, 250
42:7   8, 96
44:19   223
45:7   8
49:5   62
54:9   214, 244
56:6   53
58:13–14   53
62:4   74
62:12   74
64:7 [64:8]   62

Jeremiah
1:5   62
4:23   7
5:31   24
17:21–27   53
18:11   62
19:6   74
20:14   51
23:3   41
23:9   9
32:18   204
32:20   164
34:11   29
34:16   29
50:25   49

Ezekiel
7:2–3   191
7:5–7   191
11:5   9
12:14   62
14:12–20   203

14:14   214, 244
14:20   214, 244
19:2   146
22:26   13
27–28   86
32:8   8
33:6   238

Joel
2:8   239

Micah
3:6   8

Nahum
1:8   199

Habakkuk
2:18   62

Zechariah
7:10   239

NEW TESTAMENT

Matthew
5:21–24 168
5:38   241
6:34   130
19:3–9   81
19:6   81
24:37   215

Mark
2:13–17 42
2:23–3:6 53
5   86
10:2–9   81
10:8–9   81

Luke
1:38   104
17:26   215

John
1   16, 80
17:21   129
20   16

Acts
2   16, 272
2:6–11   272
15:20   245
15:29   245
21:25   245

Romans
5   86, 110
5:9   244
5:12–15 103

1 Corinthians
12:12–14 204
13   86, 110–11
15:20–22 103

2 Corinthians
4:4–6   42
6:17   129

Ephesians
1:7   244

Philippians
2:2   129

Hebrews
9:12–14 244
11   215
11:1   215

1 Peter
1:15–17 129
3:20   215

2 Peter
2:5   215

Revelation
6:10   245
7:14   245
8:9   245
12   86
17:6   245
18   272
19:13   245
20   86
22:1–5   131

ABOUT THE AUTHOR

BRIAN R. DOAK (PhD, Harvard University) serves as Professor of Biblical Studies at George Fox University, where he is also a faculty fellow in the Honors Program and vice president of George Fox Digital. He has won the Aviram Prize in archaeology and the George Fox University undergraduate researcher of the year award for his academic writing. His books include *Consider Leviathan: Narratives of Nature and the Self in Job*, *Heroic Bodies in Ancient Israel*, and *Ancient Israel's Neighbors*. He is also the co-editor (with Carolina López-Ruiz) of the *Oxford Handbook of the Phoenician and Punic Mediterranean*, and the author of many peer-reviewed academic articles and book chapters.

Doak has served in full-time ministry as a youth minister and associate minister (King's Chapel, Springfield, Missouri) and in various leadership capacities at churches across the United States, and he continues to teach in local church settings, at retreats, and for Bible studies. In addition, he co-hosts a nationally recognized religion and pop-culture podcast (*Weird Religion*) and has appeared as a guest expert on live radio as well as on television (*America Unearthed*, on the Travel Channel). He lives outside of Portland, Oregon, with his wife and two daughters.